JOSSEY-BASS TEACHER

Jossey-Bass Teacher provides educators with practical knowledge and tools to create a positive and lifelong impact on student learning. We offer classroom-tested and research-based teaching resources for a variety of grade levels and subject areas. Whether you are an aspiring, new, or veteran teacher, we want to help you make every teaching day your best.

From ready-to-use classroom activities to the latest teaching framework, our value-packed books provide insightful, practical, and comprehensive materials on the topics that matter most to K–12 teachers. We hope to become your trusted source for the best ideas from the most experienced and respected experts in the field.

TEACH LIKE A CHAMPION

49 Techniques that Put Students on the Path to College

Doug Lemov

Foreword by Norman Atkins

 JOSSEY-BASS
A Wiley Imprint
www.josseybass.com

Published by Jossey-Bass
A Wiley Imprint
989 Market Street, San Francisco, CA 94103-1741—www.josseybass.com

Uncommon Schools

EXCELLENCE ⟩ NORTH ★ STAR ⟨ COLLEGIATE ⟩ TRUE NORTH ⟨ PREPARATORY

Jossey-Bass books and products are available through most bookstores. To contact Jossey-Bass directly call our Customer Care Department within the U.S. at 800-956-7739, outside the U.S. at 317-572-3986, or fax 317-572-4002.

Jossey-Bass also publishes its books in a variety of electronic formats. Some content that appears in print may not be available in electronic books.

Library of Congress Cataloging-in-Publication Data
Lemov, Doug, 1967-
Teach like a champion: 49 techniques that put students on the path to college / Doug Lemov; foreword by Norman Atkins
Jossey-Bass.—1st ed.
p. cm.
Includes index.
ISBN 978-0-470-55047-2 (paper/dvd)
1. Effective teaching. 2. Academic achievement. 3. College preparation programs. I. Title.
LB1025.3.L48 2010
371.3—dc22
2009049498

Printed in the United States of America
FIRST EDITION
PB Printing 10

CONTENTS

PART TWO
HELPING STUDENTS GET THE MOST OUT OF READING: CRITICAL SKILLS AND TECHNIQUES

DVD CONTENTS

FOREWORD

If John Madden—enthusiastically drawing Xs, Os, and squiggly lines on our TV screens, diagramming games, down by down—is the explainer par excellence of professional football, Doug Lemov is the John Madden of professional teaching. For the past dozen years, he has been standing in the back of hundreds of classrooms, watching thousands of hours of teachers' game films, and analyzing their teaching moves with more enthusiasm and attention to detail than virtually anyone else in the history of American education.

He's gone about this systematically and with a tremendous sense of purpose, creating and poring over countless scatter-plot charts. When Lemov graphs schools by two variables—their academic performance on the y-axis and the poverty index of their students on the x-axis—he invariably finds a line of regression that indicates students' test scores are highly correlated with the amount of money their parents make and the zip codes where they live. If he were a sociologist, he'd conclude what far too many children growing up in poverty, even in this land of opportunity, already know from experience: demography is destiny.

Now having taught and served as a principal of a school where low-income students triumphed over their putative demographic fate, Lemov is always mining for more promising data in the service of a more urgent mission: the fight for educational equity. He is not interested in the line of regression so much as the very few dots in the upper-right-hand corner of the charts soaring several standard deviations above their predicted place on the line. These dots represent nonselective schools that serve primarily students who receive subsidized lunch and, at the same time, score better on the state test than their more affluent peers. For the past decade, Lemov has run to these schools, identified the teachers generating the remarkable results, camped out in their classrooms, and watched the tiniest details, from how they greet students at the door to how they pass out papers, from how they cold-call students to how they wait for answers. He has documented and built a database of thirty-second video clips of these moves.

What he discovered is surprising for its simplicity and portends good news for the teaching profession. He did not find magicians mixing secret alchemical teaching potions or derive the elusive DNA for charisma. And, more important, he did not unearth any truth behind the pernicious lie that the most effective teachers simply come across well because they have the easiest or brightest students. No, what he repeatedly saw and captured on video, beyond the no-shortcuts preparation and an essential mind-set of high expectations, were highly skilled individuals, working with a common, discrete set of tools, building systems of classroom culture and instruction, brick by brick.

He could see that teaching was not as easy or straightforward as the home improvement projects he was doing on the weekend, but he also knew that there was a craft to it that could be taught and learned. His big "aha" was to identify the tools that master teachers used to make their classrooms into cathedrals of learning.

He began naming and codifying these techniques—*Strong Voice, Positive Framing, Stretch It*—in a new taxonomy of effective teaching practices. In the past five years at Uncommon Schools, a nonprofit charter school management organization I founded and where Lemov has served as a managing director, creating schools in Rochester and Troy, New York, the taxonomy has gone through more than twenty-five revisions as he has observed and videotaped our "rock star" teachers in action and refined his concepts based on their work.

One of Lemov's earliest and most important insights was that he could use videotape as a window into the classrooms of the most effective teachers. On tape, he found a way to isolate the microtechniques that make all the difference in student learning. In the same way that Madden might show in slow motion replay how the left tackle blocked for the quarterback, Lemov can show how a teacher stretches students' answers in a discussion.

Uncommon Schools has trained hundreds of its own teachers using the taxonomy and videos. Moreover, Uncommon and Lemov have trained thousands of other teachers, as well as hundreds of school leaders, who in turn have trained tens of thousands of their teachers. The taxonomy has become the instructional Baedeker for the highest-performing teachers and schools across the United States. Lemov's language of *Strong Voice, Positive Framing, Right Is Right, 100 Percent,* and all the others has increasingly entered the common lexicon of new teachers in charter schools. At Teacher U, a new teacher training program created by Uncommon Schools, KIPP, and Achievement First, we are training the next generation of teachers in the tools described in the taxonomy.

For years now, various sections of the taxonomy have been passed around, teacher to teacher, as dog-eared copies or unauthorized PDFs, as if it were revolutionary *samizdat* literature. Many of us have been urging Lemov to publish the work and share it with the nation's three million teachers who will benefit from its insights. At long last, I am pleased to say, you are holding that book in your hands. *Teach Like a Champion* is essential reading for those who intend to make every moment count in their classrooms, who want to build a repertoire of skills that will help them lead all their students to meaningful achievement, who are all about getting down to the work of ensuring that demography is not destiny for our children and our nation.

Unlike Madden, Lemov is more professor than football coach; he's not a loud or in-your-face personality. At the same time, his love of teachers and Madden-like enthusiasm for their teaching shine through every page in this book. He has given teachers a tremendous gift: a beautiful set of tools that they can use to become successful (assuming, of course, that they work relentlessly!) at the world's greatest profession.

October 2009   Norman Atkins

Norman Atkins *is the founder and CEO of Teacher U; the founder, former CEO, and board chair of Uncommon Schools; the co-founder and former co-director of North Star Academy; and the former co-executive director of the Robin Hood Foundation.*

For Mike and Penny Lemov
My first teachers

ACKNOWLEDGMENTS

My friend and colleague Norman Atkins likes to start up audacious projects. He founded Newark's North Star Academy, the most successful charter school in New Jersey, and arguably one of the best public schools in the country. He founded Uncommon Schools, the network of sixteen college preparatory charter schools (so far!) in high-need school districts in New York and New Jersey. He founded Teacher U, the teacher training program and graduate school in New York City that has reinvented the process of teacher education to focus it on what gets real results in real classrooms. All in all, not a bad decade's work.

Norman wills projects into being when he believes they can help eliminate the gap between the achievement levels of poor and privileged students. And he got it into his head that one of those projects was the "taxonomy," the impromptu list I was making of what great teachers did in their classrooms. It should be a book, Norm advised. I said no in a lot of very clear ways. But Norman nagged me. For every excuse he had a solution, usually delivered with exuberance and gesticulating. And in the end I knew it would be easier to write the thing than to battle Norman's will. Now that you hold the result in your hands, it's fitting that I start with thanks to Norman for his tenacity and faith.

That said, having written this book on the techniques that champion teachers use, thanking all those inspiring and brilliant teachers should by all rights be my starting point. And as it seemed right to name names, I started in on a comprehensive list. The challenge proved daunting, though, and when I got over fifty names, I realized that to try to name all the teachers I'd learned from in writing this book would yield a list both unwieldy and unforgivable in the worthy individuals it left out, either because I somehow forgot a few or because in some cases it felt strange to be thanking people I'd barely met. Ironically, some of the teachers who were influential in writing this I watched anonymously from the back of the classroom or even on video tape. So with perhaps a hundred apologies, I've made the gut-wrenching decision to offer a blanket thank-you to all the teachers I've worked with, even though I'm chastened by the ingratitude this shows. There are so many, especially at Uncommon Schools, who have taught me every piece of insight contained in this book while also, and more important, teaching class after class of deserving students to aspire, reach, and achieve. My heartfelt thanks to all of those champions, alongside those of their students and their parents.

A second source of the inspiring success those teachers have achieved is the leadership they get from their principals in putting them in a position to succeed. And in this case I owe thanks to Stacey Shells, the founding principal of Rochester Prep, the first Uncommon School in upstate New York, as well as Paul Powell and David McBride, instructional leaders with whom I am lucky to work and from whom I have learned much.

I'm also deeply indebted to the "taxonomy team" at Uncommon—the folks whose work it is to take hours of teacher video and turn it into teacher training modules that help ensure the success of novice teachers and the continued development of veterans. On that team are Tracey Koren, Max Tuefferd, Erica Woolway, John Costello, Melinda Phelps, Katie Yezzi, and, most of all, my friend and colleague Rob Richard. Rob, who directs the taxonomy video project, is my indispensable partner in developing the material in this book (especially the DVD) and a reliable source of music recommendations for late-night drafting and editing of books.

Also, my fellow managing directors at Uncommon—Paul Bambrick, John King, and Brett Peiser—as well as chief operating officer Josh Phillips and chief executive officer Evan Rudall, have provided me with invaluable advice and insight into all aspects of the work we do, including the contents of this book. The chapters in Part Two on reading are particularly indebted to John King's constant inquiry and counsel.

This book, and the larger teacher training project of which it is a part, would have been impossible without the generous support and guidance of the Carnegie Corporation of New York and the Kern Family Foundation. Both organizations placed great faith in me, in Uncommon Schools, and in our programs. To them and to Ryan Olson, Jim Rahn, and Talia Milgrom-Elcott in particular, I am deeply grateful.

Over the five or so years I spent writing this book, I received invaluable editing support from Sophie Brickman, Karen Lytle, Jessica Petrencsik, and Jennifer Del Greco. Kate Gagnon at Jossey-Bass found a way to shape and refine the whole messy bee's nest of a project into a cohesive whole. Of the many peers and colleagues who have given me regular feedback about how to improve this work over the years, none has been more diligent and candid than Doug McCurry, co-CEO of Achievement First.

Finally my biggest debt of all is to my wife, Lisa, with whom I share the responsibility for and joy in the most important work I will ever do: raising our three children. She picked up much of my part of that so I could write. That said, thanking Lisa for her help with this book is a bit like thanking the sun. Sure, there would be no book without light to write by, but it's hard to feel as if the thank-you doesn't trivialize a gift of such magnitude. Still, you gotta try. So, Lisa, thank you for the hours squeezed out of Sunday mornings and Tuesday nights and all the extra work this meant for you. Thank you for talking ideas through with me while handing snacks and drinks into the back seat. And most of all, thank you for the sunshine.

THE AUTHOR

Doug Lemov is a managing director of Uncommon Schools and oversees its True North network, with schools in Rochester and Troy. He also trains school leaders and teachers both internally, at Uncommon's sixteen schools, and nationally. He was formerly the president of School Performance, an organization helping schools use data to drive decision making, and vice president for accountability at the State University of New York Charter Schools Institute and was a founder and principal of the Academy of the Pacific Rim Charter School in Boston. He has taught English and history at the university, high school, and middle school levels. He holds a B.A. from Hamilton College, an M.A. from Indiana University, and an M.B.A. from the Harvard Business School. Visit Doug Lemov at www.douglemov.com.

THE ART OF TEACHING AND ITS TOOLS

Great teaching is an art. In other arts—painting, sculpture, the writing of novels—great masters leverage a proficiency with basic tools to transform the rawest of material (stone, paper, ink) into the most valued assets in society. This alchemy is all the more astounding because the tools often appear unremarkable to others. Who would look at a chisel, a mallet, and a file and imagine them producing Michelangelo's *David*?

Great art relies on the mastery and application of foundational skills, learned individually through diligent study. You learn to strike a chisel with a mallet. You refine the skill with time, learning at what angle to strike and how hard to drive the chisel. Years later, when and if your work makes it to a museum, observers will likely talk about what school of thought or theory it represents. They are far less likely to reflect on the degree to which proficiency with the chisel made the vision possible. But although lots of people conjure unique artistic visions, only those with an artisan's skill can make them real. Behind every artist is an artisan. And while not everyone who learns to drive a chisel will create a *David*, neither can anyone who fails to learn it do much more than make marks on rocks.

Traveling abroad during my junior year in college, I saw Picasso's school notebooks on display at the Picasso Museum in Barcelona. What I remember best are the sketches in the margins of his pages. These weren't sketchbooks, mind you. These were notebooks like every student keeps: page after page of notes from lectures. But the sketches in the margins memorialized a teacher's face or Picasso's own hand grasping a pencil with perfect perspective, line, and shading. I had always thought Picasso was a king of abstraction, of a symbolism that made the ability to draw accurately and realistically irrelevant. His sketches, filling the margins of the pages, bore witness to his mastery of fundamentals and a habitual need to refine his skills. Even in the stray moments of his schooling, he was constantly honing the building blocks of his technique. He was an artisan first and then an artist, as the fact that he filled, by one count, 178 sketchbooks in his life further attests. Diligent mastery of the tools of the craft preceded and perhaps allowed what came after.

This book is about the tools of the teaching craft. More specifically, it's about the tools necessary for success in the most important part of the field: teaching in public schools, primarily those in the inner city, that serve students born into poverty and, too often, to a rapidly closing window of opportunity. In these schools, the price of failure is high and the challenges immense. Teachers there work in a crucible where, most often, our society's failures are paramount, self-evident, and overwhelming, but also where the kind of alchemy that changes lives can and does occur. Unfortunately this alchemy happens too rarely and often without much fanfare. But in the hands of a small number of champion teachers and visionary principals who've managed to build classrooms and schools that successfully pry the window of opportunity back open, it happens reliably and consistently. If you're reading this and you're a teacher who wants to improve your craft, my aim is to give you the tools to do that—to become one of those teachers who unlocks the latent talent and skill waiting in his or her students, no matter how many previous schools or classrooms or teachers have been unsuccessful in that task.

Throughout my career working in urban public schools as a teacher, trainer, consultant, and administrator, I've had the privilege of watching many champion teachers, often in situations that would overwhelm most of us. These outstanding teachers routinely do what a thousand hand-wringing social programs have found impossible: close the achievement gap between rich and poor, transform students at risk of failure into achievers and believers, and rewrite the equation of opportunity. And while each of these teachers is unique, their teaching holds certain elements in common. After years of observing and having read the work of Jim Collins, the author of the highly lauded books *Built to Last* and *Good to Great*, then I began to make a list of what it was these teachers did, focusing in particular on the techniques that separated great teachers not from weak teachers but from those who were merely good. As Collins points out, this is much more relevant and revealing than what distinguishes great from poor or mediocre performers since the findings provide a road map to excellence. Over time my list grew in both the number of topics and the level of specificity in each technique. Not every teacher I observed uses every one of these techniques, but in the aggregate, the techniques that I include in this book emerge as the tools excellent teachers use to separate themselves from the merely good. There *is* a tool box for closing the achievement gap, and I have tried to describe its contents in this book.

Let me say, with a humility that is reinforced every time I walk into the classroom of the colleagues I describe in this book, that I am no champion teacher. Far from it. My task has not been to invent the tools but to describe how others use them and what makes them work. This has meant putting names on techniques in the interest of helping to create a common vocabulary with which to analyze and discuss the classroom. But I want to be clear. What appears here is neither mine, especially, nor a theory. It is a set of field notes from observations of the work of masters some of whom you will meet in this book, and many others you will not, but whose diligence and skill informed and inspired this work.

SPECIFIC, CONCRETE, ACTIONABLE TECHNIQUES

When I was a young teacher, people gave me lots of advice. I'd go to trainings and leave with lofty words ringing in my ears. They touched on everything that had made me want to teach. "Have high expectations for your students." "Expect the most from students every day." "Teach kids, not content." I'd be inspired, ready to improve—until I got to school the next day. I'd find myself asking, "Well, how do I do that? What's the action I should take at 8:25 A.M. to demonstrate those raised expectations?"

What ultimately helped me learn to teach was when a more proficient peer told me something very concrete like, "When you want them to follow your directions, stand still. If you're walking around passing out papers, it looks like the directions are no more important than all of the other things you're doing. Show that your directions matter. Stand still. They'll respond." Over time it was this sort of concrete, specific, actionable advice, far more than reminders that I must have high expectations, that allowed me to raise expectations in my classroom.

My approach in this book reflects that experience. I have tried to describe these techniques in a concrete, specific, and actionable way that allows you to start using them tomorrow. I call these tools "techniques," not "strategies," even though the teaching profession tends to use the latter term. To me, a strategy is a generalized approach to problems, a way to inform decisions. A technique is a thing you say or do in a particular way. If you are a sprinter, your strategy might be to get out of the blocks fast and run from the front; your technique would be to incline your body forward at about five degrees as you drive your legs up and out ahead of you. If you want to be a great sprinter, practicing and refining that technique would help you achieve more than refining your strategy. After all, it's the technique that actually makes you run faster. And because a technique is an action, the more you practice it, the better you get. Mulling your decision to run from the front a hundred times doesn't make it any better, but practicing a hundred sprints with just the right body position does. This is why, in the end, focusing on honing and improving specific techniques is the fastest route to success, sometimes even if that practice comes at the expense of philosophy or strategy. My hope is that, with practice, you'll be able to walk to the front of any classroom and use *Cold Call* (technique 22 in Chapter Four) and *No Opt Out* (technique 1 in Chapter One) to hold your students accountable in a lesson with *Positive Framing* (technique 43 in Chapter Seven) and a high *Ratio* (technique 17 in Chapter Three). Mastering those techniques will be far more productive than being firm of convictions, committed to a strategy, and, in the end, beaten by the reality of what lies inside the classroom door in the toughest neighborhoods of our cities and towns.

HOW TO USE THIS BOOK

I've organized this collection of field notes from my observations of highly effective teachers as a how-to book and divided the techniques into two parts.

Part One contains nine chapters that delve into the essential techniques I observed in the classrooms of exceptional teachers, those whose results are most clearly effective in ensuring outstanding achievement among even the highest need students. These teachers include many of the champions from within Uncommon Schools, the organization where I am a managing director, and many others from top schools around the country where I have had the privilege to observe. The techniques are clustered into chapters organized into larger themes that are relevant to your teaching: raising academic and behavioral expectations, structuring lessons, creating a strong and vibrant student culture, and building character and trust.

The forty-nine techniques to which the book's subtitle refers appear in the first seven chapters. Chapters Eight and Nine discuss two other critical issues in teaching, pacing and questioning. The observations I've drawn from watching champions in these areas didn't break down quite as cleanly into techniques so the observations in these chapters aren't numbered. That said I believe you'll find them just as useful. Like all the material in this book, those chapters were derived from watching how champions do it. Part Two of the book focuses on critical skills and techniques for teaching reading.

The structure of the book allows you to pick and choose techniques in order to improve and master specific aspects of your technique one at a time and in the order that best suits your teaching. At the same time, the full array of techniques operates in synergy; using one makes another better, and the whole is greater than the sum of the parts. So I hope you will also find time to read the book through end-to-end and push yourself to refine some of the techniques you might not initially choose to focus on. Alternatively, reading the book through cover-to-cover might help you understand more clearly where you want to develop, either because you have talent and strong instincts for a group of techniques or because you wish you did.

As you consider how to use this book, I offer one preliminary reflection on developing people, including yourself. It's easy to slip into a "fixing what's wrong" mind-set, with yourself and with others whom you're developing or managing. And while mitigating someone's weaknesses, including your own, can be an effective development strategy, an alternative is to focus not on fixing what's wrong but on maximizing and leveraging strengths. This also applies to the excellent teachers I've observed in the course of my work: they too have weaknesses in their teaching, despite their often breathtaking results. What often makes them exceptionally successful are a core group of things they are exceptionally good at. It's plausible that developing what you're already good at could improve your teaching just as much, if not more, than working on your weaknesses, though even more likely is that a combination of the two would yield the best outcomes. Regardless, you might be tempted to skip a chapter because you are already good at the topic it discusses, but I encourage you to study that chapter with special attentiveness specifically *because* you are good it. A bit of refinement in your technique could be something you quickly and intuitively apply and could make you exceptional—or more exceptional. In other words, invest in your strengths, too. Maximizing them can be as or more powerful than eliminating all of your weaknesses.

WHAT'S GOOD IS WHAT WORKS

Many of the techniques you will read about in this book may at first seem mundane, unremarkable, even disappointing. They are not always especially innovative. They are not always intellectually startling. They sometimes fail to march in step with educational theory. But remember the track record of the lowly chisel.

In practiced hands, it creates faces that emerge out of stone and are far more striking than even the most clever and ornate tool could ever be.

One of the problems with teaching is that there's a temptation to evaluate what we do in the classroom based on how clever it is, how it aligns with a larger philosophy, or even how gratifying it is to use, not necessarily how effective it is in driving student achievement. The techniques described here may not be glamorous, but they work. As a result, they yield an outcome that more than compensates for their occasionally humble appearance.

There's evidence of the effectiveness of these tools not only in the overwhelming success of the classrooms where the teachers from whom I learned them teach, but in almost every urban school. In those schools, there are usually a few classrooms where the same students who moments before were unruly and surly suddenly take their seats, pull out their notebooks, and, as if by magic, think and work like scholars. In each of those classrooms stands one teacher—an artisan whose attention to technique and execution differentiates her from most of her peers. The data on this, in the aggregate, are pretty clear. The classroom is the unit at which demonstrably higher levels of success occur in most urban schools and school systems. The successful outlier classroom is a more frequent appearance than the successful outlier school or school system, although schools and school systems control and manage far more variables that could lead to success (for example, choice of curriculum). This is because the unit at which technique varies is the classroom, and while ideally your classroom will maximize both the best strategy *and* effective technique, you alone control your technique. So no matter what the circumstances you face on the job and no matter what strategic decisions are mandated to you, you can succeed. And this, in turn, means that you must succeed.

I've given the techniques in this book names. This may seem like a gimmick at first, but it's one of the most important parts. If there was no word *democracy*, for example, it would be a thousand times harder to have and sustain a thing called "democracy." We would forever be bogged down in inefficiency—"You know that thing we talked about where everyone gets a say . . ."—at exactly the moment we needed to rise up in action. Teachers and administrators too must be able to talk about a clearly defined and shared set of ideas quickly and efficiently with colleagues in order to sustain their work. They need a shared vocabulary thorough enough to allow a comprehensive analysis of events that happen in a classroom. What we have tends to lack both specificity and consistency. I believe that names matter and are worth using. Ideally they will allow you not so much to talk about this book but to talk about your own teaching and that of your peers in efficient, specific language.

THE IRONY OF WHAT WORKS

One of the biggest ironies I hope you will take away from reading this book is that many of the tools likely to yield the strongest classroom results remain essentially beneath the notice of our theories and theorists of education. Consider one unmistakable driver of student achievement: carefully built and practiced routines for the distribution and collection of classroom materials. I often begin teacher trainings by showing a video clip of my colleague Doug McCurry, the founder of Amistad Academy in New Haven, Connecticut, and the Achievement First network of schools, both of which have a national reputation for excellence. In the clip McCurry teaches his students how to pass out papers on the first day or two of school. He takes a minute or so to explain the right way to do it (pass across rows; start on his command; only the person passing gets out of his or her seat if required; and so on). Then his students start to practice. McCurry times them with a stopwatch: "Ten seconds. Pretty good. Let's see if we can get them back out in eight." The students, by the way, are happy as can be. They love to be challenged and love to see themselves improving. They are smiling.

Inevitably there are skeptics when I show this clip. They think this isn't what teachers are supposed to be doing during classroom time. They think it's demeaning to ask students to practice banal tasks. The activity treats students like robots, they charge. It brainwashes them when it should be setting their minds free. I ask you to consider those objections in light of the following numbers, however. Assume that the average class of students passes out or back papers and materials twenty times a day and that it takes a typical class a minute and twenty seconds to do this. If McCurry's students can accomplish this task in just twenty seconds, they will save twenty minutes a day (one minute each time). They can then allocate this time to studying the causes of the Civil War or how to add fractions with unlike denominators. Now multiply that twenty minutes per day by 190 school days, and you find that McCurry has just taught his students a routine that will net him thirty-eight hundred minutes of additional instruction over the course of a school year. That's more than sixty-three hours or almost eight additional days of instruction—time for whole units on Reconstruction or coordinate geometry! Assuming that, all told, McCurry spends an hour teaching and practicing this routine, his short investment will yield a return in learning time of roughly 6,000 percent, setting his students free to engage their minds several thousand times over.

SEE IT IN ACTION

Watch Doug McCurry teach his students how to pass out papers by watching clip 13 on the "See It in Action" DVD.

Since time is a school's most precious asset, you could put it another way: McCurry has just increased his school's scarcest resource—the time it has already bought in the form of teacher salaries—by about 4 percent. He has performed a minor miracle. Then combine this manufacture of resources with the ancillary effects of having strong habits and routines: the self-fulfilling perception of orderliness it gives to the classroom; the routine's capacity to remind students over and over that in this classroom it is always about doing things, even little things, right, and then better. Now you have a potent technique, one that is common across almost every one of the highest-performing classrooms and schools I have seen. Unfortunately, this dizzyingly efficient technique—so efficient it is all but a moral imperative for teachers to use it—remains beneath the notice of the avatars of educational theory. There isn't a school of education in the country that would stoop to teach its aspiring teachers how to train their students to pass out papers, even though it is one of the most valuable things they could possibly do.

Or consider a technique, also common to high-performing teachers, called *No Opt Out* (technique 1 in Chapter One). The technique involves going back to a student who was at first unable or unwilling to provide an answer to a question and asking him to repeat the correct answer after another student in the class has provided it. You ask James what 6 times 8 is. He shrugs and says, "I don't know." You ask Jabari what 6 times 8 is. Jabari tells you it's 48 and you turn back to James: "Now you tell me, James. What's 6 times 8?" In so doing, you eliminate the incentive for James to not try. Opting out (shrugging and saying, "I don't know") now saves him no work since he will have to answer in the end anyway. It also exposes James to a simple iteration of what successful learning looks like: you get it wrong, you get it right, you keep moving. Over time, you normalize this process and ask more and more of James. The result is powerful not only for individuals but also decisive in building a classroom culture where effort replaces the disinterested shrug as the behavioral norm. To some, this technique might be scorned as demeaning, injurious to self-esteem—even though it clearly conveys exactly the opposite—an abiding respect: "I know you can." To others it might be simply too mundane to be worthy of discussion. Either way, *No Opt Out* is unlikely to find much of a place within many current training programs.

I am not writing this book to engage in a philosophical debate, however. My goal is to tell you how great teachers walk into classrooms every day in places like Newark, New Jersey; Bedford-Stuyvesant in Brooklyn; neighborhoods like Roxbury (in Boston) and Anacostia (in Washington, DC) and prepare the students they meet there to succeed. I am writing this book to tell you how you can do it too. And I am writing this book because doing this work in places like Newark, Bedford-Stuyvesant, Roxbury, and Anacostia is too important not to do. I merely offer the observation that doing the work means being willing to embrace ideas that dissent from what's orthodox, what's been taught, or even what's expected.

THE TECHNIQUES IN CONTEXT

I hope that this book helps you to harness the power of technique to make your teaching better. At the same time it's important to put these techniques in their context. They can help you achieve the highest levels of student performance, but they are not only more powerful when used in concert with four other strategic (yes, strategy after all!) approaches that drive results, they are seriously diminished without them. You might argue that these four practices describe the most effective strategic approach. Many readers are likely familiar with these ideas. If you're an effective classroom teacher you may already use them. But given that this book describes what it takes to get from good to great, I will take a moment here to digress and describe what makes classrooms good, even if for some it may seem like a review.

Teaching Assessed Standards

If you teach in an American public school, you deal with standards every day. And while most teachers make intentional reference in each lesson to the standards they are mastering, it's worth observing the difference between a teacher who plans a daily lesson and then decides which standards that lesson addresses and a teacher who decides all the standards she'll cover for the next month, breaks them up into objectives, and then decides what activity will best accomplish that day's objective. The first teacher starts with the question, "What will I do today?" The second starts with, "How will I accomplish what I need to master today?" The first question puts the teacher at risk of being distracted by the qualities of the activity: Will it be fun? Exciting? Will it allow her to use a technique she enjoys? The second question focuses the teacher on the goal: What exactly does she want her students to be able to do when the lesson is over? Both are teaching standards, but the discipline of the second approach is more likely to yield results. Great teachers plan objectives, then assessments, then activities.

Here's a good test. When the standards written on the board at the front of the room tend to retain the distinct language of state education departments (for example, "3.M.c. Students will read various genres for comprehension and understanding . . ."), it's an indication that you may be mapping standards retroactively to lesson activities. When the standards written on the board are rewritten as more specific objectives ("Students will be able to describe two characteristics of Tula's personality and find supporting evidence in the chapters we have read"), it's a likely indication that you began with the identification and adaptation of the standard. Again this is an indicator of likely success. This may be second nature to many readers, but it's far from a universal practice.

Another key to using standards effectively is locking in on how a standard is assessed: what skills, at what level of complexity, and in what formats. This is called the *assessed standard*. My Uncommon Schools colleague Paul Bambrick-Santoyo has written powerfully about the importance of understanding assessed standards. The following excerpt is from his book, *Driven by Data*:

> Most 7th grade state math standards have a standard similar to this one in New Jersey: "Understand and use . . . percents in a variety of situations" (State of New Jersey, Department of Education, 2004). With this limited guidance, math teachers are told to teach to mastery, but it's not always clear what mastery should look like. Consider these classroom assessment questions that six different 7th grade math teachers created to measure mastery of this standard:
>
> 1. What is 50% of 20?
>
> 2. What is 67% of 81?
>
> 3. Shawn got 7 correct answers on his science test out of ten possible. What percentage of questions did he answer correctly?
>
> 4. J. J. Redick was on pace to set a college basketball record in career free throw percentage. Going into the NCAA tournament in 2004, he had made 97 of 104 free throw attempts. What percentage of free throws had he made?
>
> 5. J. J. Redick was on pace to set a college basketball record in career free throw percentage. Going into the NCAA tournament in 2004, he had made 97 of 104 free throw attempts. In the first tournament game, Redick missed his first five free throws. How far did his percentage drop from right before the first game after he missed those free throws?

6. *Chris Paul and J. J. Redick were competing for the best free throw percent-
    age. Redick made 94 percent of his first 103 shots, whereas Paul made 47
    of 51 shots. (a) Which one had a better shooting percentage? (b) In the next
    game, Redick made only 2 of 10 shots, and Paul made 7 of 10 shots. What
    are their new overall shooting percentages? Who is the better shooter?
    (c) Jason argued that if J. J. and Chris each made their next 10 shots, their
    shooting percentages would go up the same amount. Is this true? Why or
    why not? Describe in detail how you arrived at your answers.*

*Note how the level of difficulty increases with each question. For the first
question, a student could understand 50 percent as one-half and determine the
answer without actually using percentages. Questions 3–6 could be considered
attempts at real world application or critical thinking, but Question 6 requires far
more critical thinking and conceptual understanding than any other question.
Despite these drastic differences, every one of the questions is standards based.
This leads to the central point. . . . Standards are meaningless until you define
how you will assess them.*

Not all teachers spend the time to learn the full detail about what they are
accountable for (and then, ideally, how to exceed it in rigor and expectations).
As a result, not all teachers are as efficient as they could be in instilling mastery
of the skills and knowledge their students need most. Again, you may well do
this already. But if you follow the techniques described in this book but fail to
align yourself carefully to assessed standards, as Paul describes, you risk moving
very decisively in the wrong direction.

Using Data

If you teach in a public school, you probably also work regularly with an assessment system that allows you to measure your students' progress in a manner
similar to state assessments but with greater frequency (several times during the
year) and then to analyze the results. Despite the proliferation of such systems,
many teachers still leave value on the table when it comes to using data to inform
their teaching.

Teachers who are most proficient at using data examine them not only to
tell them who got what right and what wrong, but why. They analyze wrong
answers for clues to students' thinking and engage in systematic action planning
as a result. They have a process for turning results into reteaching. They use data
to understand not only how to spend their time in the classroom but how to teach
better in the time they allocate to each topic. Again, this may well be something

you already do. My point in noting it here is that it is so important that if you're not doing it, you should spend as much time thinking about how you gather and use data to understand your students and your teaching as following the guidance in this book.

Higher-Level Lesson Planning

Almost every teacher writes lesson plans. Alas, for many of us, the goal is as much to satisfy reporting requirements (you have to turn in a daily lesson plan to a certain person formatted in a certain way), so we write something to describe, not design, what we'll do in class. This points out the risk of compliance-based management systems: they can force people to comply but not to excel. As you begin reading this book, it's worth observing how powerful a tool lesson planning is in the hands of the many of the teachers profiled here. Not only do the most effective teachers plan their activities, often minute by minute, but they script their questions in advance. Julie Jackson, now principal of Newark, New Jersey's, North Star Academy Elementary School but also one of the most inspiring teachers I have ever witnessed in any classroom, told me that she would use her drive to work and her walk up the stairs to her classroom to rehearse and memorize her questions for her lesson that day. The ramifications of this are far reaching. One is that, when teaching, Julie can focus on what the students are doing each moment, not what she's going to do next. Julie is famous for her radar; legend has it that there has never been a student who has done something in her classroom without Julie's seeing it. And while her innate talents have much to do with this, the fact that her lesson plan is essentially memorized allows her to focus more of her attention on exactly who's doing what. But it doesn't stop there. After she has planned her exact questions, she anticipates the wrong answers she's likely to get and the follow-up questions she'll ask if students give them.

My point is not that everyone can or should be just like Julie (many of us would like to try) but that lesson planning over and above the norm is a key driver of student achievement. As basketball coaching legend Bobby Knight once put it, "Most people have the will to win; few have the will to *prepare* to win."

Content and Rigor

Finally, the choice of rigorous material matters, and that topic too is not addressed here. I have come to recognize this issue in part through my own folly. When I first began teaching sixth- and seventh-grade English in the inner city, I thought I had to choose material that inherently "appealed" to my students. My choices were often stereotypical: novels with adolescent themes or protagonists who faced discrimination. There is a place for these types of book, and inspiring kids with stories written right at them—books written specifically for children and teens and written about people similar to themselves—is fine for a time. But in the long run, using the content you teach to take all kids, not just inner-city kids, outside their own narrow band of experience is critical. This means challenging them with ideas outside their experience. Pandering to kids by substituting lyrics for lyric poetry or referring to a corpus of movies for examples of literary devices instead of a corpus of novels is easy in the short run but insufficient in the long run.

THE ART OF USING THE TECHNIQUES

In writing this book, I acknowledge, and in fact emphasize, that the art is in the discretionary application of the techniques. I've tried to write this book to help artisans be artists, not because I think the work of teaching can be mechanized or made formulaic. There is a right and wrong time and place for every tool, and it will always fall to the unique style and vision of great teachers to apply them. That, in a word, is artistry. Great teaching is no less great because the teacher mastered specific skills systematically than is *David* a lesser reflection of Michelangelo's genius because Michelangelo mastered the grammar of the chisel before he created the statue. Given the tools here, I believe teachers will make insightful, independent decisions about how and when to use the techniques of the craft as they go about becoming masters of the art of teaching.

You'll find many of these techniques have "See It in Action" boxes. You can see the various techniques by viewing the video clips on your DVD. These clips have the potential to help you drive practical and effective classroom results. I chose these for the book because they show great teachers using specific teaching techniques that differentiate the great from the merely good. To maximize the effectiveness of these clips, I suggest you read the description of the technique, watch the DVD, and then reflect on your own practice and how you might use it. In addition to reading the teacher biographies that follow, you can also get to know these champion teachers and what they're thinking by reading the "Behind-the-Scenes Interviews" in the book's Appendix. I hope you find these teachers as inspirational as I do.

MEET SOME OF THE CHAMPIONS

Dozens of teachers informed the field notes that became this book. Some of them are colleagues I've worked with and admired for years, some are professionals I met once or twice and who welcomed me into their classrooms or shared videotapes of their teaching with me. Sometimes they came from watching gifted and driven teachers in unanticipated, impromptu moments. In watching all of these teachers, I gradually added the layers of practical guidance that I hope make this book concrete and useful.

Still, as the work is as much theirs as my own, it's important to mention a few of the most deeply influential of them by name here. If nothing else, I hope that you will be struck by how normal they are—how they go home at the end of the day to families and relationships and hobbies a lot like yours. They change the world from their humble seven hundred square feet of linoleum not because they were born with special powers but because they have nailed the details of the craft. They were determined to become artisans, and with time and practice, they are now artists.

Julie Jackson

Julie Jackson's first classroom had thirty-five students and only twenty-nine desks. As a new Teach for America corps member in Paterson, New Jersey, straight out of college, she nonetheless earned the Teacher of the Year award. My colleague Jamey Verilli, then starting North Star Academy, a new school in Newark, New Jersey, visited her classroom. He recalls watching her teach for the first time: "Every kid was working, every kid was on task. When she asked a question, she had everyone raising their hands. Plus, it was quiet. I was incredulous." As a teacher, her results were pretty incredible too: state test scores that dwarfed those of nearby schools and nationally normed gains of twenty and thirty percentiles.

Now, as the founding principal of Newark, New Jersey's, North Star Academy Elementary school, she has become a legend. She spent countless hours prepping, rehearsing possible dialogue, and writing individual notes to every student, and she elicits the same kind of dedication from her staff. Modeling dedication comes naturally to Jackson. She leaves her own two children, Amari and Nyla, at 5:25 A.M. to ride the bus with her students and is not home until 8:00 P.M. After spending time with her family, she often flips open her laptop and e-mails until late into the evening.

Bob Zimmerli

Bob Zimmerli was the first person my colleague Stacey Shells and I interviewed when founding Rochester Prep in Rochester, New York. We arranged for him to teach a sample lesson at a school he'd never been to in another city. He showed up with nothing but a pencil. Did he need to make copies? No. Did he need time to prepare? No. Would he like to be briefed on the students he would be teaching? No; he was ready. Stacey and I looked at each other and raised our eyebrows. We braced for disaster, but thirty seconds into the lesson, we knew we were hiring him. Having never met any of the children in the room, knowing he might never see them again, having no authority but his personal magnetism, he inspired them to their core. Lacing a constant patter about values like humility, respect, and diligence into a lesson on place value in which every student not only successfully mastered the objective but could recognize that success, Bob redefined teaching for me that morning. It was truly an astonishing performance, and I haven't stopped learning from him since. And this is not just my opinion. despite that fact that more than 80 percent are eligible for free or reduced price lunch, Bob's students have scored the top math results in Monroe County (Rochester, New York, plus its elite suburbs) for the past two years.

Colleen Driggs

Colleen Driggs, who hails from the tiny upstate New York town of Holland Patent, brings a bit of that small community's sense of warmth and accountability to her classroom. Colleen's is often the first classroom visitors see at Rochester Prep, and many posit the existence of a magic elixir that keeps kids engaged and focused during her reading lessons. That or she must simply be a "natural." It was only when we videotaped Colleen in action that we started to understand. In a now famous piece of training footage, we observed her make fifteen nonverbal interventions to keep individual students on task during the five or so minutes she taught a vocabulary lesson. And she did this without interrupting the content and discussion once. It was all invisible except to the student corrected. The lesson itself was rich and fascinating, and without the video, you would never realize that it is in fact relentless hard work that drives Colleen's success. The importance of this lesson—that for outstanding teachers, the root cause of success is not some gift but work ethic, diligence, and high personal standards—is impossible to underestimate.

Darryl Williams

Darryl Williams is now principal of Brighter Choice Charter School for Boys in Albany, New York, but several years ago, I walked into his third-grade class-rooms and could not take notes fast enough. I saw *No Opt Out* for the first time. Watching him take *Strong Voice* (technique 38 in Chapter Six) to a level of speci-ficity finally allowed me to write about it. His teaching in an all-boys' classroom with a 100 percent poverty rate (his school gives automatic enrollment prefer-ence to disadvantaged students) had a masculinity that was both demanding and inspiring. He called students out, but his toughness was balanced with unmis-takable love. They would walk through fire for him. Watching him praise them and watching him on the basketball court at recess, I saw that caring and strict were, as I write in *Emotional Constancy* (technique 47 in Chapter Seven), not opposite sides of the same coin, in which you choose to be one or the other, but two separate coins. We'd all met the children of families that were neither warm nor strict, but Darryl flipped that: he was both. The more he was of one, the more he was also of the other. It is not surprising that Darryl's school is now, like his classroom once was, the highest scoring in Albany.

Sultana Noormuhammad

When I was a teacher, I was a law-and-order guy—a tape-on-the-floor-and-the-legs-of-your-desk-on-the-right-piece-of-tape kind of guy. So I wasn't quite ready for my first visit to Sultana Noormuhammad's classroom at Leadership Prep Charter School in Bedford Stuyvesant Brooklyn. She was holding a microphone, and everyone was singing about math. They were dancing too—possibly about math. Her voice rang above the happy voices with an irrepressible cheer. The sense of joy (and math) was overwhelming. And then I noticed that her students were more attentive and better behaved than mine had ever been. To be clear, Sultana can and does come down as firmly as anyone else, but she's the master of engagement, of the smile as the best teaching tool, of joy because she just can't imagine any other way to be. Perhaps no other classroom has ever caused me so much (accurate) self-criticism. And here's the best part: a few years later Sultana was promoted to dean of students at Leadership Prep (she's since become a leadership fellow and is planning to start her own school), which again underscores the connection between joy and structure.

Jaimie Brillante

Jaimie Brillante is the best lesson planner I've ever worked with. Like Julie Jackson, she plans her exact questions: which students she'll call on and what she'll do if they get answers right or wrong. She teaches writing and spends a lot of time on grammar. Her artful presentation of the content—how it all works, how ideas relate, what ways the knowledge can be made systematic—results not only in outstanding student outcomes, but almost every visitor to her class remarks on the fact that they just learned a rule of grammar that they had not known before from hearing a student explain it. One of the hidden messages of this book is the power of planning, and if one teacher above all others has helped me to see how a level of planning that exceeds any I imagined can drive results, it's Jaimie.

Roberto de Leon

I first chatted with Roberto de Leon when I noticed a Baltimore Orioles jersey draped across the back of his chair in his third-grade classroom at Excellence Boys Charter School of Bedford Stuyvesant. Though we share a loyalty to the Orioles and Baltimore, I should have realized that the shirt signified something broader about Rob's teaching. Walk into his class on any given day, and you're likely to see his kids reading aloud with costumes or masks on, or just deeply in character and with their imaginations on fire. The uniform, it turns out, was just one of many props and costumes Rob uses to make reading come to life. And come to life it does, paced by Rob's stellar results (more than ninety of his students rated as proficient on the 2008 New York State assessment), Excellence was the top-rated school in all of New York City in 2008.

DEFINING WHAT WORKS

So how did I choose the teachers I studied and the schools I frequented? And what does it mean to say they were successful in closing the achievement gap? Because my primary measure was state test scores, it's worth addressing some misconceptions about their use, if only to underscore how exemplary the work of the teachers who informed this book is. (In some cases, I also used other testing instruments such as nationally normed assessments, literacy assessments like the DIBELS, and internal diagnostic tools we use at Uncommon Schools to surpass or complement the measurement range of state assessments.)

State test results are necessary but not sufficient. Without doubt there are myriad skills and a broad knowledge base that students need to master to succeed in college, and many of these things are not measured on state assessments. But also, without doubt, there is a set of core skills that is also necessary and that many, even most, students not lucky enough to be born to privilege have not mastered.

A student of mine, the bright and passionate son of a single mother with limited English, worked his way to Williams College. It was a triumph for him and his dedicated mother, who told stories of borrowing the books from a classmate in her native Haiti so she could do her homework outside a shop that left a light on in the evenings. He was the first in his family to go to college, and here he was at arguably the best liberal arts college in the country.

During a visit early in his tenure at Williams, he showed me a paper he had written on Zora Neale Hurston. He had passionately engaged the topic with strong ideas, couched in prose that at times occluded his meaning or wound itself into syntactical knots. His subject-verb agreement was imperfect. The professor's comments were to the point: the argument was hard to follow. My student, M., should take his paper to the writing lab to solve those issues, his professor advised. His comments scarcely engaged M.'s arguments about Hurston. M. had pushed himself and made huge social, monetary, and psychological sacrifices to get to Williams. Though his analysis of Hurston was insightful, he occasionally lacked the kind of skills measured on state tests (e.g., subject/verb agreement), and they kept him from producing the kind of work he was otherwise capable of. Sadly they also allowed the professor to avoid discussing the content of his argument in the same way she did for the children of privilege.

So let us assume that students need to have both kinds of skills. They need to be able to read and discuss Shakespeare, but they also need to be able to read a passage they've never seen before and effectively make sense of its meaning, structure, and craft. They need to be able to write a short paragraph giving evidence to support a conclusion. They need to be able to solve for x. Most state tests do an effective job of measuring these skills, and while students who can demonstrate them are not yet fully prepared for college, there are no students who are prepared for college who cannot demonstrate them.

It's also worth noting that the teachers who are better at teaching the skills measured on state tests are most often also the teachers who are effective at teaching broader higher-level skills. I know this because within Uncommon Schools, when we correlate the success of our students on tougher internal assessments (essay writing assessments that are far more demanding than state tests, for example), there is a strong correlation between both the teachers and students whose results show the most growth and achievement on the two types. Furthermore, our teachers who achieve the strongest results from state assessments also have the strongest results in ensuring our students' entry into and success in college. In short, student success as measured by state assessments is predictive of their success not just in getting into college but of their succeeding there.

Finally, the correlation between success on even more straightforward assessments (nationally normed test scores) and ultimate academic success should be instructive to us. I often meet educators who take it as an article of faith that basic skills work in tension with higher-order thinking. That is, when you teach students to, say, memorize their multiplication tables, you are not only failing to foster more abstract and deeper knowledge but are interfering with it. This is illogical and, interestingly, one of the tenets of American education not shared by most of the educational systems of Asia, especially those that are the highest-performing public school systems in the world. Those nations are more likely to see that foundational skills like memorizing multiplication tables enable higher-order thinking and deeper insight because they free students from having to use up their cognitive processing capacity in more basic calculations. To have the insight to observe that a more abstract principle is at work in a problem or that there is another way to solve it, you cannot be concentrating on the computation. That part has to happen with automaticity so that as much of your processing capacity as possible can remain free to reflect on what you're doing. The more proficient you are at "lower-order" skills, the more proficient you can become at higher order skills.

So what do the scores of the teachers who inspired this book look like? Since so many of the teachers I studied are part of the organization where I work, Uncommon Schools, let me start by talking about what Uncommon's results look like in the aggregate. Uncommon runs sixteen schools in Brooklyn, Newark, and the upstate cities of Rochester and Troy, New York. Our population is almost entirely minority and overwhelmingly poor (the data change constantly, but across our schools the poverty rate is 80 percent or more. In many cases it's significantly higher: as high as 98 percent). Our students are selected at random from the districts where we work, have a higher poverty rate than the districts from which we draw, and, contrary to myth, are often the least, rather than the best, prepared students in those districts (one of the major reasons parents exercise school choice is that their students are struggling and increasingly at risk in their original schools; they are moving *from* as much as *to*).

In 2009 98 percent of our students passed the New York State Math Assessment and 88 percent the New York State English Language Arts Assessment. Since our mission is to close the achievement gap, our board of directors asks us to compare ourselves to the best measure of the other side of the achievement gap: the state white average (SWA), that is, the average score of all white students in the state, a measure that exceeds the overall state average. We recognize the limitations in using this as a comparative measure, but it is the genuinely accepted measure among policy types and funders, so we use it even though, to state the obvious, race isn't poverty and many impoverished white families stand at the far side of a yawning achievement gap while many black and Hispanic families are thinking more about how to make sure it's Yale, say, for their kids and nothing less. As the figures that follow show, our schools not only outperform the districts we serve and not only outperform the average of all students in the state, but indeed outperform SWA. After a few years with our teachers, poor and minority students who come from underperforming districts surpass the performance of students of privilege. All of us who do this work know how fragile such success is and how challenging it is to sustain, so I am loathe to crow about our organization's success. That said, my abiding respect for the work our teachers do overrides my reticence here, and I observe that Uncommon's teachers have so far closed the achievement gap.

But of course the teachers who informed this book most, those at Uncommon and at similar schools like Roxbury Prep Charter School and similar groups of schools like the Knowledge Is Power Program (KIPP) and Achievement First, are not average teachers even in those gap-closing schools. They are the best among the best. So their results are even better. At Rochester Prep, the math team, led by Bob Zimmerli and Kelli Ragin, ensured that 100 percent of the sixth- and seventh-grade students were proficient, thus outperforming every district in the county, including the top suburban districts. The English language arts (ELA) team, led by Colleen Driggs, Jaimie Brillante, Patrick Pastore, and the principal at that time, Stacey Shells, not only matched the feat of 100 percent proficiency in seventh grade but managed to prepare 20 percent of students to score advanced on the test. This is the level above proficiency. For comparison, less than 1 percent of students in Rochester City School District, from which Rochester Prep drew its students just two years earlier, scored advanced. If excellence, and not just proficiency, is the bar: the Rochester Prep ELA team's results represent a twenty-fold increase. (See Figures I.1 and I.2.)

Though it's probably true in all subjects, it's especially true in ELA that sequential teams of outstanding teachers tend to achieve the most dramatic results. By sequential, I mean effective and instructionally aligned and consistent teachers who pass their classes to one another at the end of each school year. In the case of the Rochester Prep, ELA team Driggs, Pastore, Brillante, Shells, and their peers are highly aligned in terms of techniques, not only using techniques similar to those in this book but borrowing adaptations and wrinkles from one another in a virtuous cycle of improvement (for teachers) and consistency (for students). Looking at the results they posted for seventh graders, after the entire group had taught them, presents a much clearer picture of a group of teacher's capacity to close the achievement gap.

The scatter plot in Figure I.3 shows the results of every public school in New York State on the 2009 state ELA assessment while controlling for poverty rates. Every dot on the graph is a school. Each dot's position along the x-axis (horizontal) shows the percentage of students living in poverty in that school.

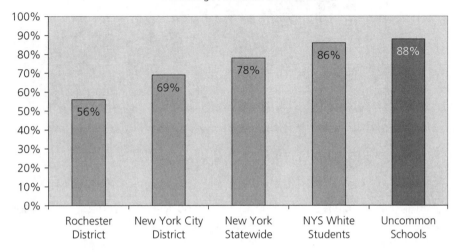

FIGURE I.1. Cumulative Results, Grades 3–8, ELA

Source: New York State Department of Education

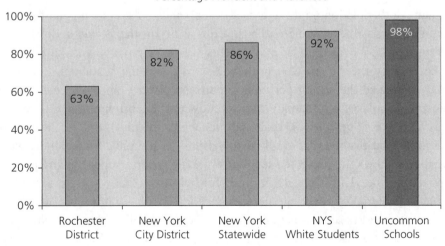

FIGURE I.2. Cumulative Results, Grades 3–8, Math

Source: New York State Department of Education

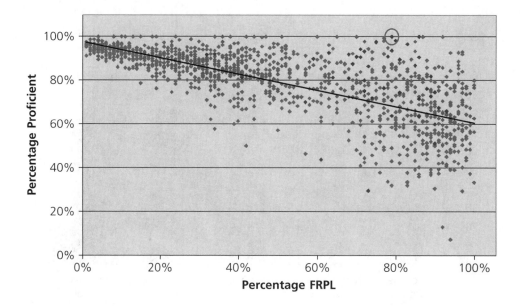

FIGURE I.3. New York State Grade 7, ELA: FRPL Versus Proficiency

Note: FRPL means free and reduced price lunch, the standard measure of poverty in the education sector.
Source: Analysis by Uncommon Schools from New York State Department of Education data.

That same dot's position on the *y*-axis (vertical) shows the percentage of students in that school scoring proficient. Thus, a dot at 50 on the *x*-axis and 50 on the *y*-axis is a school with half of its students living in poverty and half of them (not necessarily the same ones) proficient. Observing the scatter plot, you will quickly recognize the strong correlation between poverty and low performance. As poverty increases, proficiency rates go down. This correlation can be quantified using a line of best fit (the diagonal line across the plot), that is, the line that is the least total distance from all of the points on the plot. Statisticians would argue that it shows the predicted level of proficiency for a school at any point on the poverty scale. This analysis is powerful because it allows us to see a clear and accurate model of academic performance at schools with almost no students living in poverty, based on actual results of every public school in New York State. That is, it gives a much more accurate picture than SWA of the other side of the achievement gap (though it works for only a single test). Thus, on the graph, a school standing as firmly on the fortunate side of the achievement gap as possible, one with all of its students living above the poverty line, we would predict about a 96 percent proficiency rate. Rochester Prep's score of 100 percent (see the circled point) exceeds this. Great teaching, its teachers have proven, is strong enough to close the achievement gap. If you're wondering about Uncommon's other schools, our other seventh grade in 2009, Williamsburg Collegiate, scored 98.2 percent proficient and had a similar poverty rate.

PART

One

Teach Like a Champion: The Essential Techniques

CHAPTER ONE

SETTING HIGH ACADEMIC EXPECTATIONS

One consistent finding of academic research is that high expectations are the most reliable driver of high student achievement, even in students who do not have a history of successful achievement. Much of this research has been conducted to test, confirm, or debunk the famous "Pygmalion" study in which teachers were told that randomly selected groups of students had been proven through testing to be on the brink of great academic gains. Those groups of randomly selected students in fact outperformed other randomly selected groups whose teachers had not been led to expect great things, presumably because of those expectations.

One of the problems with findings about high expectations is that they often include in the definition a wide array of actions, beliefs, and operational strategies. One study defined *high expectations* as including the decision to allocate and protect more time on task in academic subjects. That's certainly good policy, but from a research standpoint, it's hard to disaggregate the effect of more time on task from expectations. It's also hard to turn that into specific action in the classroom.

So what are the concrete actionable ways that teachers who get exceptional results demonstrate high expectations? This chapter looks at five, derived from these teachers, that raise expectations and differentiate great classrooms from the merely good ones.

TECHNIQUE 1
NO OPT OUT

One consistency among champion teachers is their vigilance in maintaining the expectation that it's not okay not to try. Everybody learns in a high-performing classroom, and expectations are high even for students who don't yet have high expectations for themselves. So a method of eliminating the possibility of opting out—muttering, "I don't know," in response to a question or perhaps merely shrugging impassively in expectation that the teacher will soon leave you alone—quickly becomes a key component of the classroom culture. That's where **No Opt Out** started, though as with so many of the other techniques in this book, it soon found additional applications as a useful tool for helping earnest, striving students who are trying hard but genuinely don't know the answer. *No Opt Out* helps address both. At its core is the belief that a sequence beginning with a student unable (or unwilling) to answer a question should end with that student giving the right answer as often as possible, even if it is only to repeat the correct answer. Only then is the sequence complete.

KEY IDEA

NO OPT OUT

A sequence that begins with a student unable to answer a question should end with the student answering that question as often as possible.

In its simplest form, *No Opt Out* might look like this. It's the first day of school, and you're reviewing multiplication facts with your fifth or perhaps sixth graders. You ask Charlie what 3 times 8 is. Glancing briefly and impassively at you, Charlie mutters, "I dunno," under his breath, then sucks his teeth, and turns his head slowly to look out the window. It's a critical moment. Students all too commonly use this approach to push back on teachers when their unwillingness to try, a lack of knowledge, or a combination of the two makes them unsure or resistant. And all too often it

Reluctant students quickly come to recognize that "I don't know" is the Rosetta stone of work avoidance.

works. Reluctant students quickly come to recognize that "I don't know" is the Rosetta stone of work avoidance. Many teachers simply don't know how to respond. The result is a strong incentive for students to say, "I don't know" when asked a question. If you don't feel like working hard, those three words can save you a lot of effort. So if Charlie successfully shows you that you can't make him participate, it's going to be a long year of you gingerly (and weakly) stepping around him, of other students seeing that Charlie does what he wants, and of Charlie not learning—a lose-lose-lose situation.

If you used *No Opt Out* in this situation, you would turn to another student, Devon, and ask him that same question. Assuming he correctly answered 24, you'd now turn back to Charlie: "Now you tell me, Charlie, what's 3 times 8?" Charlie has just found—without your stopping for a time-consuming and possibly ineffective lecture—that he has to do the work anyway in your class. Later we'll look at more challenging contingencies that you may be wondering about: What if Charlie doesn't answer when you come back to him? What if Devon doesn't answer? For now, it's most important just to understand the power and necessity of coming back to a student who won't try. The moment when you circle back and ask the student to reanswer the original question is the *No Opt Out.*

No Opt Out proves to be just as powerful in situations where students are trying. Here's an example from Darryl Williams's classroom, in which a student, James, was unable to identify the subject of the sentence, "My mother was not happy." He first tried to guess: "*Happy?*" he asked. Williams persevered, repeating the question as many other teachers would do: "What's the subject?" However, as the student was still unable to answer, Williams now asked the class, "When I am asking you for the subject, what am I asking for?" The student he called on now replied, "You're asking for who or what the sentence is about." Returning to James, Williams repeated, "When I ask for the subject, I am asking for who or what the sentence is about. What's the subject?" James now answered correctly: "*Mother.*" As in all other *No Opt Outs,* the sequence began with a student unable to answer and ended with him providing the answer. The second student's answer didn't replace the original student's; it supported it. And James has seen himself succeed where just moments ago he was unable to. He has rehearsed success and practiced one of the fundamental processes of school: get it wrong; then get it right.

But let's return now to some thoughts about what you might do if things hadn't gone so well. What if James still couldn't answer, or worse, what if he had shrugged his shoulders and muttered, "I don't know," and with a bit of swagger. If James still couldn't answer, Williams might persist by asking another student, "Well, what does that mean the subject is?" The student having answered, "The subject is *mother*," Williams might then return to the original student asking him, "Okay, James, now you tell me: What's the subject of the sentence?" With only an answer to repeat, it's all but impossible for James to opt out and maintain the useful illusion that he can't answer. But in all likelihood, with any plausible gray area removed (see the box), he will answer. If he doesn't, it's a case of defiance that you can address with a consequence and an explanation: "James, you don't have to get the answers right in my class, but you will be expected to try. I'll see you here at recess."

> Much of student behavior is opportunistic and undertaken in reaction to the gray area, *"I can get away with it, so I will."* A far smaller number of students will persist in a behavior once you've made it unambiguous what you expect. Fewer still will do so when you've shown you're persistent. This is discussed further in *What to Do*.

Even more effective might be a firmer iteration of *No Opt Out* before returning to James: "Tell him again, David. What's the subject?" And then, "Let's try it again, James. What's the subject of the sentence?" Or you could repeat the answer yourself: "James, the subject of this sentence is *mother*. Now you tell me, what's the subject?" Regardless of which approach you take, the sequence ends with the original student repeating the correct answer: "The subject is *mother*."

In the case of Charlie, if Devon didn't answer and tried to mimic Charlie's impassivity, you might give the answer yourself: "Class, 3 times 8 is 24. Devon, what is it? Good. Now you, Charlie." In a minute we'll look at some of the more academically rigorous variations on *No Opt Out*. But first I want to underscore how the technique allows you to ensure that all students take responsibility for learning. It establishes a tone of student accountability, and it honors and validates students who do know the answer by allowing them to help their peers in a positive and public way.

I also want to underscore that the worst-case examples I've given above are fairly anomalous. The tone of *No Opt Out* in most classrooms is astoundingly positive and academic. Using it empowers you to cause all students to take the first step, no matter how small. It reminds them that you believe in their ability to answer. And it results in students' hearing themselves succeed and get answers right. This causes them to grow increasingly familiar with successful outcome. *No Opt Out* normalizes this process with the students who need it most.

NO OPT OUT: CLIP 1

In clip 1 on the DVD, Darryl Williams of Brighter Choice Charter School for Boys in Albany, New York, demonstrates *No Opt Out* twice. In the first instance, he calls on a student to read the word *acted*. When he isn't successful, Williams sticks with the boy, providing a cue himself until the student includes the suffix. As Williams notes, the objective for the day's lesson is to read and understand suffixes, so it's probably worth taking the time to cue the student as he does.

In the second instance, when the student is unable to read the word *performance*, Williams calls on another student and then returns to the original student: ''Read it, Jamel.'' In this case, it's not probably worth the time to break down the error as the decoding skill the student struggles with is less closely related to the day's objective. That said, Williams has still firmly established a strong accountability loop.

There are four basic formats of *No Opt Out*. I've provided examples below, with each presented as a variation of the James sequence in Williams's classroom. What's consistent across all four cases is that a sequence that begins with the student unable to answer ends with the student giving the right answer. This ensures that everyone comes along on the march to college.

- **Format 1:** You provide the answer; the student repeats the answer.

Teacher: What's the subject, James?

James: *Happy.*

Teacher: James, the subject is *mother.* Now you tell me. What's the subject?

James: The subject is *mother.*

Teacher: Good, James. The subject is *mother.*

- **Format 2:** Another student provides the answer; the initial student repeats the answer.

Teacher: What's the subject, James?

James: *Happy.*

Teacher: Who can tell James what the subject of the sentence is?

Student 2:   *Mother.*

Teacher: Good. Now you, James. What's the subject?

James: The subject is *mother.*

Teacher: Yes, the subject is *mother.*

A variation on this method is to ask the whole class, rather than one individual student, to provide the correct answer (using *Call and Response,* technique 23 in Chapter Four) and then have the initial student repeat.

Teacher: What's the subject, James?

James: *Happy.*

Teacher: On the count of two, class, tell me what the subject of the sentence is. One, two . . .

Class: *Mother!*

Teacher: What is it?

Class: *Mother!*

Teacher: James. What's the subject?

James: *Mother.*

Teacher: Good, James.

- **Format 3:** You provide a cue; your student uses it to find the answer.

Teacher: What's the subject, James?

Student 1:   *Happy.*

Teacher: James, when I ask you for the subject, I am asking for who or what the sentence is about. Now, James, see if that can help you find the subject.

James: *Mother.*

Teacher: Good, James. The subject is *mother.*

- **Format 4:** Another student provides a cue; the initial student uses it to find the answer.

Teacher: What's the subject, James?

James: *Happy.*

Teacher: Who can tell James what I am asking for when I ask for the subject?

Student 2:   You're asking for who or what the sentence is about.

Teacher: Yes, I am asking for who or what the sentence is about. James, what's the subject.

James: *Mother.*

Teacher: Good, James. The subject is *mother.*

I use the word *cue* here to mean a hint that *offers additional useful information to the student in a way that pushes him or her to follow the correct thinking process.* A hint, by contrast, could offer any information. If I ask, "Can anyone give James a hint to help him find the subject?" a student might say, "It starts with the letter *m*." This would surely help James guess the answer but doesn't teach him anything that will help him next time.

> When you ask your students to provide a cue, be sure to provide guidance as to what kind of cue would be useful. Three cues are particularly useful:
>
> - The place where the answer can be found:
>
>   "Who can tell James where he could find the answer?"
>
> - The step in the process that's required at the moment:
>
>   "Who can tell James what the first thing he should do is?"
>
> - Another name for the term that's a problem:
>
>   "Who can tell James what *denominator* means?"

So how should you go about deciding which type of *No Opt Out* to use*?* As a rule of thumb, sequences in which students use cues to answer questions are more rigorous than those in which students merely repeat answers given by others, and sequences in which students do more of the narration and intellectual work are generally preferable. At the same time, there's no way to slow down enough to cue every student in the most rigorous way toward the answer to every question that stumps somebody. You'd never get anything else done. And if you do, you risk not only losing your momentum but you allow students to co-opt the lesson by constantly feigning ignorance and cleverly taking you off task. In seeking to balance between providing cues (slow but rigorous) and providing answers (fast but more superficial), you'll probably find it helpful to go back to your objective. The closer the question you asked is to your lesson objective, the worthier of a slower and more cognitively rigorous *No Opt Out* it probably is. If it's a peripheral topic, speed through it by taking the right answer quickly from a peer, asking for a repeat of it by the original student, and moving on.

No matter what balance you strike, students in your classroom should come to expect that when they say they can't answer or when they answer incorrectly, there is a strong likelihood that they will conclude their interaction by demonstrating their responsibility and ability to identify the right answer.

TECHNIQUE 2
RIGHT IS RIGHT

Right Is Right is about the difference between partially right and all-the-way right—between pretty good and 100 percent. The job of the teacher is to set a high standard for correctness: 100 percent. The likelihood is strong that students will stop striving when they hear the word *right* (or *yes* or some other proxy), so there's a real risk to naming as right that which is not truly and completely right. When you sign off and tell a student she is right, she must not be betrayed into thinking she can do something that she cannot.

KEY IDEA

RIGHT IS RIGHT

Set and defend a high standard of correctness in your classroom.

Many teachers respond to almost-correct answers their students give in class by rounding up. That is they'll affirm the student's answer and repeat it, adding some detail of their own to make it fully correct even though the student didn't provide (and may not recognize) the differentiating factor. Imagine a student who's asked at the beginning of *Romeo and Juliet* how the Capulets and Montagues get along. "They don't like each other," the student might say, in an answer that most teachers would, I hope, want some elaboration on before they called it fully correct. "Right," the teacher might reply. "They don't like each other, and they have been feuding for generations." But of course the student hadn't included the additional detail. That's the "rounding up." Sometimes the teacher will even give the student credit for the rounding up as if the student said what he did not and what she merely wished he'd said, as in, "Right, what Kiley said was that they don't like each other and have been feuding. Good work, Kiley." Either way, the teacher has set a low standard for correctness and explicitly told the class that they can be right even when they are not. Just as important, she has crowded out students' own thinking, doing cognitive work that students could do themselves (e.g., "So, is this a recent thing? A temporary thing? Who can build on Kiley's answer?").

When answers are almost correct, it's important to tell students that they're almost there, that you like what they've done so far, that they're closing in on the right answer, that they've done some good work or made a great start. You can repeat a student's answer back to him so he can listen for what's missing and further correct—for example, "You said the Capulets and the Montagues didn't get along." Or you can wait or prod or encourage or cajole in other ways to tell students what still needs doing, ask who can help get the class all the way there until you get students all the way to a version of right that's rigorous enough to be college prep: "Kiley, you said the Capulets and the Montagues didn't get along. Does that really capture their relationship? Does that sound like what they'd say about each other?"

In holding out for right, you set the expectation that the questions you ask and their answers truly matter. You show that you believe your students are capable of getting answers as right as students anywhere else. You show the difference between the facile and the scholarly. This faith in the quality of a right answer sends a powerful message to your students that will guide them long after they have left your classroom.

SEE IT IN ACTION: CLIP 2

RIGHT IS RIGHT

In clip 2 on the DVD, Annette Riffle of North Star Academy demonstrates *Right Is Right*. She calls on a student to explain how the rules for ordered pairs on a coordinate grid work—that the x coordinate always come first. The student notes that the "x-axis has to come first and then the y-axis." Most teachers would call this answer correct, but Riffle insists on the student being all the way right and calling them the "x and y coordinates." She has the student integrate the correct terms into her answer by reanswering.

This clip also shows the power of technique 32, *SLANT* (introduced in Chapter Five), as the student tracks the speaker during her answer.

Over the years I've witnessed teachers struggle to defend right answers. In one visit to a fifth-grade classroom, a teacher asked her students to define *peninsula*. One student raised his hand and offered this definition: "It's like, where the water indents into the land." "Right," his teacher replied, trying to reinforce participation since so few hands had gone up. Then she added, "Well, except that a peninsula is where land indents into water, which is a little different." Her reward to the student for his effort was to provide him with misinformation. A peninsula, he heard, is pretty much "where the water indents into the land" but different on some arcane point he need not really recall. Meanwhile, it's a safe bet that the students with whom he will compete for a seat in college are not learning to conflate bays and peninsulas.

A better response might have been, "A bay is what you call it when water indents into land. But a peninsula is a land formation. Who can tell me what a peninsula is?" with the sequence ending with the kind of definition students get when their teachers believe they are going to college: "A peninsula is a formation where land is surrounded on three sides by water. Write that down in your notes, please. A peninsula is a formation where land is surrounded on three sides by water."

Though as teachers we are the defenders of right answers, of the standards of correctness, there are in fact four ways in which we are at risk of slipping in holding out for right and thus four categories within the *Right Is Right* technique:

1. **Hold out for all the way.** Great teachers praise students for their effort but never confuse effort with mastery. A right answer includes the negative sign if a negative sign is warranted. There no such thing as "Right! Except you need a negative sign." When you ask for the definition of a noun and get "a person, place, or thing," don't do students the disservice of overlooking the fact that the answer is incomplete: a noun is a person, place, thing, or idea.

Simple, positive language to express your appreciation for what a student has done *and* your expectation that he or she will now march the last few yards is often the best way to address such a situation and retain positive tone in your classroom. Here are some phrases to do that:

- "I like what you've done. Can you get us the rest of the way?"
- "We're almost there. Can you find the last piece?"
- "I like most of that . . ."

- "Can you develop that further?"
- "Okay, but, there's a bit more to it than that."
- "Kim just knocked a base hit. Who can bring her home?"

Another effective response is to repeat the student's words back to him or her, placing emphasis on incomplete parts if necessary:

- "A peninsula is *water* indenting into *land*?"
- "You just said that a noun is a person, place, or thing . . ."
- "You just said that a noun is a person, place, or thing, but *freedom* is a noun, and it's not exactly any of those three."
- "You just said that first you would solve the exponent and then you'd solve what's in parentheses."

2. **Answer the question.** Students learn quickly in school that when you don't know the right answer to a question, you can usually get by if you answer a different one, especially if you say something true and heartfelt about the wider world. Can't identify the setting in the story? Offer an observation about the theme of injustice in the novel instead: "This reminds me of something from my neighborhood." Most teachers can't pass up a student's taking on issues of justice and fairness, even if what they asked about was the setting. Over time, students come to recognize this.

If you're a Right Is Right *teacher, though, you know that the "right" answer to any question other than the one you asked is wrong.*

If you're a *Right Is Right* teacher, though, you know that the "right" answer to any question other than the one you asked is wrong and you'll insist that the student answer the question you asked, not the one she wished you asked or what she confused it for. You might respond with something like, "We'll talk about that in a few minutes, Daniella. Right now I want to know about the setting."

Another situation in which students answer a question other than the one you asked is when they conflate different types of information about a topic. For example, you ask for a definition ("Who can tell me what a compound word is?"), and a student replies with an example ("*Eyeball* is a compound word!"). Or alternatively, you ask them to describe a concept ("When we refer to the area of a figure, what are we talking about? Who can tell me what area is?") and a student replies with a formula to solve for the concept ("Length times width"). In the thick of the action, it's easy to miss that these are right answers but to the wrong question. And as you begin to listen for them, you'll find these kinds of exchanges far more common than you might expect.

If you ask students for a definition and get an example, try saying, "Kim, that's an example. I want the definition." After all, knowing the difference between an example and a definition matters.

3. **Right answer, right time.** Students sometimes want to show you how smart they are by getting ahead of your questions, but it's risky to accept answers out of sequence. For example, when you are teaching students the series of steps needed to solve a problem and a student you call on to provide step 3 gives the whole answer, you have a problem. Accepting her answer before you've shown all the steps required deprives the rest of your students of a full understanding of the process. It's tempting to think that it's a good thing that the class is moving ahead quickly, but it's not. It's one student. And besides, teaching a replicable, repeatable process is more important than teaching the answer to this problem. So it cheats the class if you respond favorably to one student's desire to move to the end. Instead, consider responding with something like, "My question wasn't about the solution to the problem. It was about what we do next. What *do* we do next?"

Alternatively, if you are asking what motivates a character's actions at the beginning of a chapter, you might prepare to resist accepting or engaging an answer that discusses—even very insightfully—the more dramatic events that conclude the chapter, especially if the point of the discussion of the first part is to better understand the ending when you get there. If it was really possible to jump ahead to the end and still understand the topic of the lesson, you might ask yourself why you were teaching the first part anyway! The answer, of course, is probably that the first part is important. This argues for protecting the integrity of your lesson by not jumping ahead to engage an exciting "right" answer at the wrong time.

4. **Use technical vocabulary.** Good teachers get students to develop effective right answers using terms they are already comfortable with: "Volume is the amount space something takes up." Great teachers get them to use precise technical vocabulary: "Volume is the cubic units of space an object occupies." This response expands student vocabularies and builds comfort with the terms students will need when they compete in college.

RIGHT IS RIGHT

In clip 3 on the DVD, Jason Armstrong, a math teacher at Boston's Roxbury Prep Charter School, models *Right Is Right.* In this lesson, he demonstrates three of the subtechniques in the first two minutes of his lesson with a group of sixth graders. It's hard not to notice how his use of the techniques ratchets up the level of academic expectation quickly and decisively:

Armstrong: We're going to do a couple of things with volume today. Then we're going to practice volume and then surface area. Can someone give me a definition for volume to get us started? Mark?

Mark: Volume is length times width times height.

Armstrong: You're telling me how we're going to solve for volume. If you say "length times width times height," you're giving me a calculation. What I want to know—and you probably know this too, Mark—is what volume is [a perfect example of answer my question]. What is that amount? Yeritza?

Yeritza: Volume is the amount of square cubes that takes up something.

Armstrong: Okay, but I want to refine what you said—"the amount of cubes." What should we say? What's the technical definition instead of just cubes? What were you going to say, Wes?

Wes: The amount of cubic inches that a rectangular prism or a three-dimensional figure takes up.

Armstrong: Right, any three-dimensional figure. But I don't want to just say cubic inches because it's not necessarily inches. It could be feet; it could be centimeters; it could be yards . . . [Classic all the way right here. So many teachers would have accepted these answers.]

Wes: Cubic units.

Armstrong: [writing on the overhead] So the amount of cubic units that an object takes up . . . and, Donte, I know you know the other word. What's the other word for takes up?

Donte: Occupies.

Armstrong: Yes. *Occupies.* Volume is the amount of cubic units that an object occupies. [He caps it off by stressing the technical vocabulary, *occupies.* Is it any wonder Armstrong's students are among the top-scoring math students in the state of Massachusetts?]

TECHNIQUE 3
STRETCH IT

When students finally get an answer all the way right, there's a temptation, often justified, to respond by saying "good" or "yes" or by repeating the right answer, and that's that. Just as often, though, the learning can and should continue after a correct answer has been given. So it's great to remember to respond, as many of champion teachers do, to right answers by asking students to answer a different or tougher question or by using questioning to make sure that a right answer is repeatable, that is, the student knows how to get similar right answers again and again. The technique of rewarding right answers with more questions is called **Stretch It**.

KEY IDEA

STRETCH IT

The sequence of learning does not end with a right answer; reward right answers with follow-up questions that extend knowledge and test for reliability. This technique is especially important for differentiating instruction.

This technique yields two primary benefits. First, by using *Stretch It* to check for replicable understanding, you avoid falsely concluding that reliable mastery of material has been achieved without eliminating the possibility that luck, coincidence, or partial mastery led to a right answer to the question asked. Second, when students have indeed mastered parts of an idea, using *Stretch It* lets you give them exciting ways to push ahead, applying their knowledge in new settings, thinking on their feet, and tackling harder questions. This keeps them engaged and sends the message that the reward for achievement is more knowledge.

> *Asking frequent, targeted, rigorous questions of students as they demonstrate mastery is a powerful and much simpler tool for differentiating.*

Incidentally, this also helps you solve one of the thorniest classroom challenges: differentiating instruction to students of different skill levels. We're sometimes socialized to think we have to break students up into different instructional groups to differentiate, giving them different activities and simultaneously forcing ourselves to manage an overwhelming amount of complexity. Students are rewarded with a degree of freedom that's as likely to yield discussions of last night's episode of *American Idol* as it is higher-order discussions of content. Asking frequent, targeted, rigorous questions of students as they demonstrate mastery is a powerful and much simpler tool for differentiating. By tailoring questions to individual students, you can meet students where they are and push them in a way that's directly responsive to what they've shown they can already do.

There are several specific types of *Stretch It* questions that are especially effective:

• **Ask *how* or *why*.** The best test of whether students can get answers right consistently is whether they can explain how they got the answer. Increasingly, state assessments ask these questions explicitly—one more reason for you to ask students to practice narrating their thinking process.

Teacher: How far is it from Durango to Pueblo?

Student: Six hundred miles

Teacher: How'd you get that?

Student: By measuring three inches on the map and adding two hundred plus two hundred plus two hundred.

Teacher: How'd you know to use two hundred miles for each inch?

Student: I looked at the scale in the map key.

- **Ask for another way to answer.** Often there are multiple ways to answer a question. When students solve it one way, it's a great opportunity to make sure they can use all available methods.

Teacher: How far is it from Durango to Pueblo?

Student: Six hundred miles

Teacher: How'd you get that?

Student: By measuring three inches on the map and adding two hundred plus two hundred plus two hundred.

Teacher: Is there a simpler way than adding three times?

Student: I could have multiplied 200 times 3.

Teacher: And when you do that you'd get what?

Student: Six hundred

Teacher: Very nice. That's a better way.

- **Ask for a better word.** Students often begin framing concepts in the simplest possible language. Offering them opportunities to use more specific words, as well as new words with which they are gaining familiarity, reinforces the crucial literacy goal of developing vocabulary.

Teacher: Why did Sophie gasp, Janice?

Student: She gasped because the water was cold when she jumped in.

Teacher: Can you answer with a word different from *cold,* one that shows how cold it was?

Student: Sophie gasped because the water was freezing.

Teacher: Okay, how about using one of our vocabulary words?

Student: Sophie gasped because the water was frigid.

Teacher: Very nice.

• **Ask for evidence.** As students mature, they are increasingly asked to build and defend their conclusions and support opinions from among multiple possible answers. This is especially the case in the humanities. Who's to say what the theme of the novel is, or what the author intended to show in a given scene? By asking students to describe evidence that supports their conclusion, you stress the process of building and supporting sound arguments in the larger world, where right answers are not so clear. You also give yourself grounds to avoid reinforcing poor but subjective interpretations, a task that is often challenging for teachers. You don't have to say you don't agree, just ask for the proof.

Teacher: How would you describe Dr. Jones's personality? What traits is he showing?

Student: He's spiteful.

Teacher: And *spiteful* means?

Student: *Spiteful* means that he's bitter and wants to make other people unhappy.

Teacher: Okay, so read me two sentences from the story that show us that Dr. Jones is spiteful.

• **Ask students to integrate a related skill.** In the real world, questions rarely isolate a skill precisely. To prepare students for that, try responding to mastery of one skill by asking students to integrate the skill with others recently mastered:

Teacher: Who can use the word *stride* in a sentence?

Student: "I stride down the street."

Teacher: Can you add some detail to show more about what *stride* means?

Student: "I stride down the street to buy some candy at the store."

Teacher: Can you add an adjective to modify *street*?

Student: "I stride down the wide street to buy some candy at the store."

Teacher: Good, now can you add a compound subject to your sentence?

Student: "My brother and I stride down the wide street to buy some candy at the store."

Teacher: And can you put that in the past tense?

Student: "My brother and I strode down the wide street to buy some candy at the store."

Teacher: Those were very challenging questions Charles, and look how well you handled them!

- **Ask students to apply the same skill in a new setting.** Once students have mastered a skill, consider asking them to apply it in a new or more challenging setting:

Teacher: So what's the setting of our story?

Student: The setting is in a town called Sangerville in the recent past.

Teacher: Good. I notice that you remembered both parts of setting. Can you remember the setting of *Fantastic Mr. Fox* then?

Student: It was on a farm in the recent past.

Teacher: How do you know it was the recent past?

Student: They had tractors.

Teacher: Good. But what about movies? Do movies have a setting?

Student: Yes.

Teacher: Great. I'll tell you a setting and you see if you can tell me the movie.

SEE IT IN ACTION: CLIP 4

RIGHT IS RIGHT AND STRETCH IT

In clip 4 on the DVD, Leah Bromley of North Star Academy demonstrates *Right Is Right* and *Stretch It*. Asked to draw a conclusion from a set of data comparing slope with stream depth, a student in Bromley's class replies: "The different slope affects how deep the stream is." Bromley notes that the answer is pretty close to correct but still holds out for more: "I need somebody who can make that more specific." To be right in her class, students have to explain what the effect is: "The steeper the slope, the deeper the stream is."

Now that she's gotten her class to a fully "right" answer, Leah begins asking a series of questions to stretch her students. First, "What's the opposite of that?" a question she asks to ensure that students can apply the same relationship in reverse, and then, "Now I want someone to take this one step further and use the word *erosion.*" In this case, she asks students to upgrade with more rigorous vocabulary. Then after arguably another *Right Is Right* (in which the answer has to be more concise to be right), she asks students to *Stretch It* again and explain why.

All of this cognitive work—explaining the opposite of the phenomenon, using better vocabulary to describe it, and explaining why—all happen after she's gotten a correct answer from her students. The right answer is just the beginning.

Stretch It asks students to be on their toes: to explain their thinking or apply knowledge in new ways. Just asking a quantity of tough questions isn't necessarily sufficient. In one fifth-grade classroom, a student was asked by her teacher to use the vocabulary word *passion* in a sentence. "I have a passion for cooking," she replied. "Who else can use *passion* in a sentence?" the teacher asked. "I have a passion for basketball," answered a boy. The teacher accepted with a nod where she might have stretched. Here was an opportunity to test whether the student really understood how to use the word or was just making a rote copy of a previous example. The teacher might have asked the student to use the adjective form of *passion*. Instead, she simply asked, "Anyone else?" Four or five students methodically used the same sentence structure but replaced the object noun with some other—"I have a passion for dancing," "I have a passion for riding my bike"—making it an exercise in banal copying of a basal concept, and, ultimately, low expectations.

Think of all the ways the teacher could have used *Stretch It* with her students at an equal or lesser cost of time than the activity she chose:

- "Can you rewrite your sentence to have the same meaning but start with the word *cooking*?"

- "What's the adjective form of *passion*? Can you rewrite your sentence using *passion* in its adjective form?"

- "If Marie had a passion for cooking, what sorts of things would you expect to find in her house?"

- "What would be the difference between saying, 'I was passionate about cooking,' and saying 'I was fanatical about cooking?'"

- "What's the opposite of having a passion for something?"

TECHNIQUE 4
FORMAT MATTERS

In school, the medium is the message: to succeed, students must take their knowledge and express it in a variety of clear and effective formats to fit the demands of the situation and of society. It's not just what students say that matters but

> *The complete sentence is the battering ram that knocks down the door to college.*

how they communicate it. The complete sentence is the battering ram that knocks down the door to college. The essays required to enter college (and every paper written once there) demand fluent syntax. Conversations with potential employers require subject-verb agreement. Use **Format Matters** to prepare your students to succeed by requiring complete sentences and proficient grammar every chance you get.

Teachers who understand the importance of this technique rely on some basic format expectations:

- **Grammatical format.** Yes, you should correct slang, syntax, usage, and grammar in the classroom even if you believe the divergence from standard is acceptable, even normal, in some settings, or even if it falls within a student's dialect—or more accurately, even if you perceive it to be normal within what you perceive to be a student's dialect. In fact, you may not know how a student's family or community speaks or what it views as normal or acceptable. And there is some history of young people adopting dialects or choosing to speak in a way different from the way their parents do or wish them to.

To gloss the vast sociological discourse on what's standard, whether it's the only right form of language and even whether it is in fact correct, champion teachers accept a much more limited but practical premise: there is a language of opportunity—the code that signals preparedness and proficiency to the broadest possible audience. It's the code that shows facility with the forms of language in which work, scholarship, and business are conducted. In it, subjects and verbs agree, usage is traditional, and rules are studied and followed. If students choose to switch and use the language of opportunity selectively and only in school settings, so be it. But no matter what you tell your students about how they talk elsewhere, making the determination to prepare them to compete for jobs and seats in college by asking them to self-correct in class is one of the fastest ways to help them. There may be a time and place in which to engage them in a broader sociological discourse on dialect—under what circumstances it can be acceptable to use dialect, who determines correctness, how much subjectivity there is in that determination, what the broader implications of code switching are, and so on. Given the frequency of very real errors by students and the potential cost to them of allowing those errors to persist, find simple and minimally disruptive techniques to identify and correct errors with minimum distraction. That way you can correct consistently and seamlessly. Two simple methods are especially helpful:

- *Identify the error.* When a student makes a grammatical error merely repeat the error in an interrogative tone: "We *was* walking down the street?" "There *gots to be* eight of them?" Then allow the student to self-correct. If the student fails to self-correct, use the next method or quickly provide the correct syntax and ask him or her to repeat.

- *Begin the correction.* When a student makes a grammatical error, begin to rephrase the answer as it would sound if grammatically correct and then allow the student to complete it. In the examples above, that would mean saying, "We *were*" or "It *has* to" and leaving the student to provide the full correct answer.

- **Complete sentence format.** Strive to give students the maximum amount of practice building complete sentences on the spur of the moment. To do this, you can use one of several methods when students answer you in a fragment or a single word.

You can provide the first words of a complete sentence to show students how to begin sentences:

Teacher: James, how many tickets are there?

James: Six.

Teacher: There are . . .

James: There are six tickets in the basket.

Another method is to remind students before they start to answer, as in:

Teacher: Who can tell me in a complete sentence what the setting of the story is?

Student: The setting is the city of Los Angeles in the year 2013.

And a third is to remind students afterward with a quick and simple prompt using the lowest possible disruption, as in:

Teacher: What was the year of Caesar's birth?

Student: 100 B.C.

Teacher: Complete sentence.

Student: Julius Caesar was born in 100 B.C.

Some teachers substitute a code such as "like a scholar" to remind students to use complete sentences. As in, "Who can tell me like a scholar?"

SEE IT IN ACTION: CLIP 5

FORMAT MATTERS

In clip 5 on the DVD, Darryl Williams of Brighter Choice Charter School for Boys demonstrates *Format Matters*. In both cases, he actively reinforces the language of opportunity by correcting the phrases "It gots to be" and "It got a '–ed'." Williams uses two strategies to do so. In the first case, he "punches the error," repeating, "It *gots* to be?" as a question and causing the student to self-correct. In the second case, he provides a sentence stem, "It has...," which the student completes. In both cases, Williams is effective in keeping his transaction cost low and maintaining a neutral and nonjudgmental tone.

- **Audible format.** There's not much point of discussing answers with thirty people if only a few can hear you. If it matters enough to say in class, then it matters that everyone can hear it. Otherwise class discussion and student participation appear as afterthoughts, incidental banter. Underscore that students should be listening to their peers by insisting that their peers make themselves audible. Accepting an inaudible answer suggests that what a student said didn't matter that much.

Perhaps the most effective way to reinforce this expectation is with a quick, crisp reminder that creates the minimum distraction from the business of class. Saying "voice" to students whose voice is inaudible, for example, is preferable to a five-second disruption such as, "Maria, we can't hear you in the back of the room. Would you speak up, please?" in three ways. First, it is more efficient. In the language of business, it has a low transaction cost. It costs almost nothing in terms of a classroom's most precious commodity: time. In fact, a champion teacher can offer three or four reminders about "voice" in the time a less proficient teacher can remind one student in the style used with Maria previously.

> *Transaction cost* refers to the amount of resources it takes to execute an exchange—be it economic, verbal, or something else. Your goal is to make each necessary intervention with the least distraction from the task at hand and the least time away from what you were doing, and thus with the absolute minimum of words.

Second, merely stating "voice" as opposed to offering a long-winded expectation suggests that you don't need an explanation for why you should speak up in class. The reason is self-evident, and the reminder makes it clear that speaking up is an expectation, not a favor. Third, by telling the student what to do as opposed to what she did wrong, the teacher avoids nagging, thus preserving her relationship with students and allowing her, if necessary, to remind often enough to make the expectation predictable and thus most effective in changing behavior.

This last point deserves some amplification. Once several colleagues and I watched a teacher's lesson. Four or five times during that lesson, the teacher reminded students to speak audibly but used the term *louder* as a reminder rather than the word *voice*. Her use of *louder* seemed to emphasize a lack of something; it constantly emphasized that expectations were not being met and thus "narrated the negative," an idea you will read about in *Positive Framing* (technique 43 in Chapter Seven). "Voice," by contrast, reinforces an expectation in a quick reminder that tells students what to try to achieve. My colleagues also noted that some teachers used the term *voice* with a finesse that was not achievable with the term *louder*, for example, "Jayshon, can you use your voice to tell me how I'd find the least common multiple?" or "I need someone with voice to tell me what I need to do next!"

My colleagues and I concluded that *voice* is the gold standard when working on audible format.

- **Unit format.** In math and science class, replace "naked numbers" (those without units) with ones that are "dressed." If you ask for the area of a rectangle and a student tells you it's twelve, ask for the units, or merely note that her numbers "need some dressing up" or "look a bit underdressed."

KEY IDEA

FORMAT MATTERS

It's not just what students say that matters but how they communicate it. To succeed, students must take their knowledge and express it in the language of opportunity.

TECHNIQUE 5

WITHOUT APOLOGY

Sometimes the way we talk about expectations inadvertently lowers them. If we're not on guard, we can unwittingly apologize for teaching worthy content and even for the students themselves. You won't do this when you use **Without Apology.**

APOLOGIES FOR CONTENT

When I returned to campus my junior year after studying abroad, I got last pick of the English electives and found myself in Professor Patricia O'Neill's class on British romantic poets. I couldn't imagine anything less interesting and

considered various forms of drastic action: Change majors? Find a very powerful dean somewhere and plead pathetically in various ways? Alas, I was too
busy with the other pursuits of a distracted college student to follow through.
I thus backed in to the single most interesting and engaging class I took in
college. Professor O'Neill somehow convinced me that the well-being of the
world urgently required me to stay up late reading William Wordsworth. She
permanently changed the way I think and read. And imagine: if I'd been even
vaguely organized, I'd never have taken her class. I suspect most readers have
had a similar experience, finding the thing that seemed least interesting became
life-changing in the hands of a gifted teacher.

The lesson? There is no such thing as boring content. In the hands of a
great teacher who can find the way in, the material students need to master to
succeed and grow is exciting, interesting, and inspiring, even if as teachers we
sometimes doubt that we can make it so. And even if this doubt puts us at risk
of undercutting it: watering it down or apologizing for teaching it. There are four
primary ways we are at risk of apologizing for what we teach:

*A belief that content is boring
is a self-fulfilling prophecy.*

- **Assuming something will be
boring.** Saying something like, "Guys,
I know this is kind of dull. Let's just try
to get through it," or even, "You may
not find this all that interesting," is apol-
ogizing. Think for a minute about the presumption that your students will find
something boring, even if it is genuinely uninteresting to you. Thousands of
accountants love their job and find it fascinating, whether or not anyone else
thinks they'd like the work. Someone has awakened them to its rarified joys.
Every year thousands of students take pride and joy in diagramming sentences.
A belief that content is boring is a self-fulfilling prophecy. There are teachers
who make great and exciting and inspiring lessons out of every topic that some
other teacher may consider a grind. Our job is to find a way to make what we
teach engaging and never to assume that students can't appreciate what's not
instantly familiar to them or what does not egregiously pander to them. Doing
so suggests only a small faith in the power of education.

- **Blaming it.** A teacher who assigns the responsibility for the appearance
of content in her class to some outside entity—the administration, state officials,
or some abstract "they"—is blaming it. It sounds like this: "This material is on
the test so we'll have to learn it." "They say we have to read this so. . ." If it's
"on the test" it's also probably "part of the curriculum" (though the later is a
less emotionally charged way of thinking about it). And a better way to address

it is to assume it's part of the curriculum for a reason and start by reflecting on that rationale.

• **Making it "accessible."** Making material accessible is acceptable— preferable, even—when it means finding a way in, that is, finding a way to connect kids to rigorous college prep content; it's not so great when it dilutes the content or standards. It's okay to use a contemporary song to introduce the idea of the sonnet. It's not okay to replace sonnets with contemporary songs in your study of poetry. Here are some alternatives to apology:

- "This material is great because it's really challenging!"

- "Lots of people don't understand this until they get to college, but you'll know it now. Cool."

- "This can really help you succeed" [for example, "by helping you understand how sentences work"].

- "This gets more and more exciting as you come to understand it better."

- "We're going to have some fun as we do it."

- "A lot of people are afraid of this stuff, so after you've mastered it, you'll know more than most adults."

- "There's a great story behind this!"

Content is one of the places that teaching is most vulnerable to assumptions and stereotypes. What does it say, for example, if we assume that students won't be inspired by books written by authors of other races? Or by protagonists of different backgrounds than their own? More specifically what does it say if we are more likely to assume those things about minority students? Do we think that great novels transcend boundaries only for some kids? Consider the novelist Earnest Gaines's description of the authors who inspired him to write. Gaines, who wrote several of the most highly acclaimed novels of the twentieth century, including *Autobiography of Miss Jane Pittman, A Lesson Before Dying,* and *A Gathering of Old Men,* grew up poor in rural Louisiana on the same land his family had share-cropped for generations, He was the eldest of twelve children and was raised by his aunt—the kind of kid to whom some might ascribe a limited worldview, probably without asking, and to whom few would assign a diet of nineteenth-century Russian novelists. Yet Gaines recalls: "My early influences were . . . the Russian writers such as Tolstoy, Turgenev and Chekhov. I think I've also been influenced by Greek tragedy, but not by Ellison and any black writers. I knew very early what it was I wanted to write. I just had to find out a way to do it and the . . . writers whom I've mentioned showed me this way."

Let me say that I love Ellison, just as I love Gaines, and am not suggesting we not teach his work (to all students incidentally). But imagine the loss not just to Gaines but to all of us if the teacher who first put Turgenev in his hands and inspired the spark of genius to grow into a flame had looked at the color of his skin, assumed that Gaines wouldn't find interest in anything so foreign, and thought better of Turgenev.

APOLOGIES FOR STUDENTS

Assuming something is too hard or technical for some students is a dangerous trap. At the first school I founded, the inner-city students we enrolled learned Mandarin Chinese as their foreign language. Not only did outsiders react with shock ("You're going to teach *those kids* Chinese???"), but sometimes so did their parents ("She's not gonna sit through that"). But millions of people, most of them far poorer than our poorest student, learn Chinese every year. And in the end every student did learn Chinese, much to their and their parents' enjoyment. There's a special pleasure in exploding expectations, and many of the black and Hispanic students in the school took special pleasure in using their Chinese exactly when people around them least expected it. This offers a reminder not to assume there's a "they" who won't really "get" something, say sonnets and other traditional forms of poetry, and that it's therefore better to teach them poetry through hip-hop lyrics instead. What happens when they take Introduction to Literature in their freshman year in college and have never read a poem written before 1900? Kids respond to challenges; they require pandering only if people pander to them.

The skill of not apologizing for students is critical not only in the introduction and framing of material but in reacting to responses to it. Sticking with kids, telling *them* you're sticking with them, and constantly delivering the message, "But I know you can," raises a student's self-perception. Here are some alternatives to apologizing:

- "This is one of the things you're going to take real pride in knowing."

- "When you're in college, you can show off how much you know about . . ."

- "Don't be rattled by this. There are a few fancy words, but once you know them, you'll have this down."

- "This *is* really tricky. But I haven't seen much you couldn't do if you put your minds to it."

- "I know you can do this. So I'm going to stick with you on this question."

- "It's okay to be confused the first time through this but we're going to get it, so let's take another try."

REFLECTION AND PRACTICE

1. The chapter presented five techniques for raising academic expectations in your classroom: *No Opt Out, Right Is Right, Stretch It, Format Matters,* and *Without Apology.* Which of these will be the most intuitive for you to implement in your classroom? Which will be the toughest, and what will make it difficult?

2. There are variety of reasons that a student might opt out of answering a question you asked—for example:

   - A student is actively testing or defying you.

   - A student is trying not to stand out in the classroom.

   - A student genuinely does not know the answer.

   - A student is embarrassed to not know the answer.

   - A student didn't hear you when you asked.

   - A student didn't understand what you asked.

   See how many possible reasons for a *No Opt Out* you can add to this list. How should the breadth of possible reasons listed cause you to consider or adapt the tone with which you engage students when you use *No Opt Out?*

3. One of the keys to responding effectively to "almost right" answers—reinforcing effort but holding out for top-quality answers—is having a list of phrases you think of in advance. After reflecting on which of the following phrases most match your style as a teacher, try to write four or five of your own.

   - "I like what you've done. Can you get us the rest of the way?"

   - "We're almost there. Can you find the last piece?"

   - "I like most of that."

- "Can you develop that further?"
- "Okay, but there's a bit more to it than that."
- "Satish just knocked a base hit. Who can bring him home?"

4. Here's a list of questions you might hear asked in a classroom and the objective for the lesson in which they were asked:

   - 6 + 5 = ? *Objective:* Students will be able to master simple computations: addition, subtraction, multiplication, and division.

   - Who can use the word *achieve* in a sentence? *Objective:* Students will be able to increase their vocabulary through drills that explore the use of synonyms, antonyms, and different parts of speech.

   - What do you think is the lesson of "The Three Little Pigs"? *Objective:* Students will be able to explore the moral of the story and the genre of fables in general.

   - What is one branch of the U.S. government? *Objective:* Students will be able to understand the three branches of the U.S. government and how they relate to each other and current events.

   Try to think of ten *Stretch It* questions you might ask for the one that's closest to what you teach. (This is a great activity to do with other teachers.)

5. *Format Matters:* Next time you're observing a peer's class, guess how many times you will hear answers that are given:

   - In a single word or with a sentence fragment
   - In ungrammatical syntax
   - Inaudibly

   Then count how many times they actually occur during your observation. Was the number more or less than you expected? Why?

6. *Without Apology:* Try to imagine the most "boring" content (to you) that you could teach. Now script the first five minutes of your class in which you find a way to make it exciting and engaging to students.

CHAPTER TWO

PLANNING THAT ENSURES ACADEMIC ACHIEVEMENT

The five planning techniques in this chapter are designed to be implemented before you walk in the door of your classroom. They are a bit different from the other techniques in this book in that they are not for the most part executed live in front of students. Few people will see you do them. But they set the stage for your success once you do walk in the door so they are inexplicably linked to the rest of the techniques you'll find in this book. To state the obvious, these five specific types of planning are critical to effective teaching.

TECHNIQUE 6

BEGIN WITH THE END

When I started teaching, I would ask myself while I planned, "What am I going to do tomorrow?" The question revealed the flaws in my planning method in at least two critical ways—even without accounting for my sometimes dubious answers to the question.

The first flaw was that I was thinking about an activity for my classes on the following day, not an objective—what I wanted my students to know or be able to do by the end of the lesson. It's far better to start the other way around and begin with the end, the objective. By framing an objective first, you substitute, "What will my students understand today?" for, "What will my students do today?" The first of these questions is measurable. The second is not. The only criterion that determines the success of an activity is not whether you do it and people seem to want to do it, but whether you achieved an objective that can be assessed. Instead of thinking about an activity, perhaps, "We are reading *To Kill a Mockingbird*," framing your objective forces you to ask what your students will get out of reading the book. Will they understand and describe the nature of courage as demonstrated in *To Kill a Mockingbird*? Will they understand and describe why injustice sometimes prevails as demonstrated in *To Kill a Mockingbird*? Or perhaps they'll use *To Kill a Mockingbird* to describe how important characters are developed through their words and actions.

> *Why are you teaching the material you're teaching? What's the outcome you desire? How does this outcome relate to what you'll teach tomorrow and to what your students need to have learned to be ready for the fourth or eighth or tenth grade?*

In short, there are lots of worthwhile things you can do in class and lots of ways you can approach each of them. Your first job is to choose the rationale that is most productive: Why are you teaching the material you're teaching? What's the outcome you desire? How does this outcome relate to what you'll teach tomorrow and to what your students need to have learned to be ready for the fourth or eighth or tenth grade?

The second flaw in my question was that I was usually asking it the night before the class. Beyond the obvious procrastination that implies, it shows that I was planning my lessons singly, each lesson vaguely related to the previous perhaps, but not reflecting an intentional progression in the purpose of my lessons. Of the two flaws, this was actually the more damning. I could cure the procrastination issue by planning all of my lessons the Friday before, say, but until I began to think of my lessons as parts of a larger unit that developed ideas intentionally and incrementally toward mastery of larger concepts, I was sure to be treading water. In fact, I would have been better off planning all of my objectives (only) for the trimester in advance and then procrastinating the planning of each lesson than I would have been dutifully planning a batch of activity-driven lessons the week before.

Great lessons begin with planning, and specifically with effective *unit* planning: planning a sequence of objectives, one or possibly two for each lesson, over an extended period of time (say, six weeks). Unit planning means methodically asking how one day's lesson builds off the previous day's, prepares for the next day's, and how these three fit into a larger sequence of objectives that lead to mastery. Logically, then, it also implies that if you know you've failed to achieve full mastery of one day's objective, an objective on which tomorrow's depends, you must go back and reteach the content to ensure full mastery before moving on. To be sure of mastery, great **Begin with the End** teachers often begin lessons by circling back to anything they're not sure the class mastered the day before.

The unit planning process is followed by lesson planning, which consists of:

1. Refining and perfecting the objective based on the degree to which the objective the day before was mastered

2. Planning a short daily assessment that will effectively determine whether the objective was mastered

3. Planning the activity, or, more precisely, a sequence of activities, that lead to mastery of the objective

Using this lesson planning sequence—objective, assessment, activity—disciplines your planning. It helps ensure that your criterion will not be, "Is my lesson creative?" or "Does it employ enough of the right strategies?" but, "Will it be the best and fastest way to help me reach the goal?"

Don't underestimate how critical this is. The prevalence of flawed lesson criteria is a major issue in teaching. Teachers care about earning the respect and admiration of their peers, and when teachers praise each other for their lessons, they are as likely as not to praise an artful, clever design or the loyal use of recommended methods such as group work, whether or not they yield results. Having effective lesson criteria ("Did this lesson accomplish the goal?") allows you to constantly evaluate and refine your strategy and technique, rather than flying blind.

To sum, *Begin with the End* means:

1. Progressing from unit planning to lesson planning

2. Using a well-framed objective to define the goal of each lesson

3. Determining how you'll assess your effectiveness in reaching your goal

4. Deciding on your activity

TECHNIQUE 7
4 MS

Given the importance of objectives in bringing focus, discipline, and measurability to a lesson, it's important to think about what makes an objective useful and effective. My colleague Todd McKee artfully designed four criteria for effective objectives, the **4 Ms,** and if you're able to ensure that your objectives meet those criteria, your chances of starting with an effective goal are high.

Effective objectives should be:

- **Manageable.** An effective objective should be of a size and scope that can be taught in a single lesson. It's not that you don't want your students to master the broad, rich, deep, and critically important skill of making character inferences, for example, but setting the goal that students will learn to make strong character inferences in a single hour's practice is patently unrealistic. Actually it requires weeks to establish a firm basic mastery. You'd want to revisit it constantly thereafter to build depth and context into your students' skill and to give them lots of practice. One of the most common misconceptions about objectives is that they preclude you from talking about other things during class. Of course, you should take time to discuss how you'd make effective inferences to better understand the nature of a character in a story during your lessons working toward mastery of theme, plot, use of evidence, and so forth. In fact, doing so, and knowing that your students can do so, should reinforce your effectiveness in achieving those goals.

Knowing how fast they can master information means knowing whether you need two or three weeks to master the basic skill.

Given the importance of character inference, a key part of the process necessary to do it justice is to conceptualize in your own mind the steps necessary to achieve mastery. You will have to do different things each day so that your students will master the skill. Perhaps you'll start by identifying words and actions that provide evidence of character, then practice interpreting them singularly, then practice assembling evidence and examining multiple pieces of it at once. Or perhaps you'll want to start with inferences about simple, stock characters and work your way up to more complex, nuanced ones. Either way, it would be a mistake to use the same broad objective every day for three weeks while you "work on" the skill. You would have a much greater chance of success if you built a series of day-by-day objectives that set achievable goals for each day. Not only would you make your work more strategic, but you'd also gain a better and better sense for what your students could accomplish in a day. Knowing how fast they can master information means knowing whether you need two or three weeks to master the basic skill.

- **Measurable.** An effective objective should be written so that your success in achieving it can be measured, ideally by the end of the class period. This lets you better understand in your own mind what worked in your implementation. The best teachers take this opportunity to the next logical step: they measure every lesson with an exit ticket (a short activity, question, or set of questions that students must complete and leave with you before departing; see technique 20 in Chapter Three). Even if you don't use exit tickets, setting an explicit measurable goal beforehand helps you hold yourself accountable.

Finally, setting measurable lesson objectives disciplines you in other ways. For example, it forces you to think through key assumptions. If your goal is to have students know something or understand something or think something, how will you know they have reached it? Thoughts are not measurable unless they are described or applied. Does your lesson include that? Do your lessons rely on a balance of methods for describing or applying understanding? Furthermore, if your goal is to have students feel, think, or believe something, how appropriate is that? Is it sufficient to be able to read and understand poetry without enjoying, appreciating, or loving it? Are students accountable for learning skills that can help them make up their own minds or for accepting the judgments and tastes of others?

I am a pretty fair case study of this. Although I have a master's degree in English literature, I do not *enjoy* reading poetry. In fact I usually find it almost unreadable. I'm sorry to say (to all my fantastic professors and teachers) that I have almost never achieved the objective of loving a poem. Nevertheless, having learned to analyze and sustain arguments about poetry, and having had to critique those of others, has helped me to become a more effective thinker and writer and occasionally (very occasionally, my wife might argue) a more insightful person. So in the end, I am truly glad to have studied and read poems in my literature classes. My point is that my best teachers held themselves accountable for what they could control (the quality of my thinking and sustainability of my arguments), not what they couldn't (whether I liked reading the stuff). Even though their love for the things they taught me was probably their reason for doing the work, passing that love on to me fell into the realm of what they couldn't control and so they eschewed it as their objective even if it was their motivation—an irony, to be sure, but a useful one.

- **Made First.** An effective objective should be designed to guide the activity, not to justify how a chosen activity meets one of several viable purposes. The objective comes first. The rationale for this is described in *Begin with the End*. Be aware, however, of just how many teachers who believe they are objective driven start with an activity ("We're playing Jeopardy today!" "We're reading *I Know Why the Caged Bird Sings* today") and retrofit an objective to it. You can often tell these teachers because their objectives look like learning standards (which are different and far broader) and are occasionally written on the board undigested from state documents: "3.L.6 Students will read a variety of texts for understanding." To risk beating a dead horse, you must digest the standard into a strategic series of daily objectives to ultimately achieve its broader mastery by mastering a series of component pieces.

- **Most Important.** An effective objective should focus on what's most important on the path to college, and nothing else. It describes the next step straight up the mountain.

KEY IDEA

4MS

As my colleague Todd McKee puts it, a great lesson objective (and therefore a great lesson) should be manageable, measurable, made first, and most important on the path to college.

The following objectives fail to meet at least one of the 4M criteria:

- *Students will be able to add and subtract fractions with like and unlike denominators.* This objective isn't manageable. It contains at least four different objectives for four different days (and more likely four different weeks): adding fractions with like denominators, subtracting fractions with like denominators, adding fractions with unlike denominators, and subtracting fractions with unlike denominators. Realistically, this objective is a standard, a huge one, and the topic of a unit plan.

• *Students will be able to appreciate various forms of poetry, including sonnets and lyric poetry.* What is appreciation? How will you know whether it happened? Can students understand T. S. Eliot and not like his writing, or do they have to pretend to assimilate your tastes as well? This objective isn't measurable. It's probably not manageable either.

• *Students will view scenes from the film version of* The Crucible. This objective is an activity, not an objective. Therefore it's not made first. Showing the film version of Arthur Miller's play *The Crucible* could be a home run or a waste of time, depending on what its purpose is. Will students compare the film version of *The Crucible* to Elizabeth George Speare's *The Witch of Blackbird Pond?* If so, why? To learn what? Will they compare the portrayal of colonial witchcraft in the two stories? If so, with what purpose? For example, will students better understand Speare's perspective on witchcraft by comparing it to another contemporary story? If so, that should be described in the objective: *To better understand the author's perspective on witchcraft in colonial America by comparing her portrayal to another contemporary portrayal.*

• *Students will construct a poster to celebrate Martin Luther King Jr. Day.* This objective isn't "most important." Skill at making posters won't help put students in a position to succeed through the content of their character. Understanding Dr. King's legacy certainly is deeply important, and that understanding might even be reflected in a poster, but a champion teacher would consider poster making useful only if it was the best way to reinforce that understanding. The objective should be about Dr. King.

TECHNIQUE 8
POST IT

Once your objective is complete, **Post It** in a visible location in your room—the same location every day—so everyone who walks into the room, your students as well as peers and administrators, can identify your purpose for teaching that day in as plain English as possible.

In the case of students, posting your objective is important because they should know what they're trying to do. Awareness of this fact will help them work more intentionally toward the goal. In the example of *The Crucible*, students will watch better if they know what they're looking for. You can go a step further by making the objective part of the fabric of the classroom conversation. You can underscore its importance by asking students to discuss, review, copy, or read it, as a matter of habit, at the outset or at the conclusion of the lesson. You might even make a habit of asking your students to be able to put the objective in context, to say why it matters, to connect it to what happened yesterday, and so on.

Visitors give you feedback, and feedback is more useful when the person giving it knows what you're trying to do—if they address not just whether your teaching was "good" in some abstract sense, but whether it appeared to be getting you to your goal.

In the case of visitors, for example, your fellow teachers or your supervisor, it's important because visitors give you feedback, and feedback is more useful when the person giving it knows what you're trying to do—if they address not just whether your teaching was "good" in some abstract sense, but whether it appeared to be getting you to your goal. A visitor who thinks you should be discussing more about how the characters are developed in the *Crucible* may or may not be right. Whether you should spend more time on the development of characters depends on what your purpose is, and it's to your benefit to discipline those who help you to focus on what best accomplishes the task as well. Otherwise, their advice and evaluation of your lesson fall to idiosyncratic criteria. Your department chair observes you and says you should be emphasizing character development more because, in the end, that's what she does with the *Crucible*.

TECHNIQUE 9
SHORTEST PATH

When you can think of more than one possible activity to achieve an objective, your rule of thumb should be something like Occam's razor: "All other things being equal, the simplest explanation or strategy is the best." Opt for the most direct route from point to point, the **Shortest Path** to the goal. Eschew the complex if something less clever, less cutting-edge, less artfully constructed will yield a better result. Use what the data tell you works best, but when in doubt rely on proven, direct, trustworthy methods, especially *I*/We/*You* (see Chapter Three). This seems obvious, but in a profession where teachers for years had become accustomed to flying blind—that is, not having objective criteria with which to measure the effectiveness of their lessons—a culture of nonmastery-based criteria emerged: *How clever, how artfully designed, how enjoyable to teach, how inclusive of various state-of-the-art philosophies is the lesson?* If you listen carefully, you will hear constant implicit and explicit reference to such criteria in the discussions of teachers: "I loved your lesson; the stations were so well designed, and there was so much peer interaction." The assumption in such a statement is that both of those things are inherently positive in their own right, whether they best achieve the goal and whether they make achieving the goal take twice (or half) as long.

Again, the criterion is mastery of the objective and what gets you there best and fastest. Group work, multisensory approaches, open inquiry, Socratic seminars, discussions, and lectures are neither good nor bad for a teacher to use except in how they relate to this goal. Take the shortest path, and throw out all other criteria.

Shortest Path does not necessarily mean that the shortest path you choose is an approach sustained for forty-five minutes or an hour or an hour and twenty minutes. Champion teachers are generally inclined to make their lessons motivating by switching among a series of reliable activities with a variety of tones and paces, a method discussed more fully in the section on pacing in Chapter Eight. These can be energetic and spirited or reflective and deliberate, often within the same lesson. The terrain always changes, even on the shortest path between two points.

TECHNIQUE 10
DOUBLE PLAN

At its best, lesson planning is driven by an objective that's part of a carefully planned sequence of objectives. It determines how to assess the outcome before choosing activities to get from A to B. Good lesson planning also requires specificity. Great teachers often plan their questions, and, like Julie Jackson at North Star Academy, they memorize them on their drive to school or their walk to class. But there's a final element to effective lesson planning that's often overlooked and especially powerful: **Double Plan**.

Too often teachers forget to plan what students will be doing each step of the way. What will they be doing while you're reviewing the primary causes of the Civil War?

Most lesson plans focus on what you, the teacher, will be doing—what you'll say and explain and model, what you'll hand out and collect and assign. Too often teachers forget to plan what students will be doing each step of the way. What will they be doing while you're reviewing the primary causes of the Civil War? Will they be taking notes? If so, where? On a blank sheet of paper? On a graphic organizer you've designed? Will they then review those notes and write a quick one-sentence summary? While you "explain the difference between prime and composite numbers" what will their task be? To listen carefully? To fill in a T-chart? To try to remember three key differences? To watch and listen but respond to occasional whole-class call and response questions (for example, "Prime numbers are not *what*, class?")?

Thinking about and planning for what students will do is critical. It helps you see the lesson through their eyes and keeps them productively engaged. It helps remind you that it's important to change pace occasionally during your lesson and for students to change pace, to get to do a variety of things during a lesson—write, reflect, discuss. One way to start yourself thinking this way is to make a double plan: plan your lessons using a T-chart with "you" on one side and "them" on the other. I don't know many teachers who continue to plan this way once they've gotten in the habit (the "them" is embedded naturally in their planning), but disciplining yourself to do it is a way to focus on keeping your students actively engaged.

KEY IDEA

DOUBLE PLAN

It's as important to plan for what students will be doing during each phase of your lesson as it is to plan for what you'll be doing and saying.

TECHNIQUE 11

DRAW THE MAP

There's a final piece to effective planning that almost every teacher already uses. The problem is that teachers sometimes forget they're using it or use it once per year and then forget to adapt and adjust it. That piece is the planning and controlling of the physical environment, which should support the specific lesson goals for the day rather than using the best approach to support the most lesson on average or, worse, to support ideological beliefs about what classrooms *should* look like. I refer to it as **Draw the Map**.

Teachers in many classrooms seat their students in pods of desks that face each other because they believe that students should be socialized to interact in school. This is a general (in fact, overgeneralized) belief about the nature and philosophy of schooling. With the exception of the fact that some teachers realign desks for tests, this classroom layout often doesn't change even if critical parts of the class period involve, say, taking notes on what the teacher writes on the board. This often erodes outcomes. Though students should interact in school, the time when they are supposed to be constructing a record of key information in writing may not really be the time for that. And with desks in pods, some percentage of students must now look over their shoulders to see the information they are accountable for and then swivel to write it down in front of them. Furthermore, students now must ignore the student directly across from them to attend to the teacher behind their back. If the teacher's goal is to be attended to for much of the lesson, she has created a strong disincentive for that. The classroom layout has made the primary lesson objective harder to accomplish in deference to philosophy.

What if, rather than asking whether students should interact in school or opining that they should, a teacher with this classroom layout asked:

- *When* should students interact in school?

- *How* should students interact in school? (There are lots of ways, and it doesn't take much imagination to realize it's worthwhile to avoid conflating them.)

- *What* should the way students sit signal and incentivize about the various kinds of interactions?

- *Which kinds* of interactions support which kinds of lesson objectives?

- *What other* kinds of ways can students be socialized to interact appropriately without necessarily building the classroom around that one idea every day?

It might be that a teacher wants students facing each other only for some lessons. It might be that a teacher wants interaction for only part of the lesson. It might be that asking students to turn to one another and discuss an idea will suitably accomplish the goal at exactly the moments when interaction is warranted without structuring the classroom so that some student always have their backs to the teacher. I'm giving my own biases about classroom layout away here, but you don't have to agree with me to use the technique. *Draw the Map* means making space planning part of your lesson planning.

I am in fact a big fan of rows as the default classroom structure—specifically three paired columns of rows (see Figure 2.1), mostly because I see so many teachers I watch use it. This layout is tidy and orderly and socializes students to attend to the board and the teacher as their primary focus. It allows teachers to stand directly next to any student they want to or need to as they teach in order to check work or ensure being on task. It gives every student a place to write that is directly in line between them and what they are supposed to be writing about in most cases. Teachers who want them to interact more directly ask students to "track the speaker" (look at the person who's talking) or have them turn their chairs accordingly or have them move their desks quickly to another formation.

Regardless of the layout you use, where the aisles and alleys are is at least as important as where you put the desks. You have to be able to get anywhere in the room (preferably to within a foot of any student so you can whisper in his or her ear without leaning across anyone else) without a word—while you are teaching, in fact. Once you have to say "excuse me" to ask students to

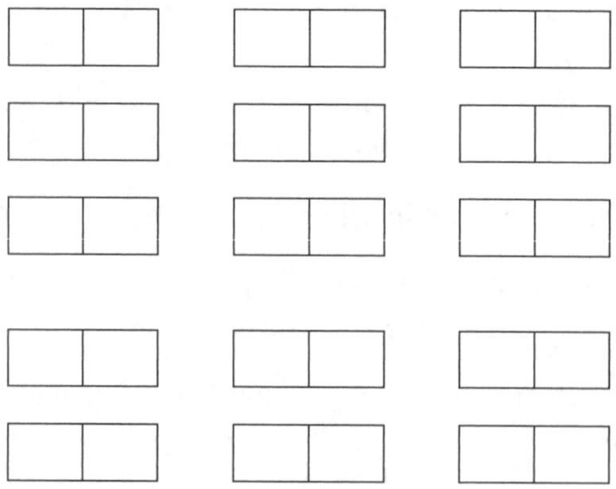

FIGURE 2.1. Paired Columns of Rows

push in a chair or resituate backpacks in order to get where you want to go, you are essentially asking permission. You have to interrupt your lesson to be where you want. You have ceded control of and full natural access to parts of the room. This will limit your ability to hold students to high behavioral and academic standards. So no matter what layout you choose, think as intentionally about aisles and alleys as about desks.

Finally, planning walls is important too. The first rule of thumb for walls in the best classrooms is that they should help, not harm. This means that they should avoid clutter and overstimulation. A few critical things should be up, and they should not distract students' attention from the primary instructional space by being too close to it. Posted items are best when they focus on useful tools: reminders of key steps in adding fractions; examples of common themes; seven types of conflict in a story; pictures representing recent vocabulary words; rules for bathroom use; phrase starters for agreeing or disagreeing with a peer during discussion. Once you've taught a key skill, posting a tool quickly after helps students review it and use it frequently. Though most teachers are frequently told to post student work, posting tools like this is at least as important.

This doesn't mean you shouldn't also post student work. You should. But be sure to post work that is both exemplary and provides a model to other students. Often there's important work to be done in making this visible. Can you make comments on posted work specific and aligned to learning goals? Can you replace writing "great job" in the margin with, "Great job starting your paragraph with a clear topic sentence," or even "Great topic sentence—clearly previews the key issue in the paragraph"? If you can, it will help make success replicable to other students.

REFLECTION AND PRACTICE

The following activities should help you think about and practice the techniques in this chapter.

1. Choose an especially large learning standard from the state in which you teach. Try to guess before you analyze it how many objectives you'd need to truly master it. Now break it up into a series of manageable, measurable objectives that flow in a logical

sequence from introduction of the idea to full mastery. Next, try to increase or decrease the number of days you have available by 20 percent. How does this change your objectives?

2. Make a building tour of your school, writing down the objectives. Score them as to whether they meet *4 Ms* criteria. Fix the ones you can, and then ask yourself where as a school you need to improve objective writing.

3. Think of a recent lesson you taught, and write out all of the actions from a student's perspective, starting in each case with an action verb: "Listened to" and "Wrote," for example. If you feel daring, ask your students if they think your agenda is accurate. Even more daring is to ask your students to make a list of what they were doing during your class.

4. Make an action plan for your classroom setup:

   a. What should your default layout be, and what would the most common other layouts look like? Will you use them enough to justify having your students practice moving from one to another?

   b. What are the five most useful and important things you could put on the walls to help students do their work? Are they up?

   c. What things are on your walls that don't need to be? Nominate five to take down.

CHAPTER THREE

STRUCTURING AND DELIVERING YOUR LESSONS

There's a consistent progression to the lessons of the champion teachers who informed this book. It's best described as "I/We/You." (As far as I know, Doug McCurry, founder of Amistad Academy Charter School, coined this phrase. Others use the terms *direct instruction, guided practice,* and *independent practice* to describe what McCurry means.) This name refers to a lesson in which responsibility for knowing and being able to do is gradually released from teacher to student. It means beginning with "I" by delivering key information or modeling the process you want your students to learn as directly as possible, then walking your students through examples or applications. In the "We" step, you first ask for help from students at key moments and then gradually allow them to complete examples with less and less assistance on more and more of the task. Finally, in the "You" step, you provide students the opportunity to practice doing the work on their own, giving them multiple opportunities to practice. Put another way, I/We/You is actually a five-step process:

Step	Lesson Segment	Who's Got the Football?	Typical Statement
1	I	I do.	"The first step to adding fractions with unlike denominators is to make the denominators equal."
2	We	I do; you help.	"Okay, now let's try it. How did we say we were going to make our denominators equal, Martin?"
3	We	You do; I help.	"Okay, Camilla, you take us through this. What's the first thing I should do?"
4	You	You do . . .	"Now that we've solved this example, try one on your own."
5	You	And do . . . and do . . . and do.	"Great, we're starting to get this. There are five more in your packet. Take six minutes and see how many you can get exactly right. Go!"

Note that the shift from one step to the next happens as soon as, but not before, students are ready to succeed given the additional independence. It's not necessarily better to get to the We and the You as fast as you can. Getting there too soon will slow you down in the long run.

The recipe may sound obvious to some, but it doesn't happen this way in many classrooms. Often students are released to independent work before they are ready to do so effectively. They are asked to solve a problem before they know how to do it on their own. They're asked to infer the best solution by "inquiry" when they have little hope of doing so in an effective and efficient way. In many cases, they independently and industriously practice doing a task the wrong way. They reflect on "big questions" before they know enough to do so productively. In other classrooms, by contrast, students get very good at watching their teacher demonstrate mastery without ever learning to do it on their own. There's lots of hard work going on, but it's all done by the grown-ups. The answer, of course, is not to choose between the poles of direct instruction and independent thinking but to progress from one to the other.

Staging that progression is tricky work, though, and the key factors in designing an effective I/We/You lesson are not only the manner and sequence in which the cognitive work is released to students, but also the rate at which the cognitive work is released. This last part requires you to check frequently for understanding, a topic discussed in this chapter at some length.

I/WE/YOU: AN OVERVIEW

I Techniques

- Technique 12—*The Hook:* When necessary, use a short, engaging introduction to excite students about learning.

- Technique 13—*Name the Steps:* When possible, give students solution tools—specific steps by which to work or solve problems of the type you're presenting. This often involves breaking down a complex task into specific steps.

- Technique 14—*Board = Paper:* Model for students how to track the information they need to retain from your lessons; ensure that they have an exact copy of what they need.

- Technique 15—*Circulate:* Move around the classroom to engage and hold students accountable.

Additional Thoughts About Good "I"

- Include both modeling (showing how to do something) and explanation (telling how to do something).

- Include student interaction even though you're driving. (You can still ask questions and engage in dialogue with students during "I.")

- Anticipate: "I knew I was becoming a teacher," champion teacher Kate Murray of Boston told me, "when I started being able to know in advance what my kids would do wrong, what the common mistakes would be. I realized I could plan for that. I could tell them what was going to confuse them before they got there, so they would be alert to the danger. I could keep them from getting tripped up or at least help them to recognize when it started to happen. From then on, my planning process included a 'what could go wrong' conversation with myself. And I planned to preteach what I knew would be the pitfalls. I put that right into my lesson plans." Amen.

"We" Techniques

- Technique 16—*Break It Down:* One of the best ways to present material again is to respond to a lack of clear student understanding by breaking a problematic idea down into component parts.

- Technique 17—*Ratio:* The goal of "we" is to push more and more of the cognitive work out to students. Feigned ignorance—"Did I get that right, you guys?" "Wait a minute, I can't remember what's next!"—and unbundling—breaking one question up into several—can be especially useful.

- Technique 18—*Check for Understanding:* Used to determine when and whether students are ready for more responsibility and when they need material presented again.

"You" Techniques

- Technique 19—*At Bats*

- Technique 20—*Exit Ticket*

- Technique 21—*Take a Stand*

Some Thoughts on Effective "You"

- Repetition matters. Students need to practice over and over. Some of them learn the skill for good the third time they do it right; some of them learn it the tenth time. Very few of them learn it the first or second.

- Go until they can do it on their own. By the end of independent practice, students should be able to solve problems to the standard they'll be accountable for, entirely on their own.

- Use multiple variations and formats. Students should be able to solve questions in multiple formats and a significant number of plausible variations and variables.

- Grab opportunities for enrichment and differentiation. As some students demonstrate mastery faster than others, be sure to have bonus problems ready for them to push them to the next level.

TECHNIQUE 12
THE HOOK

If you can introduce material in a way that inspires and excites and can get your students to take the first step willingly, then there is no content about which you cannot engender excitement, engagement, and deep learning among your students. The way in is with **The Hook**: a short introductory moment that captures what's interesting and engaging about the material and puts it out front. It can be a brief story, a riddle, a picture of the thing you'll be discussing in class. It brings Gregor Mendel's pea plants to life and makes Newton's second law of motion seem like the most important thing in the world. *The Hook* is not a plan to water down material; rather, it prepares students to be brought up to the material. It's not a lesson-long dog-and-pony show, not an hour of circumventing *Romeo and Juliet* to make it "contemporary" but the five minutes that will open the doors of Elizabethan drama. You may not need *The Hook* for every lesson, and you shouldn't confuse length in time with effectiveness: a ten-second hook can suffice as well or better than a three-minute hook.

> The way in is with **The Hook**: the short introductory moment that captures what's interesting and engaging about the material and puts it out front.

After watching dozens of teachers hook their students on every kind of content under the sun, I've broken the types of hooks into the following rough categories, with the understanding that there are almost assuredly a thousand brilliant ideas for hook that don't fit any of the categories:

- *Story.* Tell a quick and engaging story that leads directly to the material. Bob Zimmerli introduces long division with a story about a group of kids staying home without their parents and babysitting for themselves. The long division sign is the house, and they huddle by the door as numbers approach and knock from the position of the divisor. The key moment (whether to open the door) turns on the rules of divisibility.

- *Analogy.* Offer an interesting and useful analogy that connects to students' lives, for example, as I recently observed a teacher do, comparing single replacement bonds in chemistry to dancers choosing partners at the school dance.

- *Prop.* You can jazz up one of the other styles of prop with a good prop: a jacket like the one the main character in the story might have worn (or couldn't have worn: "Who can tell me why?!"); a globe and a flashlight to demonstrate the earth's rotation.

- *Media.* A picture or a piece of music or video (*very* short) can enhance your hook when planned carefully to support and not distract from your objective. Or assume the role of a someone from the book or from history. Use this cautiously as well. It too can be distracting and you can easily get carried away and waste time if you're not disciplined!

- *Status.* Describe something great: great work by a student, the reasons that Shakespeare is so highly regarded. Or mention that today you'll begin reading the works of "the author many believe is the greatest of his generation," or "the greatest to write about war," or "the greatest to write about love and relationships," or "to write in the English language."

- *Challenge.* Give students a very difficult task, and let them try to accomplish it. ("See if you can translate this line from Shakespeare into plain English!") (An example follows.) If you can't think of anything especially clever, a good game of *Pepper* (technique 24 in Chapter Four) is great challenge and works perfectly. In fact, at several schools, teachers use *Pepper* as their default if a more distinctive hook can't be found.

Here are two examples:

- On a recent September morning, Jaimie Brillante asked her students who knew what a complete sentence was. All raised their hands. Great, she said and gave them five words, asking them to take two minutes to make a sentence out of them, encouraging them to try to make the best sentence possible. As it turned out, the five words couldn't be made into a complete sentence. After a few minutes of wrestling with the brainteaser, Jaimie asked them to figure out what's missing. The answer? A subject. The surprise of the unsolvable riddle hooked her students for the hour to come.

- When Bob Zimmerli teaches place value to his fifth graders, he weaves a story about a hypothetical friend of his named "Deci" though his lesson. The houses on the right side of Deci's house are named tenths, hundredths, and thousandths; those on the left side are ones, tens, and hundreds. There's a story about Deci walking down the block to get to a burger joint and passing the different houses on hundreds and thousands street, saying the names aloud as he goes. Before they know they're learning math, his students are rapt.

Like these examples, a good hook typically has the following characteristics:

- *It's short.* It's the introduction, not the lesson, and it engages students in a few minutes.

- *It yields.* Once the ship is under sail, it quickly gives way to more the teaching part of the lesson.

- *It's energetic and optimistic.* It dwells on what's great about Shakespeare, for example, not what's hard or daunting or difficult, unless that's what's great.

A final thought on *The Hook:* you don't need one for every lesson. Colleen Driggs likes to use *The Hook* on the first lesson on a given topic. As she proceeds through the often three or four subsequent lessons with objectives that develop and advance understanding of the topic, she turns to another technique. This seems like an especially useful rule of thumb.

TECHNIQUE 13
NAME THE STEPS

Why is it that the best coaches often rise from the ranks of the almost- or not-so-great athletes, while the most gifted athletes rarely make the best coaches? Why is it that brilliant and sophisticated actors can't help others do something similar and are so often at a loss to describe how they do what they do? Meanwhile, unheralded thespians manage to unlock world-class talent in others?

One cause may be this: superstars often don't have to pay meticulous attention to the what's-next and how-to of each step. The very thing that makes them brilliant, an intuitive and lightning-quick understanding of how to handle a given problem on the stage or the court or the field, keeps the most talented from recognizing how the rest of us, for whom the intuition does not come quick as silver, learn. The rest of us, who cannot see it once and then do it ourselves beginning to end, are more likely to take complex tasks and break them down into manageable steps. We move piecemeal toward mastery and need to remind ourselves over and over what step comes next.

We move piecemeal toward mastery and need to remind ourselves over and over what step comes next.

One of my soccer coaches had been an all-world superstar as a player. As coach, he'd stand on the sidelines and shout, "Defense, you guys! Defense!!" We were pretty aware that we were on defense, though, and also pretty aware we weren't playing it especially well. He coached by offering pointers "Don't tackle there, Doug!" When I started to play for another coach I realized how a coach might also be a teacher. The other coach broke defense down into a series of steps: First, position yourself increasingly closer to your man as he gets closer to the player with the ball. Second, deny the ball if and only if you are certain you can intercept. Third, prevent your man from turning if he is facing away from the goal. Fourth, steer your man toward the sidelines if he has the ball and has turned. Fifth, tackle if you must. Sixth, otherwise keep position between him and the goal.

He focused his coaching (before the game rather than during!) on reminding us what step came next. If my man got the ball, he would gently remind me, "Don't let him turn." If I let him turn (I usually did), he would say, "Take him wide." If, as was often the case, I found myself unsuccessful, he would say, "If you must . . . ," a reminder that keeping my position between the player and the goal was more important than winning the ball. For years after I stopped playing for him I'd recall his steps ("If you must") while I played. Once I asked the second coach how he thought to teach the way he did. His reply was revealing: "That was the only way I could learn it."

If you are teaching in your area of skill and passion, you likely have more intuition (natural or learned) than your students do, and you can help them succeed by subdividing complex skills into component tasks and building knowledge up systematically. Champion teachers **Name the Steps** by habit (knowing how to do this is perhaps their superstar intuition). They traffic in recipes: the five steps to combining sentences with the same subject, the four steps to regrouping, the six parts of a great literary response. Their students learn the steps, refer to the map they provide as they are developing competence, and then leave the steps behind when they are familiar enough with the recipe to forget they are following it. Perhaps they even add their own variations and flourishes. For most, this is the path to becoming a virtuoso.

So keep in the back of your head the distinction between champion performers and champion teachers. Champion teachers help their students learn complex skills by breaking them down into manageable steps and, often, giving each step a name so that it can be easily recalled. This allows the process to take on a consistent, often story-like progression. There are not just five steps to combining sentences with the same subject, but the steps are named, given a catchy mnemonic to help students recall them in order, and posted in the classroom so they can be used and referred to over and over again.

Here are four key components, or subtechniques, that are often part of *Name the Steps* classrooms:

1. **Identify the steps.** Teaching the process makes complex skills transparent to students. For example, Kelli Ragin doesn't just teach students to round whole numbers to a given place value; she teaches them the five steps for rounding whole numbers to a given place value:

1. Underline the digit in the place you are rounding to.

2. Circle the digit to the right of the underlined digit.

3. If the circled digit is four or less, the underlined digit stays the same; if the circled digit is five or more, the underlined digit gets one more.

4. All of the digits to the left of the underlined digit stay the same.

5. All of the digits to the right of the underlined digit become zeroes.

Ragin calls the portion of the lesson where she introduces these steps her "Rules and Tools." When she names the steps, she's careful about keeping to a limited number. The reason is that people have a hard time remembering more than seven items in sequence, so having more than seven steps is a recipe for confusion. If you have too many steps to remember them clearly and easily, it's the same as having none at all. Ragin is also intentional about maintaining economy of language in her steps. As she teaches rounding, she adds wrinkles and complexity, but the part she wants her students to remember is intentionally focused and crisp.

A teacher who examines a process like the one for rounding carefully and puts them into sequential steps gives her students scaffolding. This scaffolding is powerful, and with it the students can attack any similar problem. It essentially gives them a map to refer to if they get stuck, especially if they have written the steps down in their notes, as Ragin requires. This means they'll also have the support they need to complete problems for homework no matter where they are and when they do the work. Finally, having clear and concrete steps lets Ragin post them on the walls of her classroom as a reminder. This makes the walls functional, not just decorative and motivating.

Some schools don't stop at identifying steps for specific skills; they figure out the steps implicit in broader practices and methods, such as what to do when you are stumped and can't solve a problem or what to do when you are reading and don't understand a sentence.

2. **Make them "sticky."** Once you've identified steps, name them (if possible). This is the first step to make them memorable and therefore stick in your students' minds. It's also a trick to go a step further in stickiness by creating a story or a mnemonic device around the names for you steps.

A teacher who was trying to help her students master the skill of inferring the meaning of an unfamiliar word or phrase from context clues created these steps for her students:

1. Figure out the general context of the word. What does it seem to have to do with? Words about cooking? About sports? About money? About happy things? About sad things?

2. Look for an appositive: a restatement of the word's meaning somewhere in the sentence.

3. Spot relationship words. *And, but,* and *because* tell how a word relates to other words: "I tried to stand but tumbled off the cart." "But" tells you tumbling is the opposite of standing.

In order to make this more memorable to her class so that it was as simple and easy for them to recall as possible, this teacher added a mnemonic. She simplified each step into one word and strung the first words together to make an acronym, explaining that each letter in *CAR* stands for one of the steps in solving a context clue question:

Context

Apposition

Relational words

Then to make the idea of the CAR even stickier, she made up a catchphrase: "To gather the clues, you've gotta drive the CAR!" She trained her students in a *Call and Response* (technique 23 in Chapter Four) to remind them what to do. When she called out the first half of the sentence, they'd respond with the second half:

Teacher: Looks like we need some clues here. And to gather the clues, class?!

Students: You gotta drive the CAR!!

To add to the fun and make the steps more memorable, she used lots of catchy metaphors in class. When an unfamiliar word that she wanted students to infer the meaning of appeared in the text, she might say, "Who wants to drive?!" or "I think I hear an engine running!"

In her rounding lesson, Ragin used an interesting variation on this. She recognized that the most important steps were remembering what to do if the circled digit is four or fewer or five or more. So she wrote a song to make that step especially sticky. It's sung to the tune of *Rawhide:*

Roundin', roundin', roundin', keep those numbers roundin'. Keep those numbers
    roundin'—Roundin'.

Five or more? *Kick it up!* Four or less? *Stays the same!* All the rest go to zero,
    roundin'

Roundin', roundin', roundin'.

For that extra touch of stickiness, Ragin occasionally gets out her cowboy hat when her fifth graders sing the song. After that, all she needs to do it point to it, and her kids remember what to do.

3. **Build the steps.** In designing lessons, it's essential to name steps and make them memorable. Equally as important is the understanding that designing the steps can be a key part of teaching too. A memorable lesson can be to derive the rules with students from one or several example problems through structured inquiry. For example, in her first lesson on rounding, before she's talked to her students about what to do when a series of digits carry over in sequence, as they would in 9,998 rounded to the nearest ten, Ragin gives her students a challenge problem that becomes the basis of her next lesson where she derives the steps for handling such problems. She didn't do this impromptu. The "answer" steps her students arrived at as the key to solving such problems was carefully planned in advance.

4. **Use two stairways.** Once students know the steps, classrooms can have two parallel conversations going at once: how to get an answer to the current problem and how to answer any problem like this. In other words, students can narrate the process or the problem, and the teacher switches back and forth, as in this sequence from a lesson on multiplying fractions:

Teacher: What's the next step, Paul? [process]

Paul: Multiply the numerators.

Teacher:	Okay, what are the numerators? [problem]
Paul:	The numerators are 4 and 1.
Teacher:	So the numerator in our solution is going to be? [problem]
Paul:	It's going to be 4.
Teacher:	Okay, good. So, Sasha, what do we need to do next? [process]
Sasha:	We need to multiply the denominators.
Teacher:	And the denominator is? [problem]
Sasha:	The denominator should be 2.
Teacher:	So I'm done, right Conrad? [process]
Conrad:	No, you have to reduce.
Teacher:	Perfect. So what's our final answer?" [problem]
Conrad:	The answer is 2.

You can often take advantage of this dynamic by adjusting roles, sometimes asking students to focus on explaining the process while she does the math, sometimes asking them to do the math while reminding them of the process, and sometimes doing both. Sometimes you can ask one student to concentrate on one and one student to concentrate on the other. Sometimes you can solve a problem and ask students to explain what you're doing and why. Sometimes you'll make mistakes and ask them where you went wrong or what a better way to solve would have been. In short, teaching the steps makes the process legible and easily followed in a consistent way.

TECHNIQUE 14
BOARD = PAPER

Students often have to learn how to be students as much as they need to learn content and skills, and the processes and practices of being a student also must be assimilated by modeling. This includes one of the most complex and critical aspects of being a student: learning to take notes and retain a record of one's knowledge. As a matter of habit, expecting students to make an exact replica in their notes of what you write on the board is the right starting point (hence the name of this technique: **Board = Paper**). As students grow they can begin learning to make intentional decisions about how to take notes and what to include, but that process should wait until they're totally reliable and automatic about getting what matters down right, and the best way to accomplish this goal is to start by making your overhead a mirror image of the graphic organizer you give to students to take notes on. As you fill in a blank, they fill in a blank. You fill out the projected worksheet on the board and say, "Make your paper look like mine."

Figure 3.1 shows the overhead a third-grade science teacher used during her lesson on the muscular system. Her students filled out the exact same information in hard copy at their desks, allowing her to teach them not only about muscles

The Muscular System

Your muscular system is made up of _muscles_ and _tendons_ .

Muscles _pull_ on your _bones_ to make you move.

There are two kinds of muscles in the Muscular System, _Voluntary_ and _involuntary_ muscles. You only get to choose when you move your _voluntary muscles_ .

Here are 3 examples of voluntary muscles:
Your arms
Your hands
Wiggling your nose

Here are 3 examples of involuntary muscles:
Your heart
Your eyes (blinking)
Your lungs (breathing)

There _630_ are muscles in a typical human body. Rounded to the nearest hundred that's about _600_ muscles.

Write a sentence below describing the most interesting fact about your muscular system:
When your heart beats. That's a muscle.

Re-write your sentence below adding one of the things your teacher asks you to add.
When your heart beats, it is an example of an involuntary muscle.

FIGURE 3.1.   Sample of Excellent Note-Taking

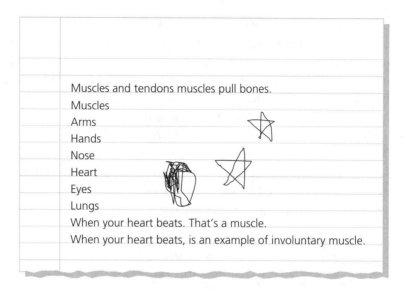

FIGURE 3.2. Student Sample to Show Poor Note-Taking

but about note taking and organizing information as well. By contrast, Figure 3.2 shows the notes a student took in another classroom where the teacher instructed students to "take careful notes on a separate sheet of paper."

Gradually students should progress in the amount of the note taking they exercise discretion over, filling out longer and longer passages of their graphic organizers on their own and finally taking notes on a separate sheet of paper as you write terms and definitions on the board exactly as you wish students to copy them down. As you introduce the skill of note taking, guide students through the process, telling them what to title their papers, when to skip a line, how to make subheadings and headings. When they can do this reliably, you can again gradually begin to divest yourself of responsibility for exact phrasing and let students own even that, but know that it may take years before students are ready to own full responsibility for such a critical piece of the process.

TECHNIQUE 15

CIRCULATE

Circulate is a technique for moving strategically around your room during all parts of your lesson. (It's not only relevant to the "I" portion, but as it's critical to think about from the outset, I'll address it here.) As a profession, we frequently talk about "proximity"—getting near students to stress accountability and eliminate behavioral problems—but teachers often expect proximity to magically work of its own accord. They know to move toward trouble but aren't always as confident in knowing how to maximize its benefits and what to do when they get there if proximity by itself proves insufficient. And of course there's a whole lot more to know about how you move around your classroom beyond just proximity:

- **Break the plane.** The "plane" of your classroom is the imaginary line that runs the length of the room, parallel to and about five feet in front of the board, usually about where the first student desks start. Many teachers are hesitant or slow to "break the plane" and move past this imaginary barrier and out among the desks and rows.

It's important, however, to try to break the plane within the first five minutes of every class. You want to make it clear to students that you own the room—that it is normal for you to go anywhere you want in the classroom at any time. Furthermore, you want to break the plane before a behavioral correction requires you to. This will show that you move where you want as a product of your decisions about teaching rather than as a product of student behavior. If you don't do these things, you risk allowing the territory beyond the plane to become the property of your students.

Just as important, when you move out into the classroom to establish proximity only when you need to (to address a behavioral situation), this action will be highly visible to all and in essence you will be telling students that things aren't going well and they've got you off your game. It also calls heightened attention to what you do when you break the plane. This will make the subtlety necessary to corrections that don't interrupt instruction (for example, via proximity) almost impossible. If instead you're constantly out and about, you'll be able to correct inconspicuously as you teach or go about what appears to be a normal routine.

- **Full access required.** Not only must you be able to break the plane, but you must have full access to the entire room. You must be able to simply and naturally stand next to any student in your room at any time and be able to get anywhere in your room easily and simply without interrupting your teaching.

Breaking the plane shows that you move where you want as a product of your decisions about teaching rather than as a product of student behavior.

This is the only way to own the room. If you can't, students will quickly establish a "no-fly zone" that they know to be safely insulated from your influence. If getting anywhere would require the shuffling and dragging aside of backpacks or the moving of multiple chairs, then ownership has already been ceded. If you have to say "excuse me" to get around chairs and backpacks and desks to reach the back corner, then you are asking permission of the students to stand in that space. This means they own it, not you. This is a price no teacher can pay. Keep your passageways wide and clear; find a better place for backpacks than on the back of chairs; seat your students in pairs so you can stand directly next to anyone at any time.

- **Engage when you circulate.** It's not enough to just stand there; you've got to work a room. If you're teaching actively (in the "I" or "We" portion of your lesson), make frequent verbal and nonverbal interventions (hands subtly on Steven's shoulders to remind him to sit up; "check your spelling" to Pamela as you gaze at her notes) as you circulate. There's nothing more awkward than a teacher walking toward a student in hopes of extinguishing a behavior only to get there and realize that proximity alone hasn't worked. Normalizing quiet, private interactions as you circulate gives you space to respond when you get there, hopefully with some of the tools described in *100 Percent, What to Do,* and *Strong Voice* (techniques 36 to 38 in Chapter Six). It's equally important to offer positive reinforcement as you circulate, again either verbally or nonverbally (thumbs up to Michael; "I like it" to Jasmine as you glance at her notes) and constructively. Finally, reading, assessing, and responding to student work as it is happening is indispensable to checking for understanding and sets a tone of accountability. Both are critical to your ability to provide academic support and rigor ("Try that one again, Charles"; "Just right, Jamel"; "You haven't shown me the third step").

- **Move systematically.** Look for opportunities to circulate systematically—that is, universally and impersonally—but unpredictably. This not only exerts accountability pressure on all students but allows you to exert pressure on the students who pose the greatest challenges for you without revealing to them that they pose a challenge. If you announce to your class, "I need everyone's eyes on me," and march directly toward Alphonse, your toughest kid, you are telling Alphonse that you are worried that he will not comply and you may not be able to control him. Alphonse may comply with that request, but inside he may be smiling, knowing that he has you rattled. Preemptively moving down each row, asking each student for his or her eyes in turn, and pausing briefly for them to meet your eyes, will ensure that you address Alphonse but you won't make your anxiety about him visible. Of course, there will also be times when he is off task and you must move right toward him, but when you are making a proactive request, do your best to treat Alphonse like just another member of the class by moving systematically.

Be aware, though, that systematic is not the same as predictable. If you always follow a predictable order of interactions as you circulate, students will know when you'll be likely to get to them and react accordingly. Avoid using the same pattern every time (left to right; clockwise around the room). Vary your pattern and skip interacting with some students (and invest heavily in time spent with others) unpredictably as you circulate.

• **Position for power.** As you circulate, your goal should be to remain facing as much of the class as possible. Then you can see what's going on around you at a glance and with minimal transaction cost. You can lift your eyes quickly from a student's paper and then return to reading in a fraction of a second. Turning your back, by contrast, invites opportunistic behavior. Think of yourself as the earth: it turns on two axes at the same time, both revolving (moving around the sun) and rotating (changing the way it faces). This may require you to consider what side of students you stand on as you circulate and to lift a student's paper off his desk and subtly reorient yourself to face more of the class as you read. Second, leverage student blind spots. The most powerful position to be in with another person is one where you can see him, he knows you can see him, and he can't see you. Standing just over a student's shoulder as you peruse his work or standing at the back of the classroom as a class discusses a topic builds subtle but pervasive control of the classroom environment in order to focus it on learning.

SEE IT IN ACTION: CLIP 6

CIRCULATE

In clip 6 on the DVD, you can see Domari Dickinson of Rochester Prep modeling *Circulate*. Notice how Dickinson interacts with her seventh graders both actively (asking them questions and offering reminders) and passively (taking work and reading it silently; using proximity).

Dickinson is also the master of the nonverbal. As she reads a student's paper, she typically stands behind the student, eliminating the distraction her own actions could provide but also keeping him in suspense by standing just over his shoulder where he can't see her but knows she's there. As she moves around the classroom, she turns to face the majority of the class while she reads so she can check on them with the simplest possible upward glance.

TECHNIQUE 16

BREAK IT DOWN

Break It Down is a critically important teaching tool, but it can be challenging to use because it is primarily a reactive strategy. You use it in response to a student error at the moment the incorrect answer happens. Most teachers recognize that when a student error occurs, simply repeating the original question is unlikely to be especially helpful unless you have reason to believe the student failed to hear you the first time. But what to do instead? As soon as they recognize an error or a guess, champion teachers conceptualize the original material as a series of smaller, simpler pieces. They then go back and ask a question or present information that bridges the part of the material that they think was most likely to have caused the error, thus building the student's knowledge back up from a point of partial understanding.

Consider a simple example. A student in Darryl Williams's classroom, reading aloud, was unable to decode the word *nature*. He hesitatingly sounded "nah . . . nah" before falling silent. Williams responded by writing the word on the board and saying, "This is the word you're trying to read." He paused briefly and drew a short horizontal line (the sign of a long vowel) above the "a." He paused again to see if the student recognized the meaning. He didn't, and Darryl proceeded to break it down one step further, saying, "long a," as he pointed to the horizontal line. This intervention was effective. With new information on the problem spot, the vowel sound, the student was able to combine the new knowledge Williams provided with the knowledge he had of the other letter sounds. He now read the word correctly.

Williams had successfully isolated the problem part within the larger error and caused the student to use his previous knowledge to arrive at a successful solution without Williams providing it. Williams might have just said, "That word is *nature*." This would have been faster for sure, but it would have left the student with little or no cognitive work to do and would have emphasized the failure rather than the success (both in terms of the student ultimately getting it right and also in terms of his using some knowledge he did have to solve the problem).

It's worthwhile to note at how many different levels even this question could be broken down because determining the degree to which to break down a problem or question is a critical decision. You never know exactly how big the gap is between the student's level of knowledge and the knowledge necessary for mastery, but in most cases, you want to

> *You never know exactly how big the gap is between the student's level of knowledge and the knowledge necessary for mastery.*

provide the smallest hint possible and still enable your student to get to the correct answer successfully. This will cause your student to apply what she knows to the greatest degree possible. It's worth thinking about some of the subtler ways that information can be broken down. For example, in the case of the student struggling to read the word *nature,* merely rewriting the word on the board, a very minimal hint, might have proven effective. Seeing the word in a new context (on the board where perhaps he'd seen it before) might have jogged his memory.

Providing such a minimal hint gets at the tension in *Break It Down,* however. While one goal is to break things down to the least degree possible, another is to do it quickly, thus managing time and pace. Meticulously adding a thin additional slice of knowledge to each previous subtle hint would be the perfect solution to the goal of causing students to do the greatest amount of cognitive work, but would likely derail instruction in a series of tedious exercises and squander time that could be used more productively. Figure 3.3, on the next page, illustrates that challenge.

As the figure suggests, *Break It Down* is a complex and challenging technique. One of the best ways to ensure success with it is to prepare for it as part of the lesson planning process by identifying potential trouble spots and drafting both anticipated wrong answers and possible cues. Another solution is to use consistent types of follow-ups. These patterns are often highly successful and are a good starting point in thinking about how to cue. Although there are probably a limitless number of ways to break down difficult information and tasks, these six offer a good starting point:

- **Provide an example.** If you got a blank stare when you asked for the definition of a prime number, you might say, "7 is one," or "7 is one, and so is 11." If you wanted to break it down further, you could cue: "7 is one but

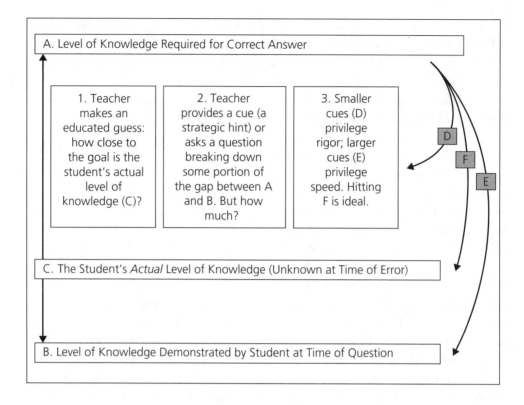

A. Level of Knowledge Required for Correct Answer

| 1. Teacher makes an educated guess: how close to the goal is the student's actual level of knowledge (C)? | 2. Teacher provides a cue (a strategic hint) or asks a question breaking down some portion of the gap between A and B. But how much? | 3. Smaller cues (D) privilege rigor; larger cues (E) privilege speed. Hitting F is ideal. |

C. The Student's *Actual* Level of Knowledge (Unknown at Time of Error)

B. Level of Knowledge Demonstrated by Student at Time of Question

FIGURE 3.3. How *Break It Down* Works

8 is not." You could take it a step further by observing, "8's factors include 2 and 4." At some point there's not much left to cue, and a technique like *No Opt Out* (technique 1)—"Who can tell David what a prime number is?"—might become more appropriate. You can also provide additional examples if the question stumping the student was originally based on categorizing an example of something. For example, a student in Jaimie Brillante's fifth-grade writing class struggled to identify the part of speech of the word *owner*. It's hard to provide an example of the word *owner*, so instead Brillante provided another, cueing: "Well, *owner* would logically be the same part of speech as other words that end in *-er. Dancer, swimmer, singer.* What are those?" she asked. "They're people," the student replied. Jaimie prompted, "And people have to be . . ." as the student chimed in, "Nouns!"

• **Provide context.** Another student in Jamie Brillante's class was stumped when asked to name the part of speech of the word *ancient*. Brillante noted that it had been a vocabulary word in another teacher's class. The student remained stumped: "I hope nobody ever calls *me* ancient," cued Brillante. Nothing. "Maybe in, like 2080, you could call me ancient, but that would be the only time it was acceptable." "Oh yeah, it's very old," the student successfully recalled. It's important to note that Brillante is using this approach with a vocabulary word she knows the student learned but is having trouble remembering.

This strategy would be far less effective if Brillante did not know whether the student knew anything at all about the word. To return to the definition of prime number, you might observe that positive integers are either prime or composite. Or you might refer to a previous conversation: "We discussed prime and composite, and we spent some time on the example of the number 8." Or: "You'll recall from our discussion last week that factors are important in deciding whether a number is prime."

- **Provide a rule.** In Christy Huelskamp's sixth-grade reading class at Williamsburg Collegiate in Brooklyn, a student guessed incorrectly that *indiscriminate* was a verb when used in the sentence, "James was an indiscriminate reader; he would pick up any book from the library and read it cover to cover." Huelskamp replied with a rule: "A verb is an action or a state of being. Is indiscriminate describing an action?" The student quickly recognized that it was modifying a noun. "It's an adjective," she said.

- **Provide the missing (or first) step.** When a student in her fifth-grade math class was unable to explain what was wrong with writing the number 15/6, Kelli Ragin cued: "Well, what do we always do when the numerator is larger than the denominator?" Instantly the student caught on. "Oh, we need to make a mixed number so I divide 6 into 15."

- **Rollback.** Sometimes it's sufficient to repeat a student's answer back to her. Many of us instantly recognize our errors when they're played back for us, as if on tape. If a student in Ragin's class had proposed reducing an improper fraction to a mixed number by multiplying the numerator and denominator, Kelli might merely repeat that back to her: "You said that I would multiply six times fifteen to reduce . . ." The degree of emphasis she places on the word *multiply* would be key in determining how much of the gap between answer and mastery Ragin was breaking down. (Emphasis on *multiply* makes the hint much bigger.) Regardless, hearing your own error is another's words is often revealing.

- **Eliminate false choices.** When Brillante's student struggled to recognize that *owner* was a noun, she could have eliminated some false choices as follows: "Well, let's go through some of the options. If it were a verb, it would be an action. Is *owner* an action? Can you or I owner? Well, what about an adjective? Is it telling me what kind or how many of some noun?"

One of our most important goals as teachers is to cause students to do as much of the cognitive work—the writing, the thinking, the analyzing, the talking—as possible. The proportion of the cognitive work students do in your classroom is known as your **Ratio.** (To my knowledge, the term was coined by David Levin, cofounder of the nationally known and high-achieving Knowledge Is Power (*KIPP* for short) schools and, in many people's eyes, one of the country's most insightful and effective teachers.) As you embrace *Ratio*, you'll find yourself rarely completing a problem at the board without input of your students: to add each column ("6 plus 8 is what, Sarah?"); to identify the next step ("What do I do with my 1, James?"); to reinforce key terms ("What's it called when I bring it to the top of the tens column, Jamar?"); and finally to check the work. When your students answer incorrectly, you'll find yourself asking a student to correct and explain the mistake ("Valerie says 6 divided by 2 is 5. What did she do wrong, Ray?"). Your goal is to give them the most practice possible, to apply what they know as much as they can, to do all the work in solving sample problems as opposed to watching you solve sample problems.

My own understanding of this complex technique was developed significantly by a conversation with Jesse Rector, principal of North Star Academy's Clinton Hill Campus, who felt that one of my favorite *Ratio* clips was disappointing. Rector observed that while students in the clip were participating actively, almost intensely, he did not think they were engaged in the deepest levels of thinking. His comments caused me to distinguish between what I'll call the "Thinking Ratio" and the "Participation Ratio." The Participation Ratio describes how much of the participating—the answering, the talking, the writing—students do.

Imagine a lesson in which students are reviewing a skill they are near to mastering or perhaps trying new and more challenging problems involving a process they're familiar with, say, figuring the volume of a rectangular prism. Your goal is to give them the most practice possible, to apply what they know as much as they can, to do all the work in solving sample problems as opposed to watching you solve sample problems. You might ask questions like, "Who can tell me the first step?" "And what's my value for width?" "Great! And what do

I do next?" "What do I need to be careful of?" "If my length increased by 1 and my width decreased by 1, would my volume stay the same?" These types of questions, which force students to apply and consolidate their knowledge, are important. But so are questions that ask students to push their depth of thinking and analyze new content. This would be more applicable when working through a problem on volume for the first time or perhaps when wrestling with a question where the right answer is a matter of opinion. In this case, the questions might sound more like, "Why might I need to multiply?" "How is volume different from area?" "When might I measure volume?" "What would happen to my volume if my width increased?" The Thinking Ratio gets more at the depth of the increased amounts of participating students do.

KEY IDEA

RATIO

A successful lesson is rarely marked by a teacher's getting a good intellectual workout at the front of the room. Push more and more of the cognitive work out to students as soon as they are ready, with the understanding that the cognitive work must be on-task, focused, and productive.

Champion teachers use dozens of methods in upping the ratio; it would be impossible to categorize them all, but what follows are ten especially effective methods for productively upping your ratio. They are organized around the rough amount of lesson structure they imply. That is, the first methods are most effective during what you might call direct instruction: teacher-led dissemination of information. The latter methods are more likely to apply during discussions with more student participation:

1. **Unbundle.** Break questions into smaller parts to share the work out to more students and force them to react to one another. Instead of, "Who can tell me the three dimensions of a cylinder?" try a sequence like this:

"How many dimensions to a cylinder, James?"

"Good. What's one dimension, Shayna?"

"And what's another, Diamond?"

"That leaves what, Terrance?"

2. **Half-statement.** Rather than speaking in complete ideas, express half of an idea and ask a student to finish it:

"So the next step is to combine sentences with a . . . tell me please, John."

3. **What's next?** The fastest way to double the number of questions students get to answer is to ask about process as often as product, that is, addressing both how to solve a step (or what the answer to a step in a problem is) and what step comes next. Incidentally, the hardest what's next question is the one for the first step in any solution: "Okay, what do I do first?"

4. **Feign ignorance.** Turn the tables, and pretend you don't know. Make the student play teacher and narrate what you might otherwise explain:

"So, now can I just add my numerators?"

"A theme is just a summary of what happens in the story, right?"

5. **Repeated examples.** Teachers often ask for examples: of a term they're defining, a concept in action, a character's trait. They less often ask students for another example, especially one that's different from the first. This technique can be especially rigorous when you set the terms for how the second example should be different. Beth Verrilli at North Star Academy asked her students to apply the word *exploited* to their reading of *Macbeth*. "Who gets exploited in *Macbeth*?" she asked, and following up by asking for yet another example with a different character. A teacher in this situation might also steer the second example: "Who gets exploited more subtly? Repeatedly? With or without knowing it?"

6. **Rephrase or add on.** Second drafts are better than first drafts because some of the most rigorous thinking goes into making ideas more precise, specific, and rich. Replicate this in the classroom by asking a student to rephrase and improve an answer she just gave or by asking another student to revise or improve a peer's answer. In a lesson on *Animal Farm,* Rochester Prep principal (and sometime reading teacher) Stacey Shells asked a student why the rations due to all of the animals on Orwell's mythical farm were reduced except those of the pigs and the dogs. The student answered, "The pigs' and the dogs' rations were not reduced because they were the higher . . . standard of life. They were the ones being treated better." Her answer was solid but weak in syntax and specificity of language. "You are correct," Shells responded, "but rephrase that." When the student struggled, Shells asked her peers, "Who can give her

a word to use that will help her make her answer better?" and a peer suggested trying to use the word *class*. The student upgraded: "The pigs and the dogs were of a higher class than all the other animals so their rations weren't reduced."

7. **Whys and hows.** Asking why or how instantly pushes more, and more rigorous, work onto students by forcing them to explain the thinking that solved (or failed to solve) the problem.

8. **Supporting evidence.** There's far more cognitive work to be done in supporting an opinion than in holding one, in testing its logic than in arguing for it. This process of stating an argument and supporting it involves extensive cognitive wrestling that can push your ratio higher. Ask your students constantly to explain how the evidence supports them. Or give them a position or a variety of opinions and ask them to assemble evidence in support.

9. **Batch process.** As your students progress in the grades and into broader discussions, it's powerful for the teacher to strategically step out of the way at times and not comment on and validate every student comment and instead allow a short series of student comments to be made directly following, and ideally in response to, one another. I've seen this described as playing volleyball rather than Ping-Pong, but I prefer the term *batch processing* because it underscores that it's still your job to process and respond to student answers. They don't go unmediated by you. They just get discussed in smaller groups rather than singly. If you prefer the volleyball analogy, fine, but I'd offer three pieces of advice based on observing champion teachers:

- *It's volleyball, not soccer.* In volleyball, teammates pass the ball a limited number of times before returning the ball over the net. In the classroom, your students should, similarly, make finite group comments in a row as you continue to steer, respond, and process. They get the ball, then, after two or three hits, you get the ball. In soccer, by contrast, the goal of the players is to maintain possession constantly. That often means sacrificing movement toward the goal in order to keep the ball from the opposition for as long as possible. In the classroom, your students are not maintaining possession for as long as they want. Structure it so the ball is expected to pass back over to you at frequent and regular intervals. You may pass it back again, but you will do so having controlled the direction, pace, and focus of play to maximize productivity. If left unmanaged, students will often revert to soccer and take the ball in whatever direction best allows them to keep it—and that almost always means failure to get to the goal.

- *Batch processing can be nonproductive until students are mature and ready for it.* If they are not intellectually prepared through years of study, they may go batting balls off in every direction. Be cautious with batch processing. Use it strategically, not as a default. Observation of champions suggests caution in using batch processing aggressively before high school.

- *Teach habits of discussion first.* Volleyball games work because everyone knows how to pass the ball and when it needs to go back over the net. They know this because they've been coached. The most effective teachers and schools I've seen do batch processing well intentionally teach "habits of discussion," as my colleagues at North Star Academy in Newark call them: basic procedures for how to interact. At North Star, teachers provide students with phrase starters to use in interacting:

  - I agree with x because . . .

  - I want to say more about what you said . . .

  - That's true because . . .

  - I understand what you're saying, but I have a different opinion [point or view] . . .

  - What evidence can you give to support your opinion?

10. **Discussion objectives.** Open-ended questioning and broad discussions can seem like the *Ratio* Rosetta stone. They almost by their nature appear to increase *Ratio.* But they can just as easily result in nonproductive *Ratio*—in students thinking or talking a lot but not thinking rigorously (people often confuse the amount of student participation for *Ratio*) or in students thinking about peripheral or suboptimal topics. The goal is to try to focus discussions on the most productive and rigorous points. Teachers who do this have a clear objective in mind for any open-ended discussion and use hints to steer their students back on task and, especially, head off distractions and unproductive topics. Often they use the former to achieve the latter, that is, they share the objective for the discussion with students so they can remind them of their purpose when they stray. Emily Crouch, who teaches at Leadership Preparatory Charter School in Brooklyn, did this in a recent lesson. She read a story about a girl and advised her students that their goal in discussing the story was to determine which of several subtly different character traits provided the best description of her. This discussion was not only rigorous and evidence based but efficient: when a student suggested a totally different trait he thought was evidenced, she reminded him that their goal was to decide from among the similar traits they'd identified at the outset, thus keeping the discussion focused and productive.

Before you set out to put these ideas into action in your classroom, I have two caveats. The first is that increased doses of cognitive work should come as soon as students are ready but not before. Releasing students to solve a problem that requires a skill they hadn't learned or mastered yet, in the hopes that they might infer that skill by trying, would result in students doing a lot of thinking but not a lot of productive thinking. I once observed a teacher who told her third graders to look through the book they were about to read to make inferences about what it was about. Alas, she had never taught them how to do that, so many flipped idly and at random through the pages, with most failing to take advantage of subtitles, chapter headings, and captions that might have informed them better. Any useful cognitive work they did was likely to be accidental.

The second caveat is that increased doses of cognitive work should be given with constant and vigilant discipline in making that work focused and productive. You want students to do larger and larger shares of the right work. Theoretically, your ratio would be perfect if you simply let students run the whole discussion and just got out of the way. You might say, "Class, your task for today is to determine the most important historical figure in nineteenth-century America. I expect you to discuss this question and report back to me in one hour." Or even better, "Class, here is a set of data about how a series of bodies in space react to one another. I'd like you to do your best to infer principles of gravitation from it. I will be here if you need me." Your ratio would be perfect: 100 percent! But your results would not. Your students would almost assuredly not get to the right answer at all. And if they did, they would certainly not get there in the most efficient way. They would waste a massive amount of time and preclude themselves from studying any number of other topics.

TECHNIQUE 18
CHECK FOR UNDERSTANDING

Good drivers check their mirrors every five seconds. They constantly need to know what's happening around them because waiting for an accident to tell them they're doing something wrong is a costly strategy. As a teacher, you should think the same way, seeking constant opportunities to assess what your kids can do while you're teaching and using that knowledge to inform what you do and how

The technique could more accurately be described as Check for Understanding and Doing Something About It Right Away. *That's not especially pithy, but it better captures the two key aspects of* Check for Understanding: *gathering and responding to data.*

you do it. Waiting until there's an accidental failure to comprehend means paying an unsustainably high price for knowledge.

I've chosen to use a term in common use to describe this technique, **Check for Understanding,** but it's a risky one to use since it leaves the equation half done. The technique could more accurately be described as *Check for Understanding and Do Something About It Right Away*. That's not especially pithy, but it better captures the two key aspects of *Check for Understanding:* gathering and responding to data.

GATHERING DATA

Questioning is data gathering. *Check for Understanding* requires you to think of the answers to your questions as data. Consider two teachers who ask their students to name a chief cause of the Civil War. In each case, three students answer incorrectly or incompletely before a fourth student gives an accurate answer. One teacher sees the answers as a story, a sequential narrative of the class's progress toward understanding that ends in success. She listens as her students wrestle with the question, and when she gets a correct answer, thinks,

Check for Understanding requires you to think of the answers to your questions as data.

"Oh, good they finally got it." The other teacher sees not so much a story written in a sequence of answers, but a set of four independent variables, four separate data points. The narrative sequence is irrelevant, and the numbers cause her concern. She thinks, "Only one out of four kids understands the causes of the Civil War. I need to circle back." The second teacher treats answers as data; she is effectively checking for understanding. In this case the technique involves using a simple but powerful analytical framework to assess answers: sampling. Sampling means asking iterations of a single question or a set of similar questions to a smaller group of students and using the answers as representative of a larger group's answers. The sample is a set of data points, each viewed independently, and explicitly used for analysis. The point is that the questions and answers may (sometimes) be the same as in any other class; the technique lies in how you think about them.

Here are four more specific ways to make your questioning more data driven:

- *Data sets.* We tend to think of any single answer as reflective of where the class is at any given time. But a single answer can come from anywhere on a curve of student mastery, from low to high, and you will often have no idea where. Not only that, but even if you knew a question was reflective of the class mean, you'd want to think of how much information is hidden by an average. What's the highest level of mastery? The lowest? How spread out are students in their level of mastery? Are most students very similar to the student at the mean or widely dispersed in their level of knowledge? No single question can resolve these critical questions. Instead you should reflect on your questions in groups and think of them, as the second teacher above did, as data sets. If you ask five students similar questions or different questions on a similar topic, assess them as a group. What's the hit rate (percentage correct)? This gives you far better information that does thinking of your questions as a progression of singular data points. By thinking of your questions as data sets, you come to realize that wrong, wrong, wrong, right is a bad sequence, not a good one. It also tells you that wrong, right is not enough data. You should keep asking so you know whether you're dealing with wrong, right, right, right or wrong, right, wrong, wrong.

- *Statistical sampling.* As you ask questions in sets, think about taking a statistical sample of the room. If you're asking your class five questions to test whether they understand how to find the least common denominator, ask a sample of students from across the spectrum of likely skill: two typically low-performing students, two middle students, and one high performer. Now you'll have better information about how far into the class the mastery you've tried to build has spread. Obviously to be able to do this *you* need to choose who answers, not the kids, so cold calling (calling on whom you want without regard to whose hand is raised) is a critical technique to use. (*Cold Call* is technique 22 in Chapter Four.)

- *Reliability.* Any right answer always poses the risk of its being a false positive—a lucky correct guess. Therefore, stop teaching when your students get it right several times in a row, not once. To ensure reliability (the likelihood of future correct answers on similar questions), respond to right answers with follow-up why and how questions as often as you can (see *Stretch It,* technique 3). This gives you the best data on whether a student would be likely to get a similar problem right the next time around. If he or she can't clearly explain it, the risk of a lucky guess is high.

- *Validity.* Make sure that the question you get a positive result to is an effective measure of what students have to master to be successful. You have to measure what you say you're measuring. Therefore, you should carefully align the questions you ask to check for understanding on the rigor and style of questions your students will ultimately be accountable for. You should make them sound like, and be at least as hard as, what students will see on the final exam, the state assessment, or whatever else your bottom-line measure is.

Especially data-driven teachers often insert a short verbal quiz into the fabric of their lesson to increase the amount and usefulness of the data they collect. James Verilli, principal at North Star Academy in Newark, New Jersey, calls this "dip-sticking." When he teaches, he samples a wide range of students on a set of similar questions about a common topic to gauge the level of mastery of the whole class.

Types of Questions

Although you can use *Check for Understanding* without changing the format of the questions you ask, thinking about answers as data will probably change your questions. You're likely to ask far fewer yes-or-no questions since with only two possible answers, they give a far higher possible rate of false positives. You're likely to have to learn to be more cognizant of "tipping"—giving the answers away in your question, as in this sequence:

Teacher: Who can tell me what the phrase "off the deep end" means?

Student: It means someone is upset?

Teacher: Well are they a little bit upset or like really, *really* upset?

Student: Really, really upset.

Teacher: Good.

In this case it's hard to imagine the student who thinks the answer is "a little bit upset." Finally, you'll probably come to rely a lot less on self-report, a method teachers use frequently—"Thumbs up if you get this, thumbs down if you don't." Aficionados of data know self-report to be chronically unreliable.

Observation

Observation is the second way to determine whether students understand a concept, and it addresses a key validity challenge. When you test for mastery using questioning, you don't take into account the fact that students can often answer correctly verbally but not in writing. Observation allows you to see written answers before you sign off. Furthermore, observation, which involves circulating when students are doing independent seat work to observe mastery levels, requires a larger total investment of time but allows you to see more data points more rapidly during that time. Like questioning, this skill does not so much involve changing activities as it does thinking of the information in front of you through the data lens. Instead of circulating to see how close to finished students are or whether they are working, you would specifically look for the number and type of errors they are making, possibly even tracking them on a short response sheet so you can organize and refer back to the data later.

One way to increase your capacity to gather useful data through observation is to standardize the format of what you're looking at. If you're looking for information in the same place on each student's paper, for example, you'll find it much more quickly and will be able to retain your concentration on comparing answers across students, not finding them for single students. Giving out packets is an effective way to do this. If you plan the work you want students to do during your lesson in advance, writing out of the problems or questions in order in a packet that each student picks up at the beginning of class, you know that when you want to see how many students can find the least common denominator of 28 and 77, it will always be at the top of the third page of every student's packet. You've minimized the number of unimportant things you have to process so you can concentrate on what's important.

You can take this a step further by providing clear spaces for work to be done or answers to be written. Incidentally, this method works in all subject areas, albeit slightly differently. If you are reading a novel, for example, you might ask students to underline the place where the protagonist's motivation is revealed and write "key indicator of motivation" in the margin. Then it would be easy for you to check for understanding even while students read. Or if you didn't want to be as prescriptive, you might ask your students to write a one-sentence summary of each page in a novel at the top of that page. Then you could choose a relevant page and quickly find and compare all summaries in your classroom to better assess the data.

> *One way to increase your capacity to gather useful data through observation is to standardize the format of what you're looking at.*

Another way to increase your capacity to gather observable data is to use "slates." You can quickly check the whole class's comprehension by giving your students tools to write down their answers and quickly hold them up to you. Some teachers use scrap paper, and others get mini dry-erase boards for their students. You can even use the worksheets or packets your students are completing by simply saying, "Show me," and then circulating to observe. The trick isn't so much in the tool you use to gather but in the way you gather and respond to the information. Be sure to observe all students' answers. Be sure that students can't cheat by observing others' answers before writing their own. Be sure your questions assess mastery effectively and not superficially. Asking students to use nonverbal signals to show their answer to a series of questions—"One finger up if you got A; two up if you got B"—can provide an effective and simpler variation on the theme. Just be aware of the ability of students to hide their lack of knowledge by piggy-backing.

KEY IDEA

CHECK FOR UNDERSTANDING

Effective *Check for Understanding* equals gathering data constantly and acting on them immediately. The second part (acting on the data quickly) is both harder to do and at least as important.

RESPONDING TO DATA

The second part of *Check for Understanding* involves responding to the data you collect. It's worth noting that all the recognition in the world won't help if it does not result in action. Generally teachers are better at checking for than acting on gaps in student mastery, so the imperative is not only to act but to act quickly: the shorter the delay between recognizing a gap in mastery and taking action to fix it, the more likely the intervention is to be effective. There are exceptions (sometimes you need to identify a small group of students to receive tutoring outside class), but it's important to recognize the timeliness of knowledge that students haven't mastered a concept. There's no sense pushing on to harder material when you know students can't do the simpler work. There's no sense reading on in the novel when there's a persistent misunderstanding about what's happening at the outset. Stop and fix it; then move on. This also makes sense because the sooner you fix it, the simpler the misunderstanding is likely to be. When an error is compounded by three days or three hours of subsequent misunderstandings, it's likely to be complex and thorny; the root cause will take time to figure out, and you will need a full lesson to reteach it. It's far better to act quickly and solve learning problems while they are simple and can be addressed with an additional problem, a short activity, or a reexplanation that takes three minutes rather than thirty-five.

You can take action in response to data in numerous ways. Teachers sometimes forget the benefit of reteaching material in a slightly different way from the first time. Repeating what you did before might work, but it assumes there aren't kids who would respond to something slightly different. This

> *The shorter the delay between recognizing a gap in mastery and taking action to fix it, the more likely the intervention is to be effective.*

doesn't mean that you go back and try a whole new method for teaching long division, for example. You really should decide on a best way to do that. But you can explain it in slightly different words or with different examples.

Here are several other actions to take in response to data telling you that student mastery is incomplete:

- Reteach using a different approach.

- Reteach by identifying and reteaching the problem step: "I think the place we're struggling is when we get to remainders, so let's work on that a little more."

- Reteach by identifying and explaining difficult terms: "I think the term *denominator* is giving us some trouble."

- Reteach at a slower pace: "Let's read that list of words again. I'm going to go really slowly, and I want you to make sure you hear me read the suffixes. Then I'm going to ask you to . . ."

- Reteach using a different order: "Let's try to put the key events in the story in reverse order this time."

- Reteach identifying students of concern: "We're going to push on to the problems in your packet now, but I want a couple of you to come work with me at the front. If I say your name, bring your packet up here [or meet me at lunch]."

- Reteach using more repetitions: "It seems that we're able to identify the genre most of the time, but let's try to get a bit more practice. I'm going to read you the first two sentences to ten imaginary stories. For each one, write down the genre you think it is and one reason for your answer."

TECHNIQUE 19

AT BATS

Many years ago at a school where I used to teach, I was assigned to coach baseball, a sport I'd played only casually and felt unqualified to coach. A friend of a friend was a master baseball coach, however, and I got an hour of his time over coffee to figure out how to organize my practices. His biggest piece of advice was both simple and enduring and is key to the **At Bats** technique: "Teach them the basics of how to hit, and then get them as many at bats as you can. Practice after practice, swing after swing after swing: maximize the number of at bats. Let them do it over and over again until they can swing quick and level in their sleep. That's the key. Don't change it. Don't get too fancy. Give them at bats." At bats, it turned out, were the key to hitting.

Sometimes the obvious truths are the best ones. And in fact this truth is reaffirmed by the data in just about every field and every situation. Want to know what single factor best predicts the quality of a surgeon? It's not her reputation, not the place where she went to medical school, not even how smart she is. The best predictor is how many surgeries of a particular type she's done. It's muscle memory. It's repetition. It's at bats—for complex surgery, hitting baseballs, solving math problems, writing sentences. Repetition is the key for a surgeon not just because it means she'll be smoothest when things go as expected but because if things go wrong, she'll have the most brainpower left over to engage in problem solving in the moment. With her clamping and cutting skills refined to automaticity, she'll calmly have all her faculties to focus on how to respond to the critical and unexpected event.

Nothing inscribes and refines a skill so that it can be reliably applied under any circumstances like at bats, so great lessons should have plenty of them. And if it's true that people master a new skill on the tenth or twentieth or one thousandth time they do it, never the first time, it's important to factor that into your lessons. Once your students get to "You," once they're doing independent work, they need lots and lots of practice: ten or twenty repetitions instead of two or three. This is especially important to remember because in a busy day, sufficient repetition is the first thing to go. We teach all the way to the part where students can ingrain the skill, and we

Want to know what single factor best predicts the quality of the surgeon you select? It's not her reputation, not the place where she went to medical school, not even how smart she is. The best predictor is how many surgeries of the type you're having that she's done. It's muscle memory. It's repetition.

stop. They try it once, and we say, "Good, you've got it!" or worse, "We're running out of time. Try it at home, and make sure you've got it!"

A lesson should end with students getting at bat after at bat after at bat. It should often begin with a few at bats on previous material ("cumulative review"). Here are the key points to remember:

- *Go until they can do it on their own.* By the end of independent practice, students should be able to solve problems to the standard they'll be accountable for, and entirely on their own.

- *Use multiple variations and formats.* Students should be able to solve questions in multiple formats and a significant number of plausible variations and variables.

- *Grab opportunities for enrichment and differentiation.* As some students demonstrate mastery faster than others, be sure to have bonus problems ready for them to push them to the next level.

TECHNIQUE 20
EXIT TICKET

End your lesson with a final *At Bat*, a single question or maybe short sequence of problems to solve at the close of class. When you collect this from students before they leave and cull the data, it's an **Exit Ticket.** Not only will this establish a productive expectation about daily completed work for students, but it will ensure that you always check for understanding in a way that provides you with strong data and thus critical insights. What percentage of your students got it right? What mistake did those who got it wrong make? Why, in looking at their errors, did they make that mistake? What about your lesson might have led to the confusion? Not only will you know how to refine the next lesson but you'll no longer be flying blind. You'll know how effective your lesson was, as measured by how well they learned it, not how well you thought you taught it.

Some thoughts on effective *Exit Tickets:*

They're quick: one to three questions. Honestly, that's it. It's not a unit quiz. You want to get a good idea of how your kids did on the core part of your objective with ten minutes of analysis afterward.

They're designed to yield data. This means the questions are fairly simple and focus on one key part of the objective. That way if students get them wrong you'll know why. (If you ask a multi-step problem you may not know which part they didn't get!) They also tend to vary formats—one multiple choice and one open response, say. You need to know that students can solve both ways.

They make great Do Nows *(see technique number 29 in Chapter Five).* After *you've* looked at the data, let your students do the same. Start the next day's lesson by analyzing and re-teaching the *Exit Ticket* when students struggle.

TECHNIQUE 21
TAKE A STAND

This technique involves pushing students to actively engage in the ideas around them by making judgments about the answers their peers provide. This can allow you to increase the number of students who participate in and process a particular part of your lesson. For example, you might ask your class to respond to an answer as Rochester Prep's Bob Zimmerli does: "two snaps if you agree; two stomps if you don't." One student answers, but every student has to decide if the answer is right, and to do that, they have to solve. Done right, this increases your ratio by a factor of about twenty-five.

Take a Stand techniques can be whole class ("Stand up if you agree with Alexis") or directed to an individual ("She said 9 times 9 is 81. That's not right, is it, Valeria?"). They can be evaluative ("How many people think Dashawn is right?") or analytical ("How could she check her work to see if she's right, Alaina?"). Finally, they can be verbal or signaled through a gesture: "Show me on your hands how big the remainder is." "Show me on your hands which answer choice you think is correct." (Some teachers have students put their heads down to ensure they can't see one another's responses when they *Take a Stand* or write on scraps of paper or small dry erase boards.)

Take a Stand helps students process more content, and it helps you check for understanding. How indicative of the rest of the class was the original student's answer? Which wrong answer did those who got it wrong choose? Furthermore, since using *Take a Stand* techniques means explicitly asking one student to evaluate another's answer—"Is he right, James?" "How many people got the same answer as Ty?"—the technique brings student answers to the forefront of class. It makes them appear to be as fundamental to the work of learning as are teacher-given answers and underscores the value teachers put on student responses.

When you ask your students to *Take a Stand*, be careful not to let the exercise become cursory. There are plenty of classrooms where teachers routinely ask students to agree or disagree or to do "thumbs up, thumbs down, thumbs sideways." The key to maximum effect is

> *When you ask your students to* Take a Stand, *be careful not to let the exercise become cursory.*

not so much asking whether students agree but following up on their answers to inform your teaching and make students accountable for mentally engaged judgments rather than empty and obligatory participation. To make the technique effective, you should, with predictable consistency (not every time, perhaps, but fairly reliably), ask students to defend or explain their positions: "Why is your thumb down, Keisha?" You can raise your hand easily enough; the key is to make sure that students are truly doing cognitive work when they do so, and to do that, you have to check up on their answers. It's also important to remember to have students take a stand both when the original answer was right and when it was wrong and to avoid letting the method you use tip students off. One teacher I know always asked students "two snaps if you agree; two stomps if you don't" when the answer was right and "raise your hand if you got the same answer" when it was wrong. This quickly took all of the intellectual work out of the exercise.

To make this technique succeed, you also have some cultural work to do in making sure that your students are comfortable exposing and discussing their own errors: stomping when others are snapping or keeping three fingers up when others have four and then in telling you openly about what they thought and why. Be sure to praise and acknowledge students as they do this. You might say, "Thank you for stomping, Tarynn. I appreciate that you took the risk of challenging us. Now let's figure out why you didn't agree," on the front end, or, after this example, "Let's have two snaps and two stomps for Tarynn for pushing us all to think."

REFLECTION AND PRACTICE

The following activities should help you think about and practice the techniques in this chapter:

1. Choose one of the following deliberately informal topics and sketch out a lesson plan that follows an I/We/You structure. In fact, you can go one step further by planning a five-step process: I do; I do, you help; you do, I help; you do; and do and do and do. You don't have to assume you'll be teaching your actual students.

   - Students will be able to shoot an accurate foul shot.

   - Students will be able to write the name of their school in cursive.

   - Students will be able to make a peanut butter and jelly sandwich.

   - Students will understand and apply the correct procedure for doing laundry in your household.

   - Students will be able to change a tire.

2. Now take your lesson and design a three- to five- minute hook that engages students and sets up the lesson.

3. Be sure to name the steps in the "I" portion of your lesson. Review them and find four or five ways to make them stickier.

4. Identify the two or three places in your lesson where students are most likely to make a error or misunderstand the lesson. Script *Break It Down* questions at varying levels of support for each of these likely error points.

5. Design an *Exit Ticket* that will allow you to accurately assess student knowledge at the end of the lesson.

CHAPTER FOUR

ENGAGING STUDENTS IN YOUR LESSONS

Great teachers engage students so that they feel like part of the lesson. They make a habit of focused involvement in the classroom. While that may already sound easier said than done with the most resistant students, it's doubly challenging since students need to be engaged in not just the class but in the *work* of class. That is, you could easily engage students in class by substituting frills for substance. The techniques reviewed in this chapter will consistently draw students into the work of class and keep them focused on learning.

TECHNIQUE 22
COLD CALL

When calling on students during class, it's natural to think about managing who gets to participate and think, "How do I give everyone a chance?" "Whose turn is it?" or "Who will give me the answer I want?" However, a more important question to ask is, "How can I adapt my decisions about which students I call on to help all my students pay better attention?" The idea, of course, is that you want everybody to pay attention and develop a system that ensures that all students think it's possible that they are about to be called on, regardless of whether they have raised their hand, and therefore think they must therefore prepare to answer. You need a system that ensures that instead of one student answering each of your questions, all of your students answer all of your questions in their minds, with you merely choosing one student to speak the answer out loud. **Cold Call** is that system.

KEY IDEA

COLD CALL

In order to make engaged participation the expectation, call on students regardless of whether they have raised their hands.

When you cold call, you call on students regardless of whether they have raised their hands. It's deceptively simple: you ask a question and then call the name of the student you want to answer it. If students see you frequently and reliably calling on classmates who don't have their hand raised, they will come to expect it and prepare for it. Calling on whomever you choose regardless of whether the student's hand is up also brings several other critical benefits to your classroom.

It's critical to be able to check what any student's level of mastery is at any time.

First, it allows you to check for understanding effectively and systematically. It's critical to be able to check what any student's level of mastery is at any time, regardless of whether he or she is offering to tell you. In fact it's most important when he or she is not offering to tell you. *Cold Call* allows you to check on exactly the student you want to check in on to assess mastery, and the technique makes this process seem normal. When students are used to being asked to participate or answer by their teacher, they react to it as if it were a normal event, and this allows you to get a focused, honest answer and therefore check for understanding reliably. This means that while using *Cold Call* to assist you in checking for understanding is critical, you'll also do best if you use it before you need to check for understanding. Your goal is to normalize it as a natural and normal part of your class, preferably a positive one.

Second, *Cold Call* increases speed in both the terms of your pacing (the illusion of speed) and the rate at which you can cover material (real speed). To understand the degree to which this is so, make an audiotape of your lesson sometime. Use a stopwatch to track how much time you spend waiting (and encouraging and cajoling and asking) for volunteers. With *Cold Call,* you no longer have a delay after you ask, "Can anyone tell me what one cause of the World War I was?" You no longer have to scan the room and wait for hands. You no longer have to dangle hints to encourage participants or tell your students that you'd like to see more hands. Instead of saying, "I'm seeing the same four hands.

With Cold Call, *you no longer have a delay after you ask, "Can anyone tell me what one cause of the World War I was?"*

I want to hear from more of you. Doesn't anyone else know this?" you simply say, "Tell us one cause of World War I, please, [slight pause here] Darren." With *Cold Call,* you'll move through material much faster, and the tedious, momentum-sapping mood when no one appears to want to speak up will disappear. These two results will increase your pacing: the illusion of speed you create in your classroom, which is a critical factor in how students engage (see Chapter Three for more on pacing).

Third, *Cold Call* allows you to distribute work more broadly around the room and signal to students not only that they are likely to be called on to participate, and therefore that they should engage in the work of the classroom, but that you want to know what they have to say. You care about their opinion. Many students have insight to add to your class but will not offer it unless you push or ask. They wonder if anyone really cares what they think. Or they think it's just as easy to keep their thoughts to themselves because Charlie's hand is always up anyway. Or they have a risky and potentially valuable thought on the tip of their tongue but aren't quite sure enough of it to say it aloud yet. Sometimes there will even be a glance—a moment when this student looks at you as if to say, "Should I?" or maybe even, "Just call on me so you've shared responsibility if this is totally off the mark."

Many people mistakenly perceive cold calling to be chastening and stressful. Once you've watched clips 7, 8, and 9 on the DVD, you'll know that it's not.

Many people mistakenly perceive cold calling to be chastening and stressful. Once you've watched clips 7, 8, and 9 on the DVD, you'll know that it's not. When it's done right, it's an extremely powerful and positive way to reach out to kids who want to speak but are reluctant to be hand raisers. It says, "I want to hear what you say," even if Charlie's hand is up for the tenth time in twelve questions.

Fourth, *Cold Call* will help you distribute work around the room not only more fully (that is, beyond the hand raisers) but more authoritatively. One of its positive effects is that it establishes that the room belongs to you. Not only will this allow you to reach out to individual students, but it will have a strong cultural effect in that it will draw out engagement. If I am pretty sure that at some point in the next few hours or day you're going to call on me to respond to our class work, I have a strong incentive to do that work in anticipation of this probability. You have made me accountable. This is an incredibly powerful force. People sometimes ask, "Which one of these techniques should I do first?" or "If I can teach my teachers to do only one, which will make the biggest difference?" For the reasons I've described above, the single most powerful technique in this book is, I believe, *Cold Call.* But while making a habit of calling on students regardless of whose hand is up is one of the most critical techniques you can use to drive universal achievement, all cold calling is not equally effective. You can do it wrong; doing it right will ensure that it has the effect you intended. The success of the technique relies on the application of a few key principles:

• **Cold Call** *is predictable.* Cold calling is superb preventive medicine but less effective as a cure. It is a way to keep students' attention from drifting, but is not as effective once they're off task. It's an engagement strategy, not a discipline strategy.

If you cold call for a few minutes of your class almost every day, students will come to expect it and change their behavior in advance.

When a stimulus is predictable, it changes behavior by anticipation, not just by reaction. If you cold call for a few minutes of your class almost every day, students will come to expect it and change their behavior in advance; they will prepare to be asked questions at any time by paying attention and readying themselves mentally. If your cold calls surprise students, they may learn a lesson ("Darn, I should have been ready!"), but this will be too late to help them. Unless they know there'll surely be a next time very soon, they won't have cause to change their behavior before you ask your question. They may also feel ambushed, caught off guard, and therefore more likely to be thinking about the past ("Why'd she do that?") than about the future ("I'm going to be ready!").

If cold calls are predictable and students begin to anticipate them, the effect will be universal. The possibility (indeed, the likelihood) of a cold call affects all students, not just those who actually get cold called. You want students to react beforehand to the reliable possibility, not after the unpredictable fact. You want them always ready for the call that might come, not deciding after the fact to be ready for the next one. And you want all of them thinking that way.

Cold calling, then, should be part of the fabric of everyday life in your class. A little bit of it every day will have a stronger effect on classroom culture than a great deal of intensive but inconsistent or unexpected cold calling. At some point in most lessons, students should be asked to participate regardless of whether they have raised their hands.

Furthermore, since the purpose of *Cold Call* is to engage students before they tune out, many teachers find that the beginning of class is the ideal time for this technique. This allows them to set the tone for the rest of the day and engage students before they can become distracted. *Cold Call* is preventive medicine. Take it daily to keep the symptoms from ever appearing.

- **Cold Call *is systematic.*** Teachers who use *Cold Call* signal that these calls are about their expectations, not about individuals. They take pains to make it clear that cold calls are universal (they come without fail to everyone) and impersonal (their tone, manner, and frequency emphasize that they are not an effort to single out any student or students). The less a cold call carries emotion, the less it seems tied to what a student has or has not done, to whether you are happy or disappointed with him, whether you think he did his homework.

The message should ideally be, "This is how we do business here." The teachers interviewed for this book use *Cold Call* with an even, calm tone and spend a minimum amount of time appearing to hem and haw about which student to call on. Questions come at students quickly, clearly, and calmly, in clusters directed to multiple students, in multiple locations around the room, rather than focused on a single student or group of students in isolation. They should take in all types of students—not just those who might become off-task or who are sitting in the back. After all, a cold call is not a punishment; it is a student's chance, as Colleen Driggs puts it, "to shine."

Some teachers emphasize the systematic nature of *Cold Call* by keeping visible charts tracking who's been called on. What could send a clearer message that everyone gets their share than a tracking system in which every name gets checked off in good time?

- **Cold Call *is positive.*** The purpose of *Cold Call* is to foster positive engagement in the work of your class, which ideally is rigorous work. One of its benefits is that students occasionally surprise themselves with what they are capable of. They do not volunteer because they do not think they can answer, but when they are forced to try, they are happily surprised to find themselves succeeding. In so doing they also benefit from knowing that you thought they could answer the question. You show your respect and faith in a student when you ask her to join the conversation. But this works only if your questions propose to ask students to contribute to a real conversation rather than to catch them out and chasten them. This is the aspect of *Cold Call* that teachers are most likely to get wrong. There's part of many of us that wants to use it as a "gotcha"—to call on a student when we know he was tuned out to show him that fact or prove some sort of a lesson to him ("What did I just say, John?" or "Isn't that right, John?"). But this rarely works since causing a student to publicly founder on purpose and with no potential benefit at stake is more likely to make him ask questions about you ("Why's she always picking on me?") than about himself.

The goal is for the student to get the answer right, not learn a lesson by getting it wrong.

A positive cold call is the opposite of a gotcha in two ways. First, it is substantive. "What did I just say?" is not a substantive question. It's a gotcha, designed to "teach a lesson" that in fact it rarely teaches. "Do you think Lincoln declared war on the South primarily to eradicate slavery?" is a real question. "What is the subject in this sentence?" is a real question. You might ask a peer such a question in the faculty room, and this shows that you respect the person of whom you are asking the question. Second, the goal is for the student to get the answer right, not learn a lesson by getting it wrong. You want your students to succeed, to feel good and maybe even a little surprised by that success, even while they are challenged and stretched by the healthy tension of *Cold Call.* Remember that *Cold Call* is an engagement technique, not a disciplinary technique. It keeps students on task and mentally engaged. Once a student is off task, the *Cold Call* opportunity has passed. Then you should use a behavioral technique.

You can ensure a positive cold call by asking questions that pertain to the lesson and suggest you are making a genuine invitation to a student to participate in the conversation. Use *Cold Call* in an upbeat and positive tone, suggesting that you couldn't imagine a world in which a student would not want to participate.

One final aspect of *Cold Call* that leads to a positive tone occasionally eludes some teachers when they aren't prepared: the question and what an answer could look like should be clear. Every teacher has had the experience of asking a student a question that in retrospect wasn't clear, where even a well-informed and engaged student wouldn't know what to say. It's doubly important to avoid this kind of question when cold calling, and many teachers address this challenge by planning their exact questions in advance and word for word as part of their lesson planning process.

- **Cold Call** *is scaffolded.* This technique is especially effective when you start with simple questions and progress to harder ones, drawing students in, engaging them on terms that emphasize what they already know, and reinforcing basic knowledge before pushing for greater rigor and challenge. This will often require "unbundling," or breaking a single larger question up into a series of smaller questions.

Consider this sequence from the classroom of Darryl Williams as he teaches his third graders to identify the complete sentences from among a list of several choices:

Williams:	Read the next choice for me, please, Kyrese.
Kyrese:	[reading from the worksheet] "Have you seen a pumpkin seed?"
Williams:	Do we have a subject, Japhante?
Japhante:	Yes.
Williams:	What's the subject?
Japhante:	"You."
Williams:	"You." Excellent. Do we have a predicate, Eric?
Eric:	Yes.
Williams:	What's the predicate?
Eric:	"Seen."
Williams:	"Seen." Excellent. Is it a complete thought, Rayshawn?
Rayshawn:	Yes.
Williams:	Is that our complete sentence?
Rayshawn:	Yes.
Williams:	So we just keep going? What do we need to do, Shakaye?
Shakaye:	We need to look at the other two [answer choices] because that might sound right but one of the other two might sound right too.

The sequence involves calling on five students in rapid succession and follows a careful progression of increasing difficulty. The first question merely asks a student to read what's in front of him. The difficulty level is low. Williams is scaffolding; anyone can get it right. The next question ("Is there a subject?") is an incredibly simple yes-or-no question designed for the student of whom it is asked to get it right. When he does, Williams comes back with the more difficult question ("What is the subject?"), but that question now comes on the heels of the student's previous success and after Williams has engaged him in the process of thinking about sentence structure. After asking another student a similar sequence, he goes on to harder questions about whether the sentence is complete and what strategy students should take next in answering the question. By breaking the basic question, "Is it a complete sentence?" into smaller parts and starting with simple questions, Williams successfully engages students and ensures their readiness when he asks more difficult questions. By parsing the question out to five students instead of one, he also ensures fuller participation and the expectation that participation is a predictable and systematic event.

A more subtle method of scaffolding is to allow students to begin answering cold calls about work that they have already done and have the answers in front of them. This again begins the sequence with something they are likely to get right. Darryl Williams began his sequence of *Cold Call* above with a request to Kyrese to "read the next [answer] choice for me." This engages the student at the outset at a level where he is almost sure to succeed: he merely has to read what's in front of him. Furthermore, a cold call that asks a student, "Please tell us your answer to the first problem, Milagros," employs scaffolding because Milagros has done the work and has an answer in front of her. She begins by merely reporting back on her work. Of course, a sequence that begins with such simple questions would ideally progress to more rigorous follow-up questions that did ask Milagros or Kyrese to think on their feet. One of the misperceptions some teachers have about this technique is that it is only a way to ask simple questions. But its questions should be as rigorous as you can make them—something students will come to take pride in as they see themselves able to handle demanding material on the spur of the moment. Starting simple doesn't mean ending that way, but it does tend to engage and motivate kids and cause students to be inspired by the building level of rigor and challenge.

Using *Cold Call* to follow up on previous comments in class underscores how much you value students' participation and insight. It also emphasizes that your students' engagement in what their peers say is as important as their engagement in what you say. There are three varieties to consider:

- *Follow-on to a previous question.* Ask a simple question using *Cold Call*—think of it as a warm-up—and then ask the student a short series of further questions (most teachers ask two to four) in which her opinions are further developed or her understanding further tested.

- *Follow-on to another student's comment.* This reinforces the importance of listening to peers as well as teacher: "James says the setting is a dark summer night. Does that tell us everything we need to know about the setting, Susan?" or "What does *exploit* mean, Stephen? Good and who gets exploited in *Macbeth,* Markeesha?"

- *Follow-on to a student's own earlier comment.* This signals that once the student has spoken, she's not done: "But, Yolanda, you said earlier that we always multiplied length and width to find area. Why didn't we do that here?"

Beyond these principles, there are several elements champion teachers apply, vary, and adapt to maximize the benefit of *Cold Call* in a wider variety of settings. These are key variations on the *Cold Call* theme:

- **Hands Up/Hands Down.** You can use *Cold Call* and continue allowing students to raise their hands if they wish, or you can instruct your students to keep their hands down. Both versions emphasize different aspects of the technique.

Taking hands allows you to continue encouraging and rewarding students who ask to participate, even if you sometimes call on those who don't have their hands raised. You merely move between taking hands and cold calling at your discretion. This continues providing incentives to students to raise their hands while also allowing you to add sophistication to your scaffolding. When you're allowing hands during your cold calling, you can, say, cold call students for the first three questions in a sequence and then save the capper, the last and potentially the toughest or most interesting question, for a volunteer, thus differentiating instruction and making academic challenge a reward in and of itself. One factor to consider in allowing students to raise their hands while you cold call is that it may cause your use of *Cold Call* to be less apparent and transparent and thus less systematic. That's because it may not always be obvious to students whether the classmate who got called on had her hand up or was cold called. Taking hands also gives you an important data point. Even if you ignore it, it tells you who thinks they know well enough to volunteer. Thus, if you want to try to call on students whose mastery is unsteady, you have a clearer idea of who to try.

You can also decide to tell students to put their hands down, that you're not taking hands, and then proceed to cold call whomever you wish. This sends a more forceful message about your firm control of the classroom, and it makes your cold calling more explicit, predictable, and transparent ("I'm cold calling now"). It also tends to make the pacing of your cold calling, and thus your lesson, even faster because you don't spend time navigating hands. Finally, hands down can be more effective for checking for understanding in two key ways. First, it reduces the likelihood of students' calling out answers in eagerness. While truly a sin of enthusiasm, calling out is corrosive to your classroom environment and specifically to your ability to steer questions to the students who need to work or those you need to assess. Second, because students who do want to answer are rendered less visible (they don't have their hands up), your decision to target your checking for understanding of more reticent students is less patently visible and therefore seems a bit more systematic.

A last caveat is that most champion teachers appear to use both hands up and hands down as a matter of habit, with their choice determined by the situation. One possible reason for this is that using only hands up is not as forceful and energetic and using only hands down is a disincentive to hand raising over the long run. With enough time, it risks convincing students not to bother raising their hands at all, since doing so is never rewarded. In that case a teacher had better really like *Cold Call* because she'll have few hands offered and few alternatives.

Using this sequence—"Question. Pause. Name."—ensures that every student hears the question and begins preparing an answer during the pause that you've provided.

• **Timing the Name.** *Cold Call* can vary in terms of when you say the name of the student you're calling on. The most common and often the most effective approach is to ask the question, pause, and then name a student, as in, "What's 3 times 9? [pause], James?" Using this sequence—"Question. Pause. Name."—ensures that every student hears the question and begins preparing an answer during the pause you've provided. Since students know a cold call is likely but not who will receive it, every student is likely to answer the question, with one student merely called on to give their answer aloud. In the example, it means that every student in the class has done the multiplication in the pause between question and name. If you say the name first, twenty-four fewer students practice their multiplication. The difference in leverage between this scenario (twenty-five students answering a question and one saying it aloud) and the alternative (one student answering a question and twenty-four watching) is so dramatic that it should be the default approach to most of your cold calling.

In some cases, calling a student's name first can be beneficial. Often it can prepare a student to attend and increases the likelihood of success. This can be especially effective with students who may not have been cold called before, students who have language processing difficulties, or students whose knowledge of English is still developing. In its most exaggerated form, this is known as a precall. In a precall, you tell a student that he or she can expect to be called on later in the lesson. It can happen privately (a teacher might say to a student before class, "Okay, Jamal, I'm going to ask you to go over the last problem from the homework today. Be ready!") or publicly ("Paul's going to give us the answer, Karen, but then I'll be asking you why!").

Another instance in which it is productive to state the name first is for clarity. For example, if you are coming out of a sequence of *Call and Response* (the following technique in this chapter), in which students have been calling out answers in unison, dropping in a name first and then asking the question makes it clear to students that you are no longer using *Call and Response* and thus avoids the awkward and counterproductive moment when some students attempt to answer in unison a question you had intended for an individual.

• **Mix with other engagement techniques.** *Cold Call* responds especially well to mixing with other engagement techniques. *Call and Response* is a perfect example: moving back and forth between whole group choral response and individual responses at a rapid energetic pace can drive up the level of positive energy dramatically. It can also allow you to ensure that students aren't coasting during *Call and Response.* To take a simple example, you could review multiplication tables with your students by asking everyone to call out answers to a few problems:

Teacher: Class, what's 9 times 7?

  Class: 63!

Teacher: Good what's 9 times 8?

  Class: 72!

Teacher: Good, now Charlie, What's 9 times 9?

  Class: 81!

Teacher: Good. What's 9 times 9, class?

  Class: 81!

Teacher: Good and, Matilda, what was 9 times 7 again?

Matilda: 63!

By toggling back and forth, you can cause individual students to review material or reinforce a successful answer by having the class repeat it.

Pepper (technique 24, later in this chapter) is another engagement technique that works well with *Cold Call*. In fact it's very similar to *Cold Call* in that it consists of rapid-fire questions that are often cold called. Finally, *Everybody Writes* (technique 25, later in this chapter) is a preparation for *Cold Call,* as it allows everyone to prethink the topic or questions you'll be addressing; this increases the likely quality of responses.

Teachers often conclude that *Cold Call* questions must be simple. In fact, *Cold Call* questions can and should be rigorous and demanding. Part of their power lies in having students feel the pride of answering demanding questions at the spur of the moment. Following is a transcript of a session of *Cold Call* executed by Jesse Rector of North Star Academy's Clinton Hill campus. Rector is an exceptional math teacher with exceptional results and a following within our organization for his craft. The rigor of his questioning shows why. See how many of the following *Cold Call* questions, asked of seventh graders in rapid-fire succession, *you'd* get correct.

Rector: I'm a square field with an area of 169 square feet. What's the length of one of my sides, Janae?

Janae: 13.

Rector: 13 what? [Asking Janae for the units is an example of *Format Matters,* technique 4.]

Janae: 13 feet.

Rector: I'm a square field with a perimeter of 48 feet. What's my area, Katrina?

Katrina: 144 square feet.

Rector: Excellent. I'm a regular octagon with a side that measures $8x$ plus 2. What is my perimeter, Tamisse?

Tamisse: $64x$ plus 16.

Rector: Excellent. I am an isosceles triangle with two angles that measure $3x$ each. What is the measure of my third angle, Anaya?

Anaya: 180 degrees minus $6x$.

Rector: Excellent, 180 degrees minus $6x$. The square root of 400 is what, Frank?

Frank: 100.

Rector: No, the square root of 400 isn't 100. Help him out.

David: 20.

Rector: That's right; it's 20. Tell him why.

David: Because if you multiply 20 by 20, you'll get 400.

SEE IT IN ACTION: CLIP 7

COLD CALL/PEPPER

In clip 7 on the DVD, Jesse Rector is modeling *Cold Call*. You'll notice that his students are standing up; this makes the fact that he's going to use *Cold Call* obvious or, in the language of the technique, "predictable." Jesse gives the lie to that notion. To prove it, just try to keep up with his seventh graders yourself in answering the questions. This is also a good example of *Pepper:* a significant quantity of questions (not necessarily cold calls, though in this case they are) asked rapidly around a given number of themes (geometry and square roots here), with little discussion in between. You can read more about *Pepper* later in this chapter. After you've done so, rewatch Jesse's video and see how he puts both techniques to work.

The first time you use *Cold Call*, your students may wonder what's going on, and with some justification. They may have never been cold called before. They may not have been in a classroom where that kind of thing happened. They might not see the connection between *Cold Call* and their getting to college, say, or they might be inclined to see it as a negative rather than a positive situation. Thus, it's a good idea to script some brief remarks—in essence, a rollout speech—to use the first time with *Cold Call*. Your brief remarks can explain the what and why. This makes the exercise rational, systematic, predictable, and, with a little skill, inspiring.

SEE IT IN ACTION: CLIP 8

COLD CALL

In clip 8 on the DVD, Colleen Driggs of Rochester Prep is modeling her rollout speech for *Cold Call.* Many teachers assume cold calls have to be stressful for students, that they'll be forced to participate when they don't want to. But your expectations of students' interest are often a self-fulfilling prophecy. As you watch Driggs, make a list of the things she says that you could borrow or adapt if you gave a rollout speech to explain cold calling to your students (and, I hope, tried to underscore what a good thing it is).

A rollout speech could be useful for any number of techniques and skills, not just *Cold Call.* A few that jump to my mind are *Right Is Right* (technique 2), *No Opt Out* (technique 1), Control the Game (Chapter Ten), and *Do It Again* (technique 39).

In this sequence Colleen quickly tells her students how to act during *Cold Call,* explains why she uses this technique, and frames the activity in a positive way: a chance to show off.

Elm City College Prep's Summer Payne introduces *Cold Call* to her kindergarteners by renaming it. To a cheery little tune, she sings: "Individual turns! Listen for your name!" And her kids, like Colleen's, love *Cold Call.* If you present it positively, yours will too.

SEE IT IN ACTION: CLIP 9

COLD CALL AND VOCABULARY

In clip 9 on the DVD, Beth Verrilli of North Star Academy demonstrates exemplary teaching of *Cold Call* and Vocabulary (discussed in Chapter Eleven).

Verrilli's class is an eleventh- and twelfth-grade Advanced Placement English class (thus the small class size). Notice how her use of *Cold Call* stresses follow-ons. She repeatedly cold calls students to respond to or give examples of a previous student's answer. This builds a level of strong accountability into a mature peer-to-peer culture that's especially useful with older students. It also boosts the rigor of the classroom and keeps the pacing strong.

In terms of Vocabulary, notice how many times students use and apply some version of the word *exploit* and use it in slightly different forms ("exploit," "exploits," and "exploited") in settings where both people (Macbeth) and abstract concepts (Duncan's trust) are exploited. If the goal of vocabulary instruction is for students to have a deep meaning of the word and the ability to apply it correctly in multiple settings (in terms of both syntax and meaning), Verrilli's students have leaped forward toward that goal in a very short span of time.

TECHNIQUE 23

CALL AND RESPONSE

The basic element of **Call and Response** is that you ask a question and the whole class calls out the answer in unison. It sounds simple, but when it is effectively used in all its variations, *Call and Response* can be an exceptional tool not only to engage students but to help them achieve.

Effective *Call and Response* can be accomplish three primary goals:

- *Academic review and reinforcement.* Having students respond as a group ensures that everyone gets to give the answer. Everyone swings at the pitch, and the number of at bats multiplies by twenty-five to thirty. When an individual student gives a strong answer, asking the rest of the class to repeat that answer is also an effective way to reinforce it. The whole class repeats the insight and reinforces for the original student how important what he or she said was.

- *High-energy fun.* *Call and Response* is energetic, active, and spirited. It feels lively, like being part of a cheering crowd or an exercise class. Generally participants like cheering in crowds and going to exercise classes because they find them energizing. *Call and Response* can make your class similarly invigorating and make students want to be there.

Students don't see Call and Response *as behavioral reinforcement, but it makes crisp, active, timely compliance a habit, committing it to muscle memory.*

- *Behavioral reinforcement.* There's an outstanding hidden benefit to *Call and Response*: students respond to a prompt as a group, exactly on cue, over and over again. And it makes this kind of on-cue compliance public. Everyone sees everyone else doing it. You ask; they do, over and over again. Students don't see *Call and Response* as behavioral reinforcement, but it makes crisp, active, timely compliance a habit, committing it to muscle memory. This reinforces the teacher's authority and command.

Although *Call and Response* is a fairly straightforward technique, it's easy to underestimate it, focusing on its most simplistic forms: asking students to repeat aphorisms and chants, for example. In fact, there are five types or levels of *Call and Response* sequence, listed next roughly in order of intellectual rigor, from least to greatest:

1. *Repeat:* In these sequences, students repeat what their teacher has said or complete a familiar phrase that he or she starts. The topic of the phrase can be behavioral ("Who are we??!! [South Side Prep!] What are we here to do? [To learn and achieve!]") or academic ("When we see a zero, the pattern . . . [stops and begins again] the pattern . . . [stops and begins again]").

2. *Report:* Students who have already completed problems or questions on their own are asked to report their answers back ("On three, tell me your answer to problem number three"). This version allows you to more energetically reinforce academic work once it's been completed.

3. *Reinforce:* You reinforce new information or a strong answer by asking the class to repeat it: "Can anyone tell me what this part of the expression is called? Yes, Trayvon, that's the exponent. Class, what's this part of the expression called?" Everyone has an additional active interaction with critical new content, and when a student provides the information, *Call and Response* reinforces the importance of the answer ("My answer was so important my teacher asked the whole class to repeat it").

4. *Review:* This asks students to review answers or information from earlier in the class or unit: "Who was the first person Theseus met on the road to

Athens, class? Who was the second person? And now who's the third?" or "What vocabulary word did we say meant not having enough of something?"

5. *Solve:* This is the most challenging to do well and the most rigorous. The teacher asks students to solve a problem and call out the answer in unison: "If the length is ten inches and the width is twelve inches, the area of our rectangle must be how many square inches, class?" The challenge is that when having a group of people solve a problem in real time and call out the answer, there must be a single clear answer and a strong likelihood that all students will know how to solve it. With those caveats in mind, this type of *Call and Response* call be highly rigorous, and students often surprise themselves at their ability to solve problems in real time.

To be effective in any form, *Call and Response* should be universal, that is, all students should respond. To ensure that this is the case, plan to use a specific signal ("Class!" "Everybody!" "One, Two . . . ," or even a nonverbal signal such as a finger point) to indicate your desire to have students respond in unison. Such a signal, called an *in-cue,* makes it clear when you are asking students to call out as a group and when you are asking for students to wait until you've identified a student to answer. This is critically important. Every student should know whether a question you've asked is:

- Rhetorical: "Is 42 divided by 7 going to be 5?"

- About to be directed to a single child: "42 divided by 7 is what, Shane?"

- Awaiting a volunteer: "Who can tell me what 42 divided by 7 is?"

- Asked in anticipation of full class call and response: "Class, 42 divided by 7 is . . ."

If students don't know how to quickly and reliably differentiate your expectations in these four cases, you will lose your ability to intentionally use any of these techniques at your sole discretion. Instead, it will fall to each member of the class to infer which of the above he or she thinks is (or would like have) applicable at any time. If that happens, you lose your ability to choose between checking for understanding with specific individual students using *Cold Call*, engaging all students, reinforcing an eager hand raiser, choosing just the student you think will be insightful, ensuring wait time for reflection before you take an answer, or any of a dozen other tricks of good teaching. In short, you need to have students know what kind of answer you expect. Furthermore, who doesn't shudder at the thought of being at a party speaking loudly over music when all of a sudden the music goes silent and they alone are left shouting their thoughts to a suddenly quiet room? For students to participate enthusiastically in *Call and Response,* they must confidently and clearly know when to sing out because everyone will be singing out and know as well they need not fear they will be the only one singing. Thus, for *Call and Response* to succeed, you must use a reliable and consistent signal and make 100 percent participation the rule. A good in-cue is the key to achieving this so it's worth spending a little more time on the topic.

There are five specific kinds of in-cues that champion teachers use.

The first kind of in-cue is count-based, for example, "Ready, set . . . ," "One, two . . . ," or "One, two, ready, you . . ." These have the advantage of giving students time to get ready to answer and, in classrooms where *Call and Response* is especially energetic, to breathe in and prepare to sing out in their loudest voice. They also help you ensure that students answer in unison and exactly on cue so these prompts can be particularly effective in building a strong, positive culture. Count-based cues are highly effective in that they can be cut short if students are not fully attentive or on-task in the lead-up to the *Call and Response.* In other words, a count of, "One two, ready, you!" can occasionally be cut off by the teacher ("One two . . . no I don't have everyone") to show students they're not ready while maintaining the anticipation of the fun that's to come. Finally, you can speed them up or slow them down as necessary to set the pace you desire.

Effective teachers may start with a longer count-based cue and gradually truncate it as students become familiar with it to save time. "One, two, ready, you!" may become simply "One, two!" The resulting saved second of class time speeds up the pace of instruction and allocates more time to teaching. That may sound trivial, but an in-cue that's a second shorter, repeated ten times a day over two hundred days, buys you half an hour of instructional time. In some classrooms, even this shorter version is sometimes replaced by a nonverbal cue to expedite it.

A second form of in-cue is the group prompt. Two common examples are, "Everybody!" and "Class!" as in, "What's the name of the answer to an addition problem, everybody?" Or, "Class, what's the greatest common factor of 10 and 16?" Using a collective term for the whole class helps foster group identity, and these prompts remind students of your expectation. Saying the word *everybody* reminds students that you expect universal participation, and should you fail to get it, allows you to repeat the sequence by merely repeating the word with slightly greater emphasis: "*every*body." Champion teachers are often strategic about whether they put the prompt before the question or after. Saying, "What's the name of the answer to an addition problem, everybody?" gives students time to hear and process the question before they answer, especially if there's a slight pause between question and prompt. This carries a slightly different emphasis from, "Everybody, what's the name of the answer to an addition problem?" The former starts with the content, the latter with the expectation about who's going to answer.

A third kind of in-cue is a nonverbal gesture: a point, a hand dropped from shoulder height, a looping motion with the finger. These have the advantage of speed and don't require you to interrupt the flow of the lesson. If used consistently, they can be powerful. They can also be challenging in that the tone has to be just right or they can seem schoolmarmish. (Imagine how a teacher snapping when she wants her class to answer aloud could sound wrong; at the same time, I have seen teachers use this method with great success.) It's also easy to slip on consistency with nonverbal signals, a tendency that can give rise to long-term challenges. Nevertheless, this is the choice of many top teachers.

A fourth kind of in-cue employs a shift in tone and volume. The teacher increases volume in the last few words of a sentence and inflects his or her tone to imply a question; students recognize this as a prompt and respond crisply. This method is by far the trickiest in-cue and the most prone to error. It's most often one that teachers begin using after mastering the simpler methods over time. It has the advantage of being seamless, fast, and natural, but you probably shouldn't use this as you are developing this skill. Furthermore, if you rely on it, you should expect a certain number of miscues to occur. In that case, you should have an in-cue of one of the above types ready as a backup to use to respond if students miss a cue.

The last kind of in-cue is specialized: it indicates a specific response to students. In many classrooms that use these, there are multiple such cues, each indicating a different response. For example, Bob Zimmerli teaches his students a song listing the multiples of all of the numbers up to 12. After he has taught them these songs, he can prompt them with specialized cues. If he says, for example, "Sevens on two. One, two . . ." his students will respond by singing, "7, 14, 21, 28, 35, 42 . . ." to the tune of a popular song. If he says, "Eights on two. One, two . . ." his students will respond with a different song and different numbers. Or, in a different example, you might teach your students to always respond to the in-cue, "Why are we here?" with the response, "To learn! To achieve!" Once the students learned that connection, you would no longer have to offer a reminder that you were expecting a response ("Ready, everyone?"). You would suddenly say, "Why are we here?" and your students would be chanting. This form of in-cue can be especially fun for teachers and students. There's something exciting about a teacher asking a seemingly innocuous question, and then suddenly the whole class is singing and chanting in unison.

Teachers have developed a wide variety of wrinkles that add value to *Call and Response* and make it useful in particular situations. Here are three especially effective ways to adapt and apply this technique:

- Combine and intersperse it with *Cold Call.* Varying group and individual accountability to answer increases students' level of attention and taps into the tension of the unexpected, making class more exciting for students.

- Jazz up your *Call and Response* by asking subgroups within the class to respond in unison to some cues. For example, ask the boys a *Call and Response* question and then the girls, the left side of the room and then the right, the front and then the back. This unexpected twist makes the technique more interesting and unexpected for students, factors that are likely to engage them more fully in class.

- Add a physical gesture: students cross their fingers in a mock addition sign as they call out the name for the answer to an addition problem: "The sum!" They point their fingers at the sky and chant, "On the roof!" when asked where the numbers they carry go in an addition problem. By sometimes including a physical gesture, teachers gain two advantages: they give students a way to be physically active in class, which keeps them alert and moving and gives them something positive to do, not just say. For students who struggle to sit still, this is a great relief. By adding a visual cue, especially one that's not random but where the gesture reflects the correct answer (the crossed fingers), the teacher is better able to watch for students who are hiding while others participate and increases his ability to assess students' level of understanding.

KEY IDEA

CALL AND RESPONSE

Use group choral response—you ask; they answer in unison—to build a culture of energetic, positive engagement.

Effectively implemented, *Call and Response* can engage all students at once in an exciting, energetic, and motivating activity that energizes the class. It is extremely useful as part of a larger engagement strategy, and it has positive ancillary behavioral effects. It builds the habit of compliance in a subtle but powerful way. When they participate in *Call and Response,* students make a habit of doing what the teacher has asked, over and over again, without even realizing they are practicing that skill. However, *Call and Response* has risks and downsides that every teacher should be aware of:

- *It can allow freeloading.* If I don't know the answer or don't want to participate, I can move my lips and fake it. If you're concerned about freeloading, consider adding a gesture to the response, which gives both an auditory and a visual way to test for participation.

- *It does not provide effective checking for understanding.* In the excitement of many students answering correctly, students who are lost can easily hide, mouthing answers or watching their peers and joining in for second and third repetitions.

- *It reinforces the behavioral culture in your classroom only if it's crisp.* If students sense that they can use their responses to test your expectations by dragging out their answers, answering in a silly or loud manner, or answering out of sync, they will. Therefore, you must make sharpening up a priority. When the response to your call is any of those, you should energetically and positively correct with something like: "I like your energy, but I need to hear you respond right on cue. Let's try that again."

TECHNIQUE 24
PEPPER

For decades baseball players have warmed up for games and practices by playing a game called Pepper. In a group of four or five players, one holds a bat, and the rest stand in a ring in front of the batter, a few yards away, gloves at the ready. One player tosses the ball to the batter. Without stopping to catch it, the batter taps it back toward the group using the bat; the nearest player fields it and, again without stopping, tosses it back to the batter, who hits the toss back to another player. The game is fast, providing dozens of opportunities to practice fielding and hitting skills in a short period of time and in a fast-paced and energetic environment. Unlike formal practice, it doesn't propose to teach new skills or game strategy; it's a reinforcement of skills.

Pepper, the teaching technique by the same name, also uses fast-paced, group-oriented activities to review familiar information and foundational skills. A teacher tosses questions to a group of students quickly, and they answer back. The teacher usually does not slow down to engage or discuss an answer; if it's right, she simply asks another student a new question. If it's wrong, she asks the same question of another student, though sometimes the same student, always keeping moving. That's *Pepper:* a fast-paced, unpredictable (in real Pepper, you never know who's going to get the ball) review of fundamentals with lots of chances for participation in rapid succession.

Pepper is a great warm-up activity. Many teachers include it as part of daily oral drill at the outset of class, but it is also effective as an upbeat interlude to bring energy to the class, or as an energetic part of a review, perhaps wrapping up to go over material one more time before an assessment. It's perfect for filling in a stray ten minutes inside or outside the classroom with productive, engaging fun.

Since one challenge of *Pepper* is that it's easily confused with *Cold Call,* looking at some of the ways *Pepper* is different is a good way to get to the next level of specificity about the technique.

First, although *Pepper* often involves *Cold Call*, it doesn't have to. With *Pepper,* you can take hands if you prefer, calling on volunteers quickly and energetically, either from the outset or after a brief period of *Cold Call* to engage students. Most typically I see it happen in the latter way: the game starts out with *Cold Call,* but as students get engaged and enthused, they begin raising their hands, often eagerly, at which point, the teacher makes a transition into a version of *Pepper* that involves almost all students in volunteering.

Second, *Pepper* almost always asks quick fundamental questions, often as review. This is different from *Cold Call*, which can involve questions at any level or type. You'd be fine cold calling a student to discuss the primary causes of the Civil War but less likely to cover that material in a game of *Pepper.* Since *Pepper* is often a means for review, teachers move from unit to unit within the game. They'll ask questions about properties of quadrilaterals for two or three minutes and then move on to a series of questions about coordinate geometry. And they often do this even if the topics are not entirely related. In a social studies class, you could spend a few minutes on map skills followed by a few minutes on the original colonies.

Third, *Pepper* is a game. (Baseball players love their version of Pepper because it's a break from practice.) Thus, classroom *Pepper* uses indicators that underscore for your class that they are playing a game. In some cases, this might mean that you ask all students to stand up, or you might call on students in a unique way—something you might not do outside the game. In *Pepper,* time is compressed, and the game has a clear end and beginning. Here are several variations that teachers use that emphasize the fun aspects of the technique:

- *Pick sticks.* A trademark of *Pepper* is its unpredictability: where each question goes, nobody knows. Many teachers take this a step further and use devices to engineer the randomization, most frequently using popsicle sticks labeled with each student's name (and why they are called *pick sticks*) pulled at random out of a can, for example, but also including other variations, such as random number generation on a laptop. In such a system, teachers are in most cases relying on apparent random assignment of participation. Whether or not students recognize it, a teacher pulling pick sticks retains the ability to steer questions as desired. One teacher's advice explains what I mean: "Remember, only you know whose name is really on the popsicle stick!" You can pick John's stick but call out Susan's name. Picking a stick has the disadvantage of taking as much time as asking a question: it slows you down by half.

SEE IT IN ACTION: CLIP 10

PEPPER AND EVERY MINUTE MATTERS

In clip 10 on the DVD, Annette Riffle of North Star Academy demonstrates *Pepper.* The most compelling aspect of this scene is not just Riffle's use of rapid-fire questions in fast succession, as *Pepper* dictates, but the way she makes efficient, or more precisely urgent, use of time. In her classroom, every minute matters (see Chapter Eight on the technique by this name)—even the minute when a student does her work at the board can be maximized.

- *Head-to-head.* A teacher using head-to-head begins by having two students stand up to answer a question. The student who gets the correct answer first remains standing to compete against a new challenger. What this technique gives up in predictability, it makes up for in the benefits of a friendly competition. In using this part of the technique, emphasize the same aspects of regular *Pepper:* fast pace, short and simple questions on fundamentals, and limited engagement with wrong answers. Competition makes it easy to get too involved in discussing and even arbitrating right from wrong ("But I said that!"). The best teachers just keep moving and don't engage such distractions. Otherwise there's too much talking about that game and not enough playing it.

- *Sit down.* This variation, usually done at the beginning of class, starts with all students standing and the teacher peppering them with the trademark quick questions. Students "earn their seats" (get to sit down) by answering correctly. Again the teacher does not engage answers except to signal with a gesture that a student may be seated. This game can be played in reverse (stand up) to determine the lining-up order for lunch, say.

Since *Pepper* is about speed, you'll rarely see teachers stopping to discuss and analyze wrong answers. They may ask other students to correct them, but the goal is almost always to keep the pace moving.

TECHNIQUE 25

WAIT TIME

Another technique to tap into the power of ideas and students that aren't the first to emerge when you ask a question is **Wait Time**—delaying a few strategic seconds after you finish asking a question and before you ask a student to begin answering it. Mary Budd Rowe, a professor of education at the University of Florida until her death in 1996, pioneered research into wait time and showed that the typical teacher allows about a second of it after a question and allows for more than one and half seconds before taking an answer.

The challenges and limitations posed by such a habit are significant. The answers you can expect to get after less than a second's reflection are unlikely to be the richest, the most reflective, or the most developed your students can generate. And taking answers after just a second systematically encourages students to raise their hand with the first answer—rather than the best one—they can think of if they want to reasonably hope to participate. Finally, this lack of wait time makes it more likely that you will waste time processing a poor answer before you get to discuss a good one. Ironically, waiting and ensuring that you spend your time on higher-quality initial answers may actually save you time.

Minds work fast, and the amount of additional time necessary to improve the quality of answers may be small. Some research has shown that when students are given just three to five seconds of wait time after a question, several key things are likely to happen:

> *Minds work fast, and the amount of additional time necessary to improve the quality of answers may be small.*

- The length and correctness of student responses are likely to increase.

- The number of failures to respond (those who say, "I don't know") is likely to decrease.

- The number of students who volunteer to answer is likely to increase.

- The use of evidence in answers is likely to increase.

But waiting is not quite as simple as merely pausing or counting to three in your mind. First, it is hard to discipline yourself to allow time to pass after a question, and doing nothing does not necessarily help you to do that well. Second, and more important, it is not necessarily apparent to students how they should respond to your waiting, especially when they have not spent significant time in schools that expect or train for rigorous reflection or that can even sustain a behavioral environment where reflection, rather than goofing off, is likely to fill the space between question and answer.

While you are training and acculturating your students to become scholars and habituate the behaviors that yield success, you should consider enhancing your use of *Wait Time* by narrating it. Teachers who use this *Narrated Wait Time* make the technique more intentional and productive—that is, more likely to result in the possible positive outcomes that can occur when *Wait Time* is used. They provide guidance to their students about what they should be doing with their three seconds to be most productive. They tacitly explain why they're waiting and tell them—for example:

1. "I'm waiting for more hands."

2. "I'd like to see at least fifteen hands before we hear an answer."

3. "I'm waiting for someone who can connect this scene to another play, ideally *Macbeth*."

4. "I'm going to give everyone lots of time because this question is tricky. Your first answer may not be the best."

5. "I'm seeing people thinking deeply and jotting down thoughts. I'll give everyone a few more seconds to do that."

6. "I'm seeing people going back to the chapter to see if they can find the scene. That seems like a great idea."

7. "I'm looking for someone who's pointing to the place in the passage where you can find the answer."

8. "I'll start taking answers is ten seconds."

9. "I'm starting to see more hands now. Four, five, seven. Great. People are really starting to get comfortable taking a risk here."

Notice the different emphasis of this narrated sequence. The first merely suggests that the teacher would like to see more students participate. The second sets a group goal for participation and, through use of *we,* makes answering the question a collective project. The third gives the students something specific and useful to reflect on: how this scene is connected to something else they have read. In other words, what would an especially useful answer look like? The fourth pushes students to double-check themselves and develop at least one second possibility. The fifth narrates practical forms of productive activity by students in the class (jotting down thoughts) and suggests to other students that they try this as well. Again, it stresses how to be productive during the wait time. The sixth chooses a similarly productive activity to engage in during wait time to generate and research ideas. This one increases the likelihood that the teacher will receive an evidence-based answer from her students. The seventh has a similar emphasis but asks students to affirm that they have done the productive work in the interim by pointing to the answer. It also increases the reliability with which the teacher can intentionally choose a correct or an incorrect answer. The eighth allows the teachers to give students an extended answer period (it could be longer if she wished) by establishing a clear end point. The ninth narrates positive behavior to normalize it (to make it seem typical) and encourages the risk of trying when you aren't sure of the answer.

The point is that top teachers use their narration of the interim period during their wait time to incent and reinforce the specific behaviors that will be most productive to their students during that time. They are teaching even while they are waiting.

SEE IT IN ACTION: CLIP 11

WAIT TIME

In clip 11 on the DVD, Colleen Driggs of Rochester Prep models *Wait Time*. She asks what genre a story her students have just read is most similar to. Her goal is to cause the students to think actively about the story and review and assess a variety of options before choosing the best answer. Work like that takes time, and students have to use their time wisely. So in addition to waiting almost twenty seconds between her question and the student she calls on, she provides guidance about how to use that precious time to be strong students:

- "You can go back and use your notes if you need to." *Message:* Make a habit of using your notes to help answer questions.

- "I'll give you some think time." *Message:* This answer should take some time and requires you to think about it.

- To one student: "Good job going back and using your notes." *Message:* Emphasizes how to use *Wait Time* productively. This is also a strong example of a key element of *Precise Praise* (technique 44 in Chapter Seven): praising replicable student behaviors.

TECHNIQUE 26

EVERYBODY WRITES

I recently watched a rigorous tenth-grade reading lesson at the highly successful Boston Collegiate High School. The teacher led her students though a discussion of Tim O'Brien's narratively complex short story, "The Man I Killed," from his book *The Things They Carried*. In the story, the narrator (perhaps O'Brien, perhaps not) describes in the first person his own inability to talk to others about killing an enemy combatant during the Vietnam War. In one of the culminating moments of the lesson, the teacher asked students an astute and demanding question: "Why would someone write a story about not being able to talk about what he did, and in so doing, talk about it? Why would he talk about not being able to talk about it?"

I was struck by two things: first by how lucky the students were to be in a classroom with a teacher who asked demanding and perceptive questions in full faith that they could answer them. Second I was struck by the students' response, which was silence. They looked somewhat blankly at the teacher, and she, in the end, stepped in and gave them a very nice summary of her thinking as to the answer. It was a fine summary but not a successful discussion, and the result was a lower ratio: the teacher did the cognitive work.

Looking at the students as they struggled with the question, I was struck by the paradox of their earnest confusion. No students rolled their eyes; none looked longingly out the window and disengaged. They wanted to answer, some of them even craning forward as if to await some insight. And then they averted their eyes in hopes that the teacher wouldn't call on them. This was a watershed moment: the teacher asked exactly the kind of question that pushes students beyond their current understanding and knowledge of literature, the kind of question that exemplified true college preparatory expectations, and she was rewarded with a great silence descending.

Is there any way around such a paradox? To answer, I have to consider what it would take for me to answer the teacher's question. The answer is that I would need a minute, even half a minute, to think and, more important, to write: to jot down my thoughts and wrestle them into words. With time to reflect and begin turning thoughts into words, I'd have the best chance of being ready to participate and, ideally, at some level of depth, because my ideas would be better and I would be more confident in them.

KEY IDEA

EVERYBODY WRITES

Set your students up for rigorous engagement by giving them the opportunity to reflect first in writing before discussing. As author Joan Didion says, "I write to know what I think."

Like Joan Didion, I often have to write to know what I think. In college, writing papers at the fringes of my understanding, I sometimes did not truly understand what my thesis was until I had written it. Only when the paper was done would my ideas have crystallized and coalesced in some organized form. In retrospect, my participation in discussions of literature would have been ten times better if they'd happened after I wrote the paper, a fact I recognized when one of the best professors I studied with required of his students a short written reflection as the entry ticket to each day's class. In that class, where everybody wrote first, the conversation started where it ended in other classes. Another of my best professors described a "notion" as something two steps shy of an idea. Like many other students, I spent a lot of time talking about notions in college, and, I'd argue, it's in the writing that the ideas emerge.

Effective teachers also set their students up to hold rigorous discussions and reach rigorous conclusions by giving them the opportunity to reflect first in writing before discussing. This is the rationale behind **Everybody Writes**, a technique in which teachers ask all students to prepare for more ambitious thinking and discussion by reflecting in writing for a short interval.

In a broader sense, most class discussions are structured, unwittingly, around the false assumption that the first ideas to be generated or the first students to raise their hands will be the ones most conducive to a productive conversation: ask a question, call on a hand. But the first answer is not always the best answer. Some students require time to generate worthy ideas or to feel confident enough in their ideas to offer to share them. Ideas get better even for the students whose hands shoot right up when they benefit from a few moments of reflection.

There are at least six benefits to *Everybody Writes:*

1. It often allows you to select effective responses to begin your discussion since you can review your students' ideas in advance by circulating and reading over shoulders.

2. It allows you to cold call students simply and naturally since you know everyone is prepared with thoughts and you can merely ask, "What did you write about, Ariel?" to kick things off.

3. It allows you to give every student, not just those who can get their hands up fast, the chance to be part of the conversation.

4. Processing thoughts in writing refines them, a process that challenges students intellectually, engages them, and improves the quality of their ideas and their writing.

5. You set standards or steer students in a direction you think especially fruitful. For example, you could advise them to write a sentence defining the vocabulary word *imperceptible* and ask them to ensure that their sentence makes it clear that *imperceptible* is different from *invisible*. Or you could ask students to describe what the Capulets think of the Montagues in *Romeo and Juliet* and then push them to understand the intensity of the hatred by asking them to write their answer in the words a member of the family would use.

6. Students remember twice as much of what they are learning if they write it down.

With all these advantages to writing, it's worth looking for every opportunity to have your students write—not just to improve their writing but to improve the quality of the thinking that informs discussions at key points in the lesson.

SEE IT IN ACTION: CLIP 12

EVERYBODY WRITES

In clip 12 on the DVD, Art Worrell of North Star Academy demonstrates *Everybody Writes*. He begins the sequence by asking his class a deep and challenging question: "What are some of the characteristics or qualities that an individual must have to change history?" This is a truly rich and important question to ask, but ask yourself what the very first student to raise his or her hand would say without reflection. What would the quality of the answer and the subsequent discussion be, and how ready would students be to ground their arguments in evidence?

Worrell anticipates this and asks all of his students to begin writing answers. He asks them to brainstorm "two to three characteristics that an individual must have." This direction is critical and underscores the power of this technique. If you take answers without asking everybody to write, you can really ask students to think of and keep only one answer in their heads. *Everybody Writes* allows Worrell to instantly increase the rigor and amount of thinking students do and also to stress the important fact that there are many answers.

Notice also Worrell's level of preparation. He has given them space in their notes packets to brainstorm. This reduces the transaction cost of the activity (no fumbling around looking for scrap paper) and ensures that students will retain a record of their thinking. And of course the proof is in the pudding: lots of volunteers to answer (and if there weren't an easy way to cold call) and high-quality answers that will lead to a rich discussion.

These six benefits work on at least three axes: they increase the quality of the ideas discussed in your class and expand the number of students likely to participate and their readiness to do so. And regardless of who actually speaks up, the exercise increases the ratio since it causes everybody to answer the question, not just those who discuss.

TECHNIQUE 27
VEGAS

"Every lesson needs a little **Vegas**," Dave Levin, founder and leader of the high-achieving KIPP schools has observed. The *Vegas* is the sparkle, the moment during class when you might observe some production values: music, lights, rhythm, dancing. *Vegas* draws students into a little bit of magic. But don't be fooled: *Vegas* isn't sparkle-for-

> Vegas *isn't sparkle-for-sparkle's sake. It reinforces not just academics generally but one of the day's learning objectives.*

sparkle's sake. It reinforces not just academics generally but one of the day's learning objectives. It's upbeat but often short, sweet, and on point. And once it's done, it's done.

Vegas can be the thirty-second interlude when students do the "action verb shimmy," sing the "long division song," or compete to see who can do the best charade for the day's vocabulary word. It's the moment when students compete to be the common denominator champion of the fifth grade or to finish as the king of Geography Mountain. It's a commercial break to remind you of the names of all of the midwestern states. It's the theatrical presentation of the story you just read, discussed in hushed tones or excited chatter or, best, a combination of the two. *Vegas* moments have to be developed and implemented with care. Otherwise they can take students off task and do as much harm as good. Here are a couple of sound design principles:

- **Production values.** Performers vary their tone and pace, occasionally whispering for emphasis, later speaking in a booming voice, sometimes speaking very slowly, sometimes racing along. Mike Taubman of North Star Academy uses this when he reads and discusses a story with his students. During a discussion of the Pied Piper fable, for example, he asked students to infer the lesson. In Taubman's hands, the drama of the story was clearly evident, even in his summary of the ending, which he used to help his class reflect on the lesson. His pace was quick and his voice loud, and he glossed the last moments of the tale: "He takes the children and hides them in a dark cave." As Taubman neared the end, he slowed down and dropped his voice, delivering the last word, *forever*, in a slow, emphatic stage whisper that broke the single word into two: "for ever." As he completed his dramatic summary, a moment of hushed silence ensued, and then almost every hand shot up into the air to explain the lesson. The simple production values he added to the retelling successfully drew his students in.

- **Like a faucet.** David Berkeley of Boston Preparatory Charter School jazzed up his study of direct objects by letting students literally "ooh" and "ahh" whenever one was mentioned. In setting up this moment of *Vegas*, Berkeley instructed his students, "It has to be like a faucet. You turn it on, then you turn it off. And when I say it's off, it's off."

Discussing the sentence, "Mom put the baby in the crib," Berkeley's *Vegas* might look like this:

Berkeley: Here is our verb, *put,* and at the end comes a phrase, *in the crib.* What kind of phrase is it, Charles?

Charles: It's a prepositional phrase.

Berkeley: And between the two, Shayna? What's that?

Shayna: It's a direct object.

Class: Oooh. Aaaah.

Berkeley: That's right, Shayna, a fabulous, brand-new direct object!

Class: Oooh. Aaah.

Berkeley: And Steven Jones, tell Shayna what her direct object [pause here for oohs and ahhs] can receive!

Steven: It can receive the action or result of the verb.

Berkeley: [Making a faucet motion to signal that the ooh-ing and ahh-ing is done] Perfect. What action gets done to or received by the baby in this sentence, Letty?

The final piece is critical. It's engaging to play the game, but if the game went on, it would distract students from the work of class and interfere with Berkeley's ability to teach because he'd get interrupted every time he said "direct object." He needs to start a fun game he can control, not give birth to a monster that takes on a life of its own. He may come back to it off and on through the lesson but cannot lose control of it. Good *Vegas* starts, is fun, and then is done; it doesn't keep cropping up when your back is turned, and it doesn't start singing when it hasn't been asked to. When that happens, you have to crack down quickly.

- **Same objective.** *Vegas* always has a specific learning objective and should have the same objective as the lesson or, at its most daring, review previously mastered but related content. Berkeley chose his *Vegas* to add some game-show-like shtick to his study of direct objects, but its object was to help his students focus on and recognize when direct objects appeared in sentences. It supported rather than distracted from his purpose.
- **Chorus line.** In *Vegas,* everyone in the show is singing the same tune and doing the same steps at exactly the same time. In classrooms, everyone has to know the rules. If it's a song, everyone has to know the words and the steps. If it's a multiplication showdown, students have to know when to stand, how to play, what to do if they lose, and so on, and everyone has to follow those rules. If you allow students to sing any song they want or make up a cheer on the spot, you are asking for trouble.
- **On point.** In any group activity, participants can subtly express their disdain for the activity and its leader by participating corrosively: singing off-key, or too loud, or overdoing the dance, or testing a lewd gesture. Good *Vegas* has to be vigilantly managed so that as soon as it is off-point, it is immediately corrected and standards of excellence are reinforced. For tips on how to do that, you'll want to read up on behavior management techniques like *What to Do* (technique 37), *Do It Again* (technique 39), *Positive Framing* (technique 43), *100 Percent* (technique 36), and *Strong Voice* (technique 38).

REFLECTION AND PRACTICE

1. Many of the teachers I work with think that of all the techniques in this book, *Cold Call* is the one with the greatest and fastest capacity to shift the culture of your classroom. Why do you think they feel so strongly about it?

2. Take a lesson plan for a class you're getting ready to teach, and mark it up by identifying three places where it would be beneficial to use *Cold Call*. Script your questions, and write them into your lesson plan. Make some notes about which students you'll cold call.

3. Take that same lesson plan, and mark it up to add two short sessions of *Call and Response*. Again, script your questions. Try to ask questions at all five levels, and note the in-cue you'll use.

4. Mark up your lesson one more time, this time identifying a place where all of your students will write answers to your question before discussion. Be sure to consider where they will write and what the expectations will be. (Will you collect their work? Are complete sentences required?)

5. Make a short list of what you want your students to do or think about when you use *Wait Time*. Write yourself two or three five-second scripts that you can practice and use while teaching to reinforce effective academic behaviors and discipline yourself to wait.

CREATING A STRONG CLASSROOM CULTURE

The techniques in Chapter Five (as well as those in Chapters Six and Seven) focus on building classroom culture—making your room, a place where students work hard, behave, model strong character, and do their best. Before I describe the specific methods champion teachers use to build strong classroom culture, it's worth taking a few pages to understand it and the factors that drive it more deeply because it's more complex than it first appears and because the techniques you'll read about will make more sense when studied in the context of a bit more clarity about what culture consists of.

THE FIVE PRINCIPLES OF CLASSROOM CULTURE

Building a classroom culture that sustains and drives excellence requires mastering skills in five aspects of your relationships with students. These five aspects, or principles, are often confused and conflated. Many educators fail to consider the difference between them; others use the names indiscriminately or interchangeably. However, since you must be sure to make the most of all five in your classroom, it's worth taking a moment to distinguish them.

THE FIVE PRINCIPLES OF CLASSROOM CULTURE

Discipline

Management

Control

Influence

Engagement

Discipline

When most people use the word *discipline,* they refer to the process of administering consequences and punishments. It's a verb: "I discipline you." I prefer to use it as Ronald Morish does it in his excellent book, *With All Due Respect:* as a noun that refers to the process of teaching someone the right way to do something or to the state of being able to do something the right way: "I have discipline" or "I teach discipline." This sense of the word is also captured in the meaning of self-discipline: the ability to make oneself do things all the way through and in the form of the word that refers to a body of ideas or method of thinking (as an academic discipline). This reminds us that at the core of this definition of discipline is teaching—teaching students the right and successful way to do things.

> *Too often teachers have not taken the time to teach their students, step by step, what successful learning behavior looks like.*

Ironically many teachers forget this element, even though it's most closely aligned to how they define their job. They expect to teach the content but not necessarily the habits and processes of being a successful student and community member. They set up systems of reward and consequence to hold students accountable. They exhort students to do their best, assuming all the while that they know how to do what's best. But all too often teachers have not taken the time to teach their students, step by step, what successful learning behavior looks like, assuming instead that students have inferred it in previous classrooms or doubting the value of having a right way to do things, like sitting in class, taking notes, and following directions. As my colleague Doug McCurry says, "If they're not doing what you asked, the most likely explanation is that you haven't taught them."

Teaching with discipline implies a front-end investment in teaching your charges how to be students, and that requires a fair amount of planning. How will your students sit, line up, enter the classroom, and take notes? It also means investing in a whole lot of practice and deciding implicitly how good is good enough to meet standards as part of planning your discipline. The results of emphasizing and investing in this definition of discipline can be stunning, however, because it turns out that there are a lot of kids on the margins of classroom culture who want to do what's expected of them. They are just waiting to be taught.

Management

Management, by contrast, is the process of reinforcing behavior by consequences and rewards. What we typically call "disciplining" is often really management: giving consequences. Some teachers see this as the whole game, and with what at first may appear to be significant justification. Effective classrooms need management systems. But because management is the element of school culture that has the most visible short-term results, it's easy to fail to recognize its particular reliance on the other four elements and its limitations without them. While it makes operating an achievement-focused classroom more direct and efficient and while this added efficiency and clarity is critical, management cannot sustain itself without the other four elements of positive culture. Without them, management, even in the best systems, ultimately suffers from diminishing marginal returns: the more you use it, the less effective it is.

When schools or teachers over-rely on management, a death spiral ensues: students become desensitized to consequences and Machiavellian about rewards; more of each is required to achieve the same or lesser effect; students become increasingly insensitive to the larger doses, and the larger doses signal to students either the desperation of their teacher or that they are problem kids, not successful kids, and the currency of management becomes less rational and more negative.

Strong management is not only a positive part of an effective classroom culture, but a necessary part, but effective management must operate in combination with the other four elements, or it will soon become ineffective management. Teach students how to do things right, don't just establish consequences for doing them wrong. To truly succeed you must be able to control students, that is, get them to do things regardless of consequence, and to inspire and engage them in positive work. You also are building relationships with students that are nontransactional; they don't involve rewards or consequences, and they demonstrate that you care enough to know your students as individuals. And you recognize that they are excellent classroom managers in part because of these skills.

Control

Control is your capacity to cause someone to choose to do what you ask, regard-less of consequences. It's a dirty word to many people. There has to be something wrong with controlling someone else. It's undemocratic, they think, and coer-cive. The intention to control another person seems especially reprehensible in a teacher, they say, because teaching is to help people think for themselves. How-ever, a bit of context should make it clear that all of us exert control over other people's actions and that we do it because it's the right thing to do, especially for teachers. In many cases, benign, enlightened control is a very good thing: a teacher reliably gets students to ask why and how questions when reading his-tory, gets them to be suspicions of claims not supported by evidence, and reliably gets students to work hard, value learning, and respect their peers.

In fact, my definition of control is "the capacity to cause someone to choose to do what you ask, regardless of consequences." It does not imply a lack of subjectivity in the people you cause to do what you ask. They still choose. Controlling merely involves asking in a way that makes them more likely to agree to do it. If you've done any reading in the emerging field of behavioral economics, for example, Cass Sunstein and Richard Thaler's popular and fascinating *Nudge,* you'll recognize that no choices are entirely neutral. Looking someone in the eye and speaking firmly is clearly exerting control. Meekly looking down and using a pleading tone of voice is not. But there is no way to ask that does not fall somewhere on the spectrum between the two. It's important to note that the way I use *control* in this chapter is limited to a narrow range of social and behavioral interactions in the classroom, for example, sitting down when asked to.

> *Teachers who have strong control succeed because they understand the power of language and relationships: they ask respectfully, firmly, and confidently but also with civility, and often kindly. They express their faith in students.*

The biggest paradox about control is that it is more than a necessary evil. It often supports freedom. I know this as a parent. I can give my children the freedom to run ahead of me on a side-walk and explore on their own only if I have successfully taught them the rules for crossing the street (that is, if I have "disciplined" them to know how to stop at the curb). But I also must know for certain that if they neared a driveway with a car unexpectedly backing out and I called to them to stop, they would, instantly and without fail. In addition to my other tools, I must also have control or I cannot be effective as a parent, either in protecting my children or in affording them opportunities to grow. The more I have the power to exercise responsible control, the more freedom I can give my children, ideally in ways that truly matter.

Teachers who have strong control succeed because they understand the power of language and relationships: they ask respectfully, firmly, and confidently but also with civility, and often kindly. They express their faith in students. They replace vague and judgmental commands like "calm down" with specific and useful ones like, "Please return to your seat and begin writing in your journal." These actions evince clarity, purposefulness, resolve, and caring. If you can get students to do what you are delegated with helping them to achieve, you are doing your job, and you've also saved your consequences for when you need them most. So getting comfortable with the obligation to exert control is part of preparation for success.

Influence

Ideally all teachers connect to their students and inspire them to want for themselves the things the class is trying to achieve. Inspiring students to believe, want to succeed, and want to work for it for intrinsic reasons is influencing them. It's the next step beyond control. Control gets them to do things you suggest; influence gets them to want to internalize the things you suggest. Although less visible than getting kids to behave, getting them to believe—to want to behave positively—is the biggest driver of achievement and success because it happens when kids want it for themselves and when it is real. It happens without you there, without your managing it. Belief, as the history of every powerful idea from democracy to faith demonstrates, is a powerful and lasting motivator. If influence is the process of instilling belief, maximizing it should be an intentional goal of every teacher's classroom culture.

Engagement

Champion teachers give students plenty to say yes to, plenty to get involved in, plenty to lose themselves in. They get students busily engaged in productive, positive work. This gives them little time to think about how to act counterproductively and lots that seems important and interesting to focus their energy on.

No matter what they may be thinking, what they're doing is positive. This can have a powerful ancillary effect. One of Karl Marx's more obscure but insightful ideas is the base-superstructure theory: that people's beliefs and values (the "superstructure" of a society) are a product of the "base" (the everyday realities of their life). What you do all day shapes what you believe rather than vice versa. This can apply to your students' daily role in school. Are they owners? Drudges? Serfs? Craftspeople? Happy entrepreneurs? The apparently mundane daily interactions they have shape what they believe about and value in their school lives more than the other way around. People act (or are compelled to act) a certain way and then explain their actions using ideology.

"Sometimes you gotta change from the outside in!"

Other social critics have made this same point, though more succinctly. For example, the 1990 film *My Blue Heaven,* in which an ex-mafioso (Steve Martin) teaches a straitlaced cop supervising him in the federal witness protection program (Rick Moranis) to find pleasure and verve in daily life. As Martin ushers Moranis into the changing room to try on a slick suit he's convinced him to buy, he advises through the dressing room door: "Sometimes you gotta change from the outside in!"

Kids too often change from the outside in. They see themselves being enthusiastic and start to feel enthusiastic. They see themselves lost in their work and start to think they are productive, contributing members of society and begin to believe and act accordingly more frequently. Champion teachers keep their students positively engaged not just so that they are too busy to see opportunities to be off task but because after a while, they start to think of themselves as positively engaged people. This is why engagement matters.

The Synergy of the Five Principles

The techniques described in the following chapters rely on all five of these aspects of classroom culture to varying degrees. Some require more of one than another, but because the synergy of the five makes each one stronger, the techniques an effective teacher uses ideally leverage all five. A teacher who uses only one or two will ultimately fail to build a vibrant classroom culture. A teacher who uses only control but not discipline, for example, will produce students who never learn to do things on their own and always need firm directives to act. A classroom in which the teacher does not have control and tries to address students who "don't" exclusively through management of consequences will overuse the consequences, accustom students to the consequences, and erode their effectiveness in his own and other classes. A teacher who engages and influences without control and management will build a vibrant but inefficient culture that allows some students to opt out of learning, and a teacher who does these without teaching discipline will not adequately prepare students to succeed once they leave the microcosm of their classroom because they will not have had sufficient practice in or knowledge of how to sustain successful habits of scholarship.

While the techniques in this book make varying use of one or several of these principles (for example, technique 38, *Strong Voice*, is heavily focused on Control while technique 44, *Precise Praise*, is mostly about influence), the rest of this chapter focuses almost exclusively on Discipline and on the Systems and Routines that are the hidden foundation of any classroom culture.

TECHNIQUE 28
ENTRY ROUTINE

The first routine that affects classroom culture is the one for how students enter. Like all others, this is a routine whether you realize it (and shape it intentionally) or not. Unlike *Threshold* (technique 41 in Chapter Six), which immediately precedes students' entry into the room and focuses on setting behavioral norms and expectations, **Entry Routine** is about making a habit out of what's efficient, productive, and scholarly after the greeting and as students take their seats and class begins.

A typical routine begins with students entering the room and picking up a packet of materials from a small table just inside the door. In some cases, especially at the lower elementary grades, packets might already be at students' desks. A couple of key points maximize the effectiveness of this part of the entry routine.

- It's far more efficient to have students pick up their packets from a table than it is for you to try to hand the packets to them at the door. That only slows you down and forces you to multitask when your mind should be on setting behavioral expectations and building relationships. It's also far more efficient to have students pick up their packets from a table than it is for you to try to hand them out to them later while they sit and wait for them.

- Students should know where to sit. Milling around looking for a seat or deciding where to sit or talking about deciding where to sit ("Can I sit next to him? Will he think I'm flirting?") are all examples of wasted time and energy. Assign seats, or allow students to sign up for regular seats.

- Whatever students need to do with homework (put it in a basket, place it on the front left corner of their desk, pass it to a proctor), they should do the same way every day without prompting.

- A *Do Now* (the following technique) should be in the same place every day: on the board or in the packet. The objectives for the lesson, the agenda, and the homework for the coming evening should be on the board already, also in the same predictable place every day.

TECHNIQUE 29
DO NOW

Students should never have to ask themselves, "What am I supposed to be doing?" when they enter your classroom, nor should they be able to claim not to know what they should be doing. You want students to know what to do and to know there is no ambiguity here. Those two goals—being clear with students about what to be working on and eliminating the excuses that lead to distraction—are the rationale for **Do Now**, a short activity that you have written on the board or is waiting at their desks before they enter.

The *Do Now* means that students are hard at work even before you have fully entered the room. They are both productive during every minute and ready for instruction as soon as you start. They have done the anticipatory set and are thinking about what's coming.

An effective *Do Now,* which can bring incredible learning power to a room, should conform to four critical criteria to ensure that it remains focused, efficient, and effective:

1. Students should be able to complete the *Do Now* without any direction from the teacher and without any discussion with their classmates. Some teachers misunderstand the purpose of the *Do Now* and use a version of the technique that requires them to explain to their students what to do and how to do it: "Okay, class, you can see that the *Do Now* this morning asks you to solve some typical problems using area. Remember that to solve area problems, you have to multiply." This defeats the purpose of establishing a self-managed habit of productive work.

2. The activity should take three to five minutes to complete.

3. The activity should require putting a pencil to paper, that is, there should be a written product from it. This not only makes it more rigorous and more engaging, but it allows you to better hold students accountable for doing it since you can clearly see whether they are (and they can see that you can see).

4. The activity should preview the day's lesson (you are reading *The Jacket,* and the *Do Now* asks students to write three sentences about what they'd do if they thought someone stole their little brother's favorite jacket) or review a recent lesson (you want your kids to practice all of the standards they've mastered recently so they don't forget them).

Beyond that, a *Do Now* works because of consistency and preparation. If there isn't a *Do Now* in the same place every single day, students can claim plausible deniability. That said, a *Do Now* doesn't need to be written on the board. If you do post it on the board, you can write it in advance on a large piece of newsprint and tape or use a magnet to affix it to the board before students walk in, thus saving precious moments when you would otherwise be transcribing the *Do Now* onto the board.

For example, a fifth-grade English teacher might use a *Do Now* to review a vocabulary word from the previous week. Because the important thing is for students to be able to do the work on their own, she would have already set the precedent that students could and should use their notes as necessary:

In your notebook:

1. *Define scarce.*

2. *Explain how it means more than just having a small amount of something.*

3. *Use scarce in a sentence that tells about a time when something being scarce affected you or your family.*

4. *Name the noun form of scarce.*

This example is from a math class:

1. *Solve to find the width of a rectangle with an area of 104 square centimeters and a length of 13 centimeters. Show your work.*

2. *Give the possible dimensions of at least two other rectangles with the same area but different dimensions.*

TECHNIQUE 30

TIGHT TRANSITIONS

TRANSITIONS FOR STUDENTS

Having quick and routine transitions that students can execute without extensive narration by the teacher—that is, **Tight Transitions**—is a critical piece of any highly effective classroom. By transitions, I mean times when students move from place to place or activity to activity, for example, when they line up for lunch. Your students spend a lot of time in transition—by necessity—and when they're in transition, they are not learning. The transitions in high school (putting materials away before a test, say) look different from the transitions in elementary school (moving to the carpet from desks, say). Still, they occur at all levels of school and have an immense if generally underacknowledged influence on the learning that happens before and after. If you were able to cut a minute apiece from ten transitions a day and sustained that improvement for two hundred school days, you would have created almost thirty-five hours of instructional time over the school year. Practically speaking you would have added a week to your school year.

Messy transitions are also an invitation to disruptions and conflicts that continue to undercut the classroom environment even after class has started.

You can read all day long and well into the night about the need for more resources in public education but every teacher has, at his or her fingertips, an opportunity to increase the scarcest and most important resource that money buys by a significant amount. Furthermore, the time that's wasted in poor transitions often winds up being especially critical. It's often the difference between getting through an exciting lesson and running out of time—an outcome that means failing to complete critical summative activities like recapping and reviewing the lesson or introducing homework. Losing the last three minutes of a lesson undercuts the whole lesson. Messy transitions are also an invitation to disruptions and conflicts that continue to undercut the classroom environment even after class has started. In short, the price of poor transitions is high, and since only consistently effective procedures ensure smooth and speedy transitions, teachers should seek to practice doing it the same way every time until students can follow through as a matter of habit.

By the end of the first week of school, every student should know and understand procedures like how to line up and move from place to place without having to be told. In an effective classroom, transitions take less than thirty seconds, and often far less. To engineer effective transitions in your classroom, start by mapping the route. There is one right way to line up, one path each student follows on the way to the reading area, the door, or some other place. Your students should follow the same path every time. Then they need to practice under your watchful eye, often multiple times a day. You instincts will tell you that you are wasting time, but the opposite is true. Look at it as making an investment. Save hours and hours over the course of the year by investing an extra five or ten minutes for the first few days of school.

When you teach students to transition effectively, scaffold the steps in the transition. That is, teach them to follow their route one step at a time. One especially effective way to do this is to number your steps. You might announce to a class of third graders: "When I say one, please stand and push in your chairs. When I say two, please turn to face the door. When I say three, please follow your line leader to the place to line up." Once you've done that, you merely have to call the number for the appropriate step. But in calling the number (or not calling it), you can control the pace of the transition, slowing it down as necessary to ensure success and accountability, speeding it up as students are ready, and ultimately dispensing with the numbers and merely saying, "When I say *go*, please line up," and observing as your students follow the steps. You should expect such a process to take several weeks to instill completely.

Another effective way to teach transitions is to use a method called point-to point movement or, when transitions cause you to move around the building, point-to-point walking. You identify a location or an action, and students move to that point and stop, as in, "Please walk to the end of the hallway and stop there, Jason." The key is that as you instruct students to complete a step in the transition, you set not only a beginning but a stopping point in advance so that the activity never gets out of your control. You know students will walk only to the end of the hall. If they aren't quiet enough, you can call them back right away rather than watch them wend around the corner and out of sight, barely within your influence, never mind control.

With point-to-point and other scaffolding methods, your goals are both speed and orderliness. You need to get your students to be fast. This is an area that many teachers forget when the success of control goes to their heads. They ratchet down on every step and accept slow and orderly transitions because they make them feel as if they are in control. Both to challenge your students and set goals for them and also to discipline yourself to focus on speed, practice transitions against the clock, preferably with a stopwatch, forever trying to get your students to be a little faster. "We did this in sixteen seconds yesterday; let's shoot for twelve today!"

Also control what your students say during transitions. If your transitions are quick enough, there's no reason they can't be silent, thereby avoiding distractions from students arguing and squabbling and focusing them on the transition more clearly.

As an alternative, you might do as Sultana Noormuhammad does at Leadership Preparatory Charter School and have your students sing their transitions. One morning they stood behind their desks as a student led them through their fight song, an adapted version of the fight song of their namesake, Indiana University, in which students sing about their willingness to do homework and work hard. Before the song ends, they're marching to the reading area, in perfect rows unwinding counterclockwise around their table groups and singing at the top of their lungs as they take their place in line. Their song ends as they sit on the carpet, ending the transition free of distraction, right on cue and with the mood high. Five seconds later, teaching has begun. And although Noormuhammad's students are kindergartners, if you think older kids can't sing their transition think again, this time of the armed forces, where soldiers routinely sing songs as they move from place to place for much the same purpose: to keep their mood up, focus them on the task, and avoid distractions.

Finally, you'll need consistent enforcement. When your students start testing to see if they really have to follow the rules of the road, they should always find that they do. *Do It Again* (technique 39 in Chapter Six) is especially effective in helping students practice doing transitions correctly since you are always right in the middle of something you can try over again and since transitions are the ideal time for group responsibility.

MOVING MATERIALS

The necessity (and most of the rules) for efficient transitions applies just as much when materials rather than people are moving from place to place. Invest at the outset in teaching one right way to do it. Work with a stopwatch, and practice over and over. Gain time for instruction by making these times in your day speedy and seamless. For passing and collecting papers, books, and other materials to and from students, there are a couple of additional rules of thumb:

- Generally pass across rows, not up and back. This avoids the need for turning around 180 degrees in chairs, an action that creates a golden opportunity for hard-to-see, hard-to-manage face-to-face interactions in which one person always has his or her back to you.

- Distribute materials in groups: to the student at the end of each row, to each table.

SEE IT IN ACTION: CLIP 13

TIGHT TRANSITIONS AND POSITIVE FRAMING

In clip 13 on the DVD, Doug McCurry models *Tight Transitions.* I discuss this clip in the Introduction to the book as well because of the incredible return on Doug's invested time in teaching his students to pass out papers. What's equally powerful about the clip is the students' response. Far from being annoyed and frustrated by being asked to pass papers back and forth to achieve a faster time, they love the challenge and are literally on the edge of their seats. Much of the key to accomplishing this alchemy is Doug's *Positive Framing* (technique 43 in Chapter Seven), specifically his constant use of challenge.

TECHNIQUE 31
BINDER CONTROL

Certain freedoms are overrated: the freedom to lose papers, for example, or the freedom to take notes on a grubby, torn half-sheet of paper that ultimately becomes buried at the bottom of a backpack. Care enough about and demonstrate the importance of what you teach to build a system for the storage, organization, and recall of what your students have learned. The technique for this is **Binder Control**. Have a required place for them to take notes; have that

Care enough about and demonstrate the importance of what you teach to build a system for the storage, organization, and recall of what your students have learned.

place be in a required binder, which is ideally provided by you and which you may even require to remain in the classroom at night so it won't get lost, damaged, or disorganized on the way to and from school. Your students can take home what they need that night in a homework folder, which can be color-coded so you and parents can readily identify it. Each night students can put everything they need for that night's assignment in the folder and leave the binder in the classroom.

Have a required format for organizing papers within the binder so everybody is using the same system and you can check to make sure everyone has and can find what they need. You might, for example, assign a number to all materials you expect students to keep in the binders and have students enter them into a table—for example, 37: notes on subject-verb agreement; 38: subject-verb agreement worksheet; 39: subject-verb agreement homework; and 40: worksheet for subject-verb agreement with compound subject.

That way when you say, "If you don't remember, check your notes," you know every student has the notes, and you can even tell them where in their binders they can find them. "They should be at number 37." Finally, you can ensure that students have a full and complete packet when reviewing for tests: "You'll need to take home items 32 to 45 from your binder to prepare for this test."

To ensure that students follow through, take the time to have students put their materials away during class: "Please add number 37, notes on subject-verb agreement, to your table of contents, and file these notes away on my signal. I want to hear your binders popping open on three"

TECHNIQUE 32
SLANT

No matter how great the lesson, if students aren't alert, sitting up, and actively listening, teaching them is like pouring water into a leaky bucket. Many teachers and schools practice lining up for fire drills and make sure everyone knows the routine for finding the right bus at the end of the day, but they rarely think about how to teach the behaviors and skills that help students concentrate, focus, and learn.

Five key behaviors that maximize students' ability to pay attention are in the acronym SLANT (the acronym was originally used by the first KIPP schools):

Sit up.

Listen.

Ask and answer questions.

Nod your head.

Track the speaker.

Some schools use variations of the **SLANT** technique, for example, STAR (**S**it up, **T**rack the speaker, **A**sk and answer questions like a scholar, and **R**espect those around you) or S-SLANT (which adds "smile").

One of the best aspects of the acronym is that it serves as shorthand. Teachers remind students to be attentive and ready learners by urging them simply and quickly to SLANT. The use of a consistent acronym is quick and efficient. Even better, SLANT can be broken apart when necessary. Teachers can remind their students about the "S" in SLANT or the "T" in it. In the best classrooms, the word is deeply embedded in the vocabulary of learning, as a noun ("Where's my SLANT?") and a verb ("Make sure you are SLANTing").

Since SLANTing is such a critical part of a high-performing classroom, you may want to develop nonverbal signals that allow you to reinforce and correct SLANTing without interrupting what you're otherwise doing: hands folded in front of you to remind students to sit up straight; pointing to your eyes with two fingers to remind students to track.

TECHNIQUE 33

ON YOUR MARK

No coach in the world would let players enter the huddle without a helmet on or catch a fastball without a glove. You can't hope to win if you're not standing at the starting line with your shoes tied when the race begins. You should think the same way about learning in your classroom: every student must start class with books and paper out and pen or pencil in hand. This must be the expectation in every class, every day. A coach doesn't start practice by telling kids to get their shoes on; kids show up with their shoes on. So don't ask your students to get ready as class begins; use **On Your Mark** to show them how to prepare before it begins and then expect them to do so every day.

How to Ensure Students Are on Their Marks When Class Starts

1. *Be explicit about what students need to have to start class.* Make it a small and finite list (fewer than five things) that doesn't change:

   - Paper out

   - Desk clear (of everything unnecessary to the lesson)

   - Pencil sharp and ready ("in the pencil tray")

   - Homework (in the upper right-hand corner of your desk)

   At North Star Academy in Newark, principal Jamey Verilli refers to students' work stations, or just "stations," which they set up as part of their entry routine. On the wall is a diagram of how materials should look when a station is set up: books upper left, homework upper right, blank paper in the center. And nothing else.

2. *Set a time limit.* Be specific about when students need to have the everything ready. If you're not clear about when students need to be ready, your efforts to hold those who aren't accountable will result in arguments when students say they "were doing it" or "were about to."

3. *Use a standard consequence.* Have a small and appropriate consequence that you can administer without hesitation—perhaps loss of some privilege or doing some work to help the class stay prepared. Students who weren't on their marks might lose points in a token economy, have to sharpen all of the pencils in the pencil tray at lunchtime, or come to "homework club" ten minutes before school to make sure they have everything they need for the coming day.

4. *Provide tools without consequence (pencils, paper) to those who recognize the need before class.* There's a difference between not having a pencil and getting your pencil ready before class, only to realize the tip is broken or that you accidentally left it in math class. Part of preparation is recognizing in advance that you need something. Give students the incentive to take responsibility for getting what they need by allowing them access to the tools for them to succeed without consequence as long as they recognize this need

before you've started class. You might have a coffee can full of sharpened pencils that students can take if they trade in their old one and a stack of clean looseleaf paper on the corner of your desk. Students could help themselves to these during *Entry Routine*. Once class starts, the consequence for not being *On Your Mark* would apply.

5. *Include homework.* Homework is the most important thing most students will do all day that isn't directly supervised by a teacher. It cannot be left to chance. Make turning it in part of the routine students follow to be ready for the day. It should be turned in and checked for completeness at the start of class. There should be a separate consequence of not doing it—usually coming to "homework club" after school or during gym to complete the work that hasn't been done.

TECHNIQUE 34

SEAT SIGNALS

The bathroom is the last bastion of the unconverted. Given the opportunity, some students (especially those who can least afford it) will find creative ways to maximize their time there, particularly during the time of day when they can least afford it. For other students, a long, slow walk to the pencil sharpener can be an opportunity for unique displays of deportment not necessarily designed to reinforce their classmates' learning. An impressive degree of distraction can be created by enterprising students out of their seats at the wrong time or at their own discretion.

Furthermore, managing requests for bathroom and the like—justified or not, approved or not—can become a distraction from teaching. Conversations about who's next and when can eat up precious minutes. And you risk the scenario in which, at the critical moment in your lesson that you ask some key question, a student with his hand eagerly in the air would like to go to the bathroom. Your momentum and train of thought are shot. In short, you can't afford not to develop a set of signals for common needs, especially those that require or allow students to get out of their seats. You need **Seat Signals**.

This system should meet the following criteria:

- Students must be able to signal their request from their seats.

- Students must be able to signal requests nonverbally.

- The signals should be specific and unambiguous but subtle enough to prevent them becoming a distraction.

- You should be able to manage both their requests and your response without interrupting instruction (with a nod yes or no, for example, or five fingers for "in five minutes").

- You should be explicit and consistent about the signals you expect students to use, posting them on the wall so students can see them and disciplining yourself to require them by responding only when they are used.

These signals, adopted from their use in top classrooms, tend to work:

- "Can I use the bathroom, please?" Hand up; two fingers crossed.

- "I need a new pencil": Hold pencil up, wait for exchange. Generally having presharpened pencils that students take or that you deliver to kids in exchange for broken or dull pencils is a far better system than letting kids sharpen them; it's quicker and less disruptive. If you're sure you want to let them sharpen, try hands together in fists, one rotating like a crank gesture for "I need to sharpen my pencil."

- "I need a tissue": Left hand pinching nose.

- "I need to get out of my seat" (to get something that dropped on the floor): One finger held up rotated in a circular motion.

It also makes sense to consider making clear rules about when students can ask for certain freedoms that require seat signals. For example, you do not want to consider bathroom requests at critical parts of your lesson. Instead, allow bathroom visits only at certain times during class, say, the last fifteen minutes. Or you could tie the degree of freedom students have to your behavior management system. For example, if you use colored cards (green, yellow, red) for each student to track his or her level of behavior, as many schools do, you might offer anyone on green the right to ask for the bathroom anytime after the first fifteen minutes of class, while those on yellow can go only during the last ten minutes.

If you use a system that limits access to the bathroom, you're ensuring that you'll get "emergency" requests—some real, some not—so you must be prepared for that. A good solution is to establish a separate bathroom emergency signal that students can use when bathroom visits are not approved. Students would have to "buy" the right to go in such an emergency situation through some reasonable compensation. You could allow students to purchase the right for some other price, for example, say, twenty math problems or ten minutes of classroom service (cleaning desks, picking up trash).

TECHNIQUE 35
PROPS

Effective systems and routines can also make your classroom more productive by harnessing public praise. **Props**—also called "shout-outs" and "ups"—are public praise for students who demonstrate excellence or exemplify virtues. Everyone responds to praise, to a crowd cheering for them and rooting them on. Making sure that it happens, inspires, and is reliably on-message is one of the most productive things you can do in your classroom. What better reward is there for trying a tough question, persevering, finding your own mistake, or explaining to your peers how to solve a problem than receiving the public praise of the class? If you can consistently enable classmates to deliver resounding praise to their peers in two seconds flat, you can build a culture that valorizes achievement and effort without sacrificing order or time on task. Your students hear the command—"Two stomps for Imani!"—and respond automatically and thunderously: every foot stomping twice (and only twice) in unison before it's back to learning.

The key is investing the time at the outset to teach students to give props the right way: crisply, quickly, and enthusiastically. Ensuring that you teach your students to deliver *Props* that meet the following criteria will go a long way to ensuring your success:

- *Quick.* You should be able to cue a prop in one second. If you say, "Two claps for David" and the response is any slower than that, take the time to teach your students to do it right by doing it again and doing it faster: "When we give up our claps, it's because someone did something great, so I want to hear them right away. Let's give that one more time and see if we can do it in less than a second." Similarly, the *Prop* itself should be fast because you don't have time to waste and because there's nothing less energizing than an exhortation that starts strong but peters out. Be short so the energy level stays high. The routine for *Props* should take less than five seconds from beginning to end. The transition back to the task at hand is immediate.

- *Visceral.* Teachers often assume a *Prop* has to be verbal and carry a message. To the contrary, *Props* are usually better when they rely on movement and sound, especially percussive sound. *Props* that don't use much in the way of words are less likely to get tiresome; their half-life is longer because there's no phrase to wear out. A quick, "Oh, yeah," is fine but something like, "On the way to college!" is likely to get old (and show its age) quickly. Furthermore, there's something fun and muscular about the thunder of group percussion. Students like noise and rhythm. Some will drum on anything in your class if given the chance. Embrace that. Make sure your *Props* involve movement and controlled but emphatic noise such as the stomping of feet or clapping of hands.

- *Universal.* When you *give Props,* everybody joins in. It's up to you to set and enforce this expectation.

- *Enthusiastic.* The tone is fun and lively. It should be a break—brief and fun—from hard work. Resist the temptation to make it too grown-up; it doesn't have to narrate values and express a mission-aligned personal credo. If it is a little bit of silly, it will reinforce moments when students have already demonstrated those things. *Props* are the exclamation point, not the sentence. Just make it fun enough for students to want to join in. One easy way to increase students' enthusiasm is to let a student choose the *Prop* from among the various ones you've developed as a class.

- *Evolving*. Let your students suggest and develop ideas for *Props.* They will constantly renew the systems with fresh and funky ideas and will participate more vigorously because they will have helped invent them. And if they are forever thinking of new ones, *Props* will never get tired, boring, and obligatory.

Here are six ideas for *Props* (most of them stolen from great teachers, who themselves borrowed them or invented them with the help of students):

- "The Hitter." You say, "Let's give Clarice a Hitter." Your kids pretend to toss a ball and swing a bat at it. They shield their eyes as if to glimpse its distant flight. Then they mimic crowd noise suitable for a home run for some fraction of a full second.

- "The Lawnmower." You say: "Let's give Jason a Lawnmower." Your kids reach down to pull the chord to start the mower and yank upward twice. They make engine sounds, grip the imaginary handles, and smile for some fraction of a full second before the *Prop* ends.

- "The Roller-Coaster." You say: "Oh, man, that answer deserves a Roller-coaster." Your kids put their open hands in front of them pointing upward at forty-five degrees, palms down. They "chug, chug, chug" (three times only) with their hands mimicking a roller coaster slugging its way up the last steep hill. Then they shout "Woo, woo, woo" three times as their hands mimic a coaster speeding over three steep hills after the big drop.

- "Two Hands." You say: "Jimmie, lead us in a No Hands." Jimmie calls out, "Two hands!" Your kids snap twice with both hands while chanting, "Ay, ay!" Jimmie calls out, "One hand!" Your kids snap twice with one hand while chanting "Ay, ay!" Jimmie calls out, "No hands!" Your kids do a funky impromptu dance for exactly one second.

- "Hot Pepper." You say: "An answer like that deserves a Hot Pepper." Your kids hold up an imaginary hot pepper, dangling it above their mouths. They take a bite and make a sizzle sounds "tssssss" for exactly one second.

- "Two Snaps, Two Stomps." You say: "Two snaps, two stomps for Jimmie P.!" or a variation on the sounds. Your kids deliver two snaps and two thundering stomps that end perfectly on cue.

REFLECTION AND PRACTICE

1. Script the steps and expectations for the five most critical routines in your classroom.

2. Make a poster outlining everything your students need to have to be prepared at the beginning of class. Post it on your wall. Practice referring students to it (nonverbally perhaps) before class begins.

3. Make a list of the three most common requests students make while you are teaching. Determine an appropriate nonverbal signal they can give you to request each of them. Make a poster showing each. Practice pointing at the poster and asking students to return to their seat if they do not ask for and receive your nonverbal approval for one week. Do not always give them your approval if the request comes during key instructional time.

CHAPTER SIX

SETTING AND MAINTAINING HIGH BEHAVIORAL EXPECTATIONS

This book began with a study of the techniques champion teachers use to raise academic expectations and make classrooms places of rigorous and intentional learning. And, of course, that is and should be the goal of schooling. That said, all of the techniques in the first chapters of this book won't serve you very well if you can't establish high behavioral expectations. It's one of the responsibilities of the job to bring order and respect sufficient to protect all students' right to learn to your classroom. Even if you don't want to be the kind of teacher who's "strict," I hope you will recognize the non-negotiable aspects of a strong behavioral environment and also that the techniques in this chapter can be mastered by anyone (some of the best practitioners I know are quiet and reserved in both nature and manner) and can be adapted in any of a thousand individual styles.

TECHNIQUE 36
100 PERCENT

There's one suitable percentage of students following a direction given in your classroom: **100 Percent**. If you don't achieve this, you make your authority subject to interpretation, situation, and motivation. Students have cause to ask themselves: "Did she mean that? For everyone? Do I feel like going along with her today?"

The assertion that the standard, not the goal, is 100 percent compliance may sound terrifying and draconian: a power-hungry plan for a battle of wills or the blueprint for an obedience-obsessed classroom where little but grinding discipline is achieved. The classrooms of champion teachers belie this expectation, however. They finesse their way to the standard with a warm and positive tone. They are crisp and orderly; students do as they're asked without ever seeming to think about it. Yet the culture of compliance is both positive and, most important, invisible. Not only can these two characteristics be part of a classroom with maximum order, but in the end, they must. Discipline that is most often positive and invisible (that is, a matter of habit) is, arguably, the only sustainable variety.

KEY IDEA

100 PERCENT

There's one acceptable percentage of students following a direction: 100 percent. Less, and your authority is subject to interpretation, situation, and motivation.

While champion teachers regularly achieve *100 Percent* in a crisp, decisive, and nearly invisible way, those who don't are often unaware of which and how many students do what they ask when they ask it. Many teachers who fail to approach the 100 percent standard stop noticing whether they are achieving full compliance. Remedying this is the first step to achieving the highest behavioral expectations: to wield power justly but firmly, you must be keenly aware of how students respond to your directions. The first step is to notice.

One morning, a third-grade teacher wanted to address her class. She raised her hand in the practiced signal for silence: students are expected to quietly raise their hands as well, and on the morning in question, about three-quarters of her class did so, with the room becoming quiet enough for her to speak and be heard.

Should she proceed?

Many teachers, maybe even most, would do so, but if they did, they would overlook the quarter of their students who had failed to comply with an explicit direction. Some might argue, "They're not in the way; move on," but that lends tacit approval to the noncompliance. Unless she wants to send the message that following an explicit direction is optional, she shouldn't begin until all hands are raised.

There's an important distinction to make here. If the teacher had only asked for silence, it would be okay to proceed once the room was quiet, but the teacher asked students to do two things: be quiet and respond to her signal. Only some students did that, so she should wait before proceeding, and use the methods in the *100 Percent* technique to achieve full compliance, and as quickly and positively as possible.

However, before I discuss the how, it's worth thinking about why. The danger of moving on without compliance risks allowing a toxic culture of "only the good kids do what they're asked" to develop. It causes students to see noncompliance as an option, to contemplate a choice between compliance with the teacher or the freedom of their untrammeled peers. It's not much of a choice, and in many classrooms, the culture of noncompliance spreads quickly to previously supportive students. Furthermore, when a teacher makes minor requests discretionary, getting everyone to oblige her when she needs it most will require her to risk either an authority-weakening bout of pleading or a pitched and public showdown with some of her students—probably her toughest ones. She will have to reset unproductive expectations. This is a bad place to be, and many teachers get there before they realize they're on the way.

I've chosen the example of a teacher with her hand raised for silence because it is a commonly used—or, rather, misused—device and because it shows the ease with which teachers learn to ignore noncompliance.

The teacher in the example was asking for two different things—in fact, two things that are not necessarily related. Students have four possible actions in response: raise their hands and not be silent, be silent and not raise their hands, raise their hands and become silent, or neither raise their hands nor become silent. Including raising hands in the command means more variables and more outcomes to attend to. It may well be that raising hands helps achieve silent attentiveness, but the teacher should at least ask: Is there a less invasive way to achieve silent attentiveness? Do I want to take the time right now to manage two compliance variables fully? She might consider whether it would be more effective to have students quietly sit up straight, with their eyes on her, to show they are ready to listen rather than raise their hands. This would still give her students an attention routine and herself a visual way to check for compliance. However, the visual check of eye contact is subtler than raised hands and eliminates the issue of marginal compliance. It can be done more quickly and is arguably better preparation for what life asks of attentive people: eye contact and alertness.

So there are a lot of reasons that being serious about students' doing what you asked can cause you to reconsider what you ask for. Ideally the process of reflecting will cause you to be more efficient in classroom processes. But whatever you choose, you must take your own commands seriously. If you ask, they should do it.

The example raises a second point about compliance. If the correct percentage of follow-through is 100 percent, so is the correct extent of follow-through. Tolerating marginal compliance, especially when public, will also have a corrosive effect. When the teacher in the example starts to get hands in the air from her students, she will set expectations, again whether she recognizes it or not, about what follow-through looks like and how much is enough. Students will be consciously or unconsciously asking themselves versions of the following questions:

- "Is it okay to just raise my hand halfway?"

- "Can't I rest my elbow on the desk?"

- "Is there some way to do this and not look like I am trying to be her pet?"

- "Is it okay to lift my hand the minimum conceivable amount (say, with a slight articulation of the wrist) and demonstrate to my friends that I am only humoring this teacher because I have graciously decided it is not worth my time to disrespect her publicly?"

The most sustainable form of compliance is one that for both students and teachers is clearly an exercise that will help students achieve, not an empty exercise in teacher power.

The answer to these should be no. The message should be, "What we do, we do right because it helps us on the path to college." Excellence is *the* habit: what you do, you should do well, and the easiest way to do it well is to do it well every time. If the teacher has set raising hands as the expectation, she should stand by it. This may again cause her to reconsider whether this is the setting in which she wants to enforce what a hand in the air should look like. Again, the more seriously you take compliance, the more you should reflect on the justness and discretion of your commands. Ultimately the most sustainable form of compliance is one that for both students and teachers is clearly an exercise that will help students achieve, not an empty exercise in teacher power. It happens that in most top classrooms, there's lots of learning how to do routines and rituals right. There needs to be a clear signal for quiet attentiveness, and the teacher needs to be able to see it as well as hear it. But it also needs to stand the test of alignment with the end goal.

SEE IT IN ACTION: CLIP 14

100 PERCENT AND WHAT TO DO

In clip 14 on the DVD, Ashley Buroff of Rochester Prep models *100 Percent* and *What to Do* (described later in this chapter). She starts with a simple and clear *What to Do* direction: "Track me." She then takes a moment to, in *100 Percent* parlance, "be seen looking." As she asks her students to lift their packets into the air to rip the last page off (and in so doing making students' compliance eminently visible to her), she again gives a series of concrete observable directions: "Go ahead and lift your packets up into the air holding the *Do Now* in one hand and the rest of the packet in the other." It's hard to misunderstand that one. She caps with an anonymous individual correction: "Still waiting on everybody." As you can see (and so can the students), the compliance rate is a clear 100 percent.

PRINCIPLES OF 100 PERCENT COMPLIANCE

Three principles are key to ensuring consistent follow-through and compliance in the classroom. These principles are critical not just to ensuring *100 Percent* but to ensuring that a healthy classroom climate endures, that the pace of class is crisp, and that academics remain the

Your goal is to get 100 percent compliance so you can teach. You want the intervention to be fast and invisible.

primary focus. The first principle, using the least invasive intervention possible, serves as a rule of thumb for mastery of this technique.

Use the Least Invasive Form of Intervention

Your goal is to get 100 percent compliance so you can teach. Getting this compliance at the cost of constant, time-consuming disruptions to make sure everyone's on task ironically serves to stop the progress of the task and cause the death spiral: all the disruptions to keep people on task result in no task, and thus everyone inherently is off task. The students "on the bubble," the ones you've fought hardest to engage, start to look around at what else is going on to engage in. Disaster. You want the intervention to be fast and invisible.

In the following potential interventions, the goal is to have a correction be as near to the top of the list as possible:

- **Nonverbal intervention.** Gesture to or eye contact with off-task students while doing something else, preferably teaching the others. By many measures, teachers interrupt their own lessons more than students do, so using nonverbal correction while teaching keeps your lesson on rails.
- **Positive group correction.** Quick verbal reminder to the group about what students should be doing and not what they shouldn't be doing: "We're following along in our books"; "You should be tracking the speaker." It is used just as student attention appears on the brink of wandering.
- **Anonymous individual correction.** Quick verbal reminder to the group, similar to positive group correction, except that the anonymous individual correction makes it explicit that not everyone is where they need to be: "We need two people." "Homeroom Morehouse, please check yourself to make sure you've got your eyes on the speaker."
- **Private individual correction.** When and if you have to name names (you will have to, especially when you are setting expectations early in the year), seek to correct privately and quietly. Walk by the off-task student's desk. Lean down confidently to get as near to him as possible and, using a voice that preserves as much privacy as is possible, tell the corrected student what to do quickly and calmly. Then talk about something else. Something like, "Quentin, I've asked everyone to track me, and I need to see you doing it too," will suffice on the first interaction. If you need to return, it's time for a consequence. Again you want to do this privately: "Quentin, I need you to track me so you can learn. I'm going to have to [move your card to yellow, take two scholar dollars, ask you to come in and practice at recess]. Now please show me your best."

SEE IT IN ACTION: CLIP 15

100 PERCENT

In clip 15 on the DVD, Jaimie Brillante of Rochester Prep is demonstrating the private individual correction. Notice how she makes her intervention an exercise in purpose, not in power: the reason she's talking to her student is that she wasn't able to answer correctly. The goal is for her to succeed academically, not pay attention to Brillante or to do what Brillante asked. Notice how she focuses other students on a clear task before addressing. She even gets tissues for another student to make her approach less obvious and thus the interaction more private. Finally, notice the calm, firm, nonjudgmental tone. Brillante is careful to tell her students how to solve the problem.

Want to know more? Check out the interview with Jaimie Brillante in the Appendix of this book.

• **Lightning-quick public correction.** You will be forced at times to make corrections of individual students during public moments. Your goals in making an individual verbal correction should be to limit the amount of time a student is "onstage" for something negative and focus on telling the student what to do right rather than scolding or explicating what he did wrong (when possible) to normalize the positive behavior of the majority of the class by pointing that out too. Something like, "Quentin, I need your eyes," is quick, confident, and effective. Your correction might add, "Quentin, I need your eyes. Looking sharp, back row!" In rare cases you may wish to emphasize your attentiveness to Quentin's accountability (to Quentin and his classmates) by adapting the sequence as follows: "Quentin, I need your eyes. Looking sharp, back row! Thank you, Quentin. Much better."

When the interactions follow a sequence, the narration of them should generally gather positive momentum. They end on the positive ("much better") and allow you to describe to your class the progress toward excellence (Quentin was off task, but now he's on). Although you are making a correction, your narration emphasizes that things are getting better.

Notice the importance of speed. I recommend using the longest of the above sequences only occasionally and avoiding anything longer if possible.

Finally, notice the practical utility of the correction. Merely saying Quentin's name, as many teachers might do, doesn't provide Quentin with any guidance about how to meet your expectations. This is a critical point, discussed further in *What to Do.*

● **Consequence.** The ideal is to solve a case of noncompliance quickly, successfully, and with the least possible disruption to the whole class. In the long run, it makes a teacher stronger when he or she only occasionally uses external consequences. Solving issues without external consequences reinforces the teacher's intrinsic power. However, if a situation cannot be addressed quickly and successfully without a consequence, the consequence must be given so that instruction is not interrupted. As with other interventions, consequences should be delivered quickly and in the least invasive, least emotional manner. Ideally a teacher has a scaled series of consequences from which to choose, so she can match the significance of the response to the disruption and, in so doing, ensure her own ability to administer it quickly, decisively, and without wavering. This is discussed further in *No Warnings* (technique 42, later in this chapter).

SEE IT IN ACTION: CLIP 16

100 PERCENT

In clip 16 on the DVD, Bob Zimmerli of Rochester Prep demonstrates *100 Percent*. Notice in particular his:

● Positive group corrections: *"Every*body." "All hands down; show me SLANT now!"

● Anonymous individual correction: "I still need three people. You know who you are. I need two people."

● Lightning quick public correction: "I don't have Marissa, but I *do* have Jasmine!"

Zimmerli's students are "rolling their numbers." That is, they are learning to do repeated addition with a given number so they can learn and check their multiplication tables. Notice how the use of fingers in number rolling allows Zimmerli to more readily see who's participating. He's made compliance visible. You could argue he's doing something similar when he asks his students to "track [look at] this paper," and then moves across the front of the room. If he sees their heads swivel, he knows they're paying attention, yet another way to make compliance visible.

Want to know more? Check out the interview with Bob Zimmerli in the Appendix to this book.

One common misperception about the six levels of intervention is the belief that they represent a process or a formula: that teachers always progress methodically through each of the levels, trying all five types of correction in sequence before giving a consequence. Nothing could be further from the reality. The goal is to be as close to the top of the list as possible and when possible, but your fidelity should be to what works, not to the list. Sometimes go straight to the fifth level, sometimes go back and forth among the levels, and occasionally allow five interventions to an off-task individual before assigning a consequence. In fact, using levels 1 to 5 implies that the students to whom the interventions are directed are making (or appear likely to be making) a good-faith effort to comply with expectations. Behavior that is deliberate has earned a consequence.

Another common misperception is that ignoring misbehavior—or addressing it by praising students who are behaving—is the least invasive form of intervention. But ignoring misbehavior is the most invasive form of intervention because it becomes more likely that the behavior will persist and expand. The goal is to address behavior quickly—the first time it appears and while its manifestation is still minimal and the required response still small.

Ignoring misbehavior is the most invasive form of intervention because it becomes more likely that the behavior will persist and expand.

Rely on Firm, Calm Finesse

Achieving compliance is an exercise in purpose, not power. Students need to follow directions quickly and completely so that they can be assured of having the best chance to succeed. Although that often involves absolute responsiveness to their teachers, this responsiveness is the means, not the end. "I need your eyes on me so you can learn," is a more effective statement than, "I asked for your eyes on me because when I ask you to do something, I expect you to do it." While you should expect students to do something when you ask them to, it's not really about you in the end; it's about them and their path to college. Command obedience not because you can or because it feels good but because it serves your students. Make that distinction evident in your language, tone, and demeanor.

100 Percent teachers stress the universality of expectations. Their language reinforces this: "I need everyone's eyes" stresses universality better than, "I need your eyes, Trevor," though using Trevor's name may occasionally be necessary, "I need everyone's eyes, Trevor," takes a more direct approach to Trevor while still stressing that the standard is universal. Similarly, *100 Percent* teachers are strategically impersonal. Many teachers think their job is to individualize every decision to the specific needs and people in every situation. In cases of behavioral expectations, this is likely to result in their feeling particularly picked on, especially when they don't like the decisions. Reinforcing expectations with a bit of impersonality ("That's not how we do it here"; "In this classroom we respond respectfully to peers") reminds students that your decisions are not personal.

100 Percent teachers catch it early, before the rest of the class, and sometimes even the students in question, know it's an "it."

> *Asking for eyes on you is better than asking for attention, because you can see it when you have it. Asking for pencils down* and *eyes on you is better yet, since it gives you two things you can see.*

Emphasize Compliance You Can See

You can emphasize compliance in a number of ways:

- **Invent ways to maximize visibility.** Find ways to make it easier to see who's followed your directions by asking students to do things you can see. Asking for eyes on you is better than asking for attention, because you can see it when you have it. Asking for pencils down *and* eyes on you is better yet, since it gives you two things you can see and because the second thing you've asked for—pencils down—is far easier to see in a quick scan of the room than is eye contact. Averted eyes are subtle and time-consuming to see; a pencil in hand in a room of pencils on desks is easily discerned. This makes it easier for you to see compliance and results in your students' recognizing that it is far harder not to comply, requiring a willfulness that few students are willing to pursue.

- **Be seen looking.** When you ask for compliance, look for it consistently and be seen looking for it. Every few minutes, scan the room with a calm smile on your face to ensure that everything is as it should be. When you give a direction, remember to pause and scan the room. Narrating your scan—"Thank you, Peter. Thank you, Marissa. Eyes right on me, front row"—reinforces that when you ask, you both look to see who's done it and consistently see what individuals do.

- **Avoid marginal compliance.** It's not just whether your students do what you've asked but whether they do it right. A certain number will complete a task only as fully as you show them you expect it completed. They'll rightly want to know what exactly "eyes on me" means. Eyes near you? Eyes on yours for a fleeting second? Eyes locked on yours while you're talking? The difference among these three interpretations is night and day.

- **Leverage the power of unacknowledged behavioral opportunities.** Students can gain valuable practice behaving in a constructive and positive manner without even being aware that they are doing so. For example, they can practice making a habit of following their teacher's directions. In a classroom where the teacher uses fun, high-energy *Call and Response* (technique 23) teaching, students practice doing what they're asked, right on cue, over and over again. They don't recognize that they are practicing following commands, just that they're having fun. And they see their peers doing this as well, which normalizes follow-through and compliance with the teacher. Over time this has a powerful effect. Students not only build up muscle memory of repeated on-cue compliance, but they come to expect that instant compliance from their peers and associate it with positive feelings. They are learning to buy in and behave without even being aware that they are doing so.

Teachers who find lots of opportunities for students to practice doing what they ask when they aren't concerned about behavior ensure a greater likelihood of their success when they are.

TECHNIQUE 37
WHAT TO DO

Some portion of student noncompliance—a larger portion than many teachers ever suppose—is caused not by defiance but by incompetence: by students' misunderstanding a direction, not knowing how to follow it, or tuning out in a moment of benign distraction. Recognizing this means giving directions to students in a way that provides clear and useful guidance—enough of it to allow any student who wanted to do as asked to do so easily. The name for this technique is **What to Do**, and using it makes directions routinely useful and easy to follow.

In schools we spend a lot of time defining the behavior we want by the negative: "Don't get distracted." "Stop fooling around." "That behavior was inappropriate." These commands are vague, inefficient, and unclear. They force students to guess what you want them to do.

Four primary characteristics of *What to Do* help reinforce accountability among students. In addition, a critical guiding principle emphasizes differentiating between defiance and incompetence. Consistently making this crucial distinction will have a pervasive effect on your classroom culture and relationship with students.

What to Do starts, logically, with your telling students what to do—that is, with *not* telling them what *not* to do. In schools we spend a lot of time defining the behavior we want by the negative: "Don't get distracted." "Stop fooling around." "That behavior was inappropriate." These commands are vague, inefficient, and unclear. They force students to guess what you want them to do. What's the "it" in, "Cut it out," for example? Assuming I don't want to get distracted, if all you tell me is not to do that, what should I now assume the alternative is and how would I have known that?

Even when we don't define behavior by the negative, we are often insufficiently helpful. When you tell a student to pay attention, ask yourself if she knows how to pay attention. Has anyone ever taught her? Does she know your specific expectations for paying attention (having her eyes on the speaker, say)? Has anyone ever helped her learn to avoid and control distractions and distractedness? The command "pay attention" provides no useful guidance because it fails to teach.

One of our primary jobs is to tell students what to do and how to do it. Telling students what to do rather than what not to do is not only far more efficient and effective but it refocuses us, even in moments that are about behavior, on teaching. It expresses the belief that teaching can solve problems. However, just telling kids what to do is not quite enough. To be effective, directions should be specific, concrete, sequential, and observable:

- **Specific.** Effective directions are specific. They focus on manageable and precisely described actions that students can take. Instead of advising a student to pay attention, for example, I might advise him to put his pencil on his desk or keep his eyes on me. This provides useful guidance that he can take action on and pay attention to doing. It is easy to remember, solution oriented, and hard to misunderstand.

- **Concrete.** Effective directions are not just specific; they involve, when possible, clear, actionable tasks that any student knows how to do. If I tell my student to pay attention, he may or may not know how to do that, but if I tell him to put his feet under his desk, I have asked him to do something no student can misunderstand or not know how to do. If he appears to struggle, I can get more concrete: "Turn your body to face me. Bring your legs around. Put them under your desk. Push in your chair." These are real things: physical, simple, commonplace. There is no gray area in this command and no finesse or prior knowledge required to follow through. And the elimination of such gray area allows me to better understand the intention of my student.

- **Sequential.** Since a complex skill like paying attention is rarely equated with a single specific action, effective directions should describe a sequence of concrete specific actions. In the case of my student who needs help paying attention, I might advise him, "John, put your feet under your desk, put your pencil down, and put your eyes on me." In some cases, I might add, "When I write it on the board, that means you write it in your notes."

- **Observable.** I was careful to give John not just a sequence of specific steps to follow. I described observable actions: things that I could plainly see him do. This is critical. Since my directions focused on a series of steps that were specific and simple enough that any student could reasonably be expected to do them, the observational component of my directions left John with little wiggle room in terms of his accountability. If I tell him to pay attention, I can't really tell whether he has done so and therefore cannot hold him accountable very effectively. He will protest, "But I *was* paying attention." Consciously or unconsciously, students sense and exploit this lack of accountability. However, if I tell John, "Put your feet under your desk, put your pencil down, and get your eyes on me," I can see perfectly well whether he has done it. *He* knows perfectly well that I can see whether he has done it and is therefore more likely to do it.

What to Do allows you to distinguish between incompetence and defiance by making your commands specific enough that they can't be deliberately misinterpreted and helpful enough that they explain away any gray areas. However, it's worth considering a bit more the capacity to distinguish between incompetence and defiance. If I ask John to pay attention or sit up or get on task and he doesn't, knowing whether he will not or cannot matters deeply. If he cannot, the problem is incompetence. If he will not, the problem is defiance. I respond to these situations differently.

Psychological studies suggest that learned helplessness—the process of giving up because you believe your own choices and actions are irrelevant—generally results from a perception that consequences are random.

If the issue is incompetence, my obligation is to teach John. If I punish him for not complying when he is unable to do so, the consequence will seem unjust: I will punish him for what he doesn't understand or can't do. This will erode my relationship with John and teach him that consequences are disconnected from his actions. If they happen for reasons he does not fathom, they are random to him. Psychological studies suggest that learned helplessness—the process of giving up because you believe your own choices and actions are irrelevant—generally results from a perception that consequences are random.

But if John will not do what I ask, the issue is defiance, and my obligation is to provide a consequence. Unless I act clearly and decisively in the face of a challenge to my authority, John will establish a precedent of impunity. He and his classmates will now know that John, and arguably anyone else who's willing to, can successfully challenge me for the rest of the year. When I let go of my authority in this way, I am abdicating my responsibility to protect the environment in which the rest of the students live and learn—and thus their right to a quality education. If I respond to defiance with teaching, I am just as bad off as if I respond to incompetence with punishment.

Therefore, you must distinguish between incompetence and defiance, responding to incompetence with teaching and defiance with consequence. Confusing one for the other—and many teachers routinely fail to distinguish them—has damaging consequences in both cases, and this is why making the distinction reliably and consistently has such far-reaching ramifications for your classroom. Making the distinction well is probably the most important part of *What to Do;* arguably it is one of the most important tools for building classroom culture. By giving concrete, specific, observable directions—simple and clear enough that anyone of good faith could do them if they wanted—you can make the distinction consistently and fairly. You can task students who are struggling with actions that allow you know the difference so you can teach when you should teach and exert your authority when you must.

What to Do, *Version 2*

When students fail to follow a direction and you know the cause is incompetence or believe that you need further data to determine whether it is, revising the initial direction, this time by breaking it down into an even more specific sequence of steps, can help. Let's say I task my students: "Take out your folders. Find your homework. Place it at the corner of your desk." Two students fail to do this. They take out their folders but go no further. While the rest of my class completes the task, I might say to them, "Open your folder, and look in the left-side pocket for your assignment. Take it out, and place it on your desk. Now close the folder. Good. And put it away." This reteaches the part of the task that was difficult for the students: providing more guidance where they were unclear (perhaps they didn't know where to look in their folders; perhaps they weren't sure whether I meant they should place their homework or their folders in the corner of their desks). If that reteaching is unnecessary, it reinforces the students' accountability for following through. Yes, I am babying them a little, but I am being very clear that I am aware of the noncompliance, am not rattled by it, and intend to address it. Either way I am more likely to cause the successful completion of the task or, if not, to reveal more clearly a case of minor defiance that I can handle with a consequence and the confidence that the decision to do so was just. Since this allows me to administer my consequences without doubt or hesitation, it allows me to administer them with absolute consistency.

Repeating a *What to Do* with greater specificity can also be used in crisis situations. As a dean of students, I was once called to a classroom where a teacher had tried to send a student to the office. The student, volatile and often defiant, had refused to move or to acknowledge the teacher when she had been asked to leave. Instead she put her head down and ignored all directions. With the entire classroom watching me, I bent down next to her desk and said, quietly and firmly, "Christina, come with me please." She didn't move a muscle. I was glad I made the initial command quietly and preserving a modicum of privacy but I knew time was running out. By luck or instinct—I was not yet aware of the *What to Do* technique—I said, "Christina, push your chair back from your desk, and stand up beside it." Lo and behold, that's exactly what Christina did. "Good," I said. "Now follow me to the door."

After that, I used the technique in a variety of crises and found it one of my most reliable tools, especially when confronting a group of students who needed redirection and were actively reading my level of calm and willingness to assert my authority. I found it helped me to know what to say in situations where I might otherwise be nervous. Knowing that I would rely on a clear *What to Do* allowed me to approach tough situations calmly and with a confidence that increased my likelihood of success: "Gentlemen, please pause your conversation for a moment. I am teaching on the other side of this door. Please pick up your things, walk to the end of the hall, open the doors, and step outside. You may continue your conversation there."

TECHNIQUE 38

STRONG VOICE

Some teachers have "it": they enter a room and are instantly in command. Students who moments before seemed beyond the appeal of reason suddenly take their seats to await instructions. It's hard to say exactly what "it" is and why some teachers have it. Much of it is surely intangible and nontransferable, a manifestation of the unique power of individuals and their ability to earn respect and credibility, build relationships, and exude confidence and poise. But even if I can't tell you exactly how to bottle "it," I can describe five concrete things that "it" teachers consistently use to signal their authority. These are five techniques anyone, even the seemingly meekest and mildest of novices, can use. Using them will put you in a position to establish control, command, and the benign authority that makes the use of excessive consequences unnecessary. Mastering these skills may not make you the "it" teacher, but having a **Strong Voice** will surely get you a lot closer.

Generally *Strong Voice* teachers follow five principles in their interactions with students—or at least in the interactions where they are trying to establish control: Economy of Language, Do Not Talk Over, Do Not Engage, Square Up/Stand Still, and Quiet Power. They also have a default register——a tone and demeanor they employ in their interactions—that maximizes the power of these five principles.

THE FIVE PRINCIPLES OF STRONG VOICE

Economy of Language

Do Not Talk Over

Do Not Engage

Square Up/Stand Still

Quiet Power

- **Economy of Language.** Fewer words are stronger than more. Demonstrating economy of language shows that you are prepared and know your purpose in speaking. Being chatty or verbose signals nervousness, indecision, and flippancy. It suggests that your words can be ignored. When you need your directions followed, use the words that best focus students on what is most important, and no more. Don't dilute urgent issues with things that can wait. Rather than asking students to identify the top priority of the five points you made in your directions to them, make just one point. Then you can be sure your students will hear it. Avoid initiating distractions and excess words. When you need to be all business, be clear and crisp. And then stop talking.

- **Do Not Talk Over.** If what you're saying is truly worth attention, then every student has the right and the responsibility to hear it. And if what you're saying is not that important, maybe you shouldn't be saying it, at least to the whole class. When you need them to listen, your words must be far and away the most important in the room, so make a habit of showing that they matter. Before beginning, wait until there is no other talking or rustling. By ensuring that your voice never competes for attention, you will demonstrate to students that their decision to listen isn't situational (that is, you do it if it seems as if maybe it really matters this time). Moreover, controlling who has the floor is the mark of your authority and a necessity to your teaching. If you repeat ten instructions per day at half a minute per instruction, you will waste two full days of school per child over the course of the year. You cannot afford to talk over students.

In some cases, you may need to start in order to stop, that is, start a sentence and break it off to show that you will not go on until you have full attention. Using this self-interrupt to make the fact that they are stopping obvious avoids the ironic necessity of talking over students to tell students you won't talk over them. Typically a teacher might plan to address his class with some direction like this: "Sixth grade, I need your binders out so you can write down the homework correctly." However, if students were inattentive or if there was noise or talking persisting after his first word or two, he would cut off his own sentence, ideally at the most noticeable place, and remain silent for a few seconds before starting again: "Sixth grade, I need your. . ." If the low-level muttering and distractions did not entirely disappear, he might initiate another self-interrupt, this time with a bit less of the direction given: "Sixth grade, I. . ." During these interruptions he might stand stock-still to demonstrate that nothing could continue until attentiveness was restored.

Of all the situations in which a student is likely to try to change topics, the moment in which you ask her to take accountability for her actions is among the most likely.

- **Do Not Engage.** Once you have set the topic of conversation, avoid engaging in other topics until you have satisfactorily resolved the topic you initiated. This is especially important when the topic is behavioral follow-through.

Of all the situations in which a student is likely to try to change topics, the moment in which you ask her to take accountability for her actions is among the most likely. Commonly a student will reply with an excuse or a distraction. Suppose, for example, that you say to David, who is pushing Margaret's chair with his foot, "Please take your foot off Margaret's chair." David might reply, "But she's pushing me!" or "But she keeps on moving into my space!" Many teachers might struggle in such a situation by engaging the distraction David has proposed: what Margaret was allegedly doing. Saying, "Margaret, were you doing that?" or even, "I'm not really concerned with what Margaret was doing," is a way of responding to David's choice of topic, not making him engage yours. A better response would be to say, "David, I asked you to take your foot off Margaret's chair," or even, "Right now, I need you to follow my direction and take your foot off Margaret's chair." These responses are better because they make explicit reference to the fact that you initiated a topic of conversation and expect it to be addressed and because it doesn't require you to announce that you "don't care" what Margaret did, which isn't exactly the message you want to convey.

Another possible reply from David might be, "But I wasn't doing anything!" Again, the best strategy is not to engage his topic. After all you wouldn't have corrected him if you'd had a question in your mind about whether David's foot was where it should be. The best reply is, "I asked you to take your foot off Margaret's chair. Once you've done that, you don't need to say anything more."

If you did have a question, an effective strategy would be to say, "David, if your foot is on Margaret's chair, I need you to put it under your own desk and keep it there." If he distracts with, "But she was . . . ," your response is simple. He's admitted that his foot is on her chair, and now you merely repeat your request that he remove it. If he says, "It wasn't on her chair," then you can simply reply, "Good. Then it shouldn't be hard for you to keep it under your desk for the duration of class." If you think David is likely to test you, you could add, "I'll keep an eye on it so I can help you practice that at recess if you need the help."

A better original direction to David would have been to tell him where to put his foot rather than where not to put it. After all, there's no guarantee that the next place he finds for it will be much better or that he won't move it back. So an ideal original command might be something like, "David, please put your feet under your desk and face me." This command also puts you in a better place if he removes his foot and claims, "But my foot wasn't on Margaret's chair" or "My foot isn't on Margaret's chair." Because you have initiated the topic of where his foot should be rather than where it shouldn't be, you can merely repeat your request: "I asked you to put your foot under your desk and to face me. Let me see you do that now."

This is certainly about your authority, but it's not only about your authority. Engaging in this topic allows David to defer consideration of his own accountability. Students will often seize on this opportunity to convince themselves that they were not in fact behaving in a negative manner. Ask yourself if you want your kids to get the message that you can change the topic or blame someone else if you haven't done your job. Ask yourself if you want them to be able to fool themselves into thinking it was all okay. Thus, insisting that you control the topic of behavioral conversations ensures accountability by students in your interest, that of their peers (whose interests you represent), and their own.

Refusing to engage establishes a tone of focused accountability in your classroom. Students can't change the topic. They need to act first and explain later. It also means that the issues of who is bugging whom are more easily delayed until a time when instruction is not happening.

Here's another useful example:

Teacher: (to James, who was talking) James, you are talking. Please move your card to yellow.

James: It wasn't me!

Teacher: Please move your card to yellow.

James: Shanice was talking! Not me!

Teacher: I asked you to move your card. Please get up and move your card to yellow.

It may be reasonable for the teacher to discuss who was talking with James (it also may not be), but it needs to be the expectation that the latter conversation doesn't happen until James has first done what his teacher asked. He can dissent or seek redress. Until he has obeyed the initial request, there is no other conversation.

A final situation in which it's critical not to engage is when students call out answers. Engaging with the answer, even if you say, "Right, but please don't call out," sends the message that if what you call out is interesting enough, the right answer when no one else can seem to get it, or said loud enough or repeated often enough, then the rules don't apply. This will rapidly put you in a place where you are faced with constant calling out. No matter how fascinating the comment or how needed the right answer, if you engage when it is called out, you will erode your ability to control future conversations in your classroom. No matter how intriguing the answer, it's better in the long run to remind students of what to do—"In this class, we raise our hands when we want to speak"—without engaging the answer.

- **Square Up/Stand Still.** In every comment, you speak nonverbally as well as with your words. Show with your body that you are committed to each request. When you want to express the seriousness of your directions, turn, with two feet and two shoulders, to face the object of your words directly. Make sure your eye contact is direct. Stand up straight or lean in close (ironically this shows your level of control by demonstrating that you are not shy or afraid; you don't crouch down to a dog you fear will bite you, after all). If the student to whom you are speaking is more than a few feet away, move toward him.

When giving directions that you want followed, stop moving and don't engage in other tasks at the same time. If you are passing out papers while you direct students, you suggest that your directions aren't that important. After all, you're doing other things at the same time too. At times it may even help to strike a formal pose, putting your arms behind your back to show that you take your own words seriously and therefore that they, like you, are formal and purposeful.

- **Quiet Power.** When you get nervous, and are worried that students might not follow your directions, when you sense that your control may be slipping away, your first instinct is often to talk louder and faster. When you get loud and talk fast, you show that you are nervous, scared, out of control. You

When you get loud and talk fast, you show that you are nervous, scared, out of control. You make visible all the anxieties and send a message to students that they can control you and your emotions.

make visible all the anxieties and send a message to students that they can control you and your emotions—that they can make you anxious and upset, make you put on a show that's much more entertaining than revising a paper or nailing coordinate geometry, say. When you get loud, you also, ironically, make the room louder and thus easier for students to successfully talk under their breath. Though it runs against all your instincts, get slower and quieter when you want control. Drop your voice, and make students strain to listen. Exude poise and calm.

SEE IT IN ACTION: CLIP 17

STRONG VOICE

In clip 17 on the DVD, Sultana Noormuhammad of Leadership Prep Bedford Stuyvesant demonstrates *Strong Voice*. While she's reading about penguins with her kids, there's an interruption (what sounds like a hiccup). Noormuhammad responds with a self-interruption, reinforcing the expectation that she will not talk over voices or other distractions. She emphasizes the importance of student attention by "squaring up" to face the noise and remaining absolutely still for a second. She leverages economy of language, eschewing the lecture that might come with her intervention. In this case, it's pretty clear why she stopped. It also shows how important it is to "catch it early" (the "it" being off-task behavior, as discussed in *100 Percent*). When you catch it early, you can correct with a much smaller and less invasive intervention, often one that doesn't require a discussion with the whole class: "Class, when I am talking, I need you to . . ." That may help set expectations, but it also calls lots of attention to noncompliance and thus normalizes it. Little fixes, like the one Noormuhammad uses here, often don't require narration.

Note a visible contrast between her formal register in the moment of her *Strong Voice* intervention and her warmer and chattier style when she's discussing content with her students.

FORMAL POSE: THE DEFAULT REGISTER OF *STRONG VOICE* TEACHERS

Imagine three interactions between colleagues at work. The workplace may be a school but it doesn't have to be. In the first interaction, a woman tells her colleague about her recent weekend. Maybe they're in the lunch area at work. "Oh my gosh, it was such a great weekend," begins the first. She's recounting a trip with some friends to a nearby city. As she does so, her eye contact drifts away from and comes back to her colleague, as if she was gazing out at some latent image of the weekend projected on a nearby wall. Her hands move as she describes it. "We were in this funky coffee shop with old records up the walls," she says, as her hands make a sweeping gesture alluding to the locations of said vinyl. She stands with her hips to the side, reclining against a wall perhaps. She's squinting slightly. Her weight is on one foot. Her words run together in a pitter-patter-like rhythm. All of these things—her inconsistent eye contact; her use of extensive, sweeping gestures; her asymmetrical, relaxed posture; her words running into one another as if each was not so critical in its own right but part of a larger narrative—suggest casualness, informality, a sense of ease. *We're just talking here,* she seems to say. *You can interrupt me anytime. If you have to walk away in the middle to do something else, that's okay too.*

Register is the word I'll use to describe the tenor of a conversation, encompassing eye contact, body position, gestures, facial expression, and rhythm of language. The register of this conversation is casual, and many teachers use something like it in the classroom. It's fine to do so if you're aware of what it signals: *We're just talking here. You can walk away at any time. I'm telling you a story as I talk, and you just need to get the general gist of it.* The problem is that teachers often deliver an important message in a casual register that ultimately undercuts it. There may be times when you can tell a student, "I need you to sit up" in a casual register, but using it generally suggests discretion for the listener: you are telling a story; the listener just needs to get the general gist and can walk away at any time. "Sit up if you feel like it" is what the casual register says. And if it contradicts the words the teacher is using, it's likely to win out.

Now imagine a second conversation in which our speaker suddenly adjusts to a more formal register. She stands up straight and holds her body symmetrical. She looks directly at her colleague. Her chin rises slightly. She puts her hands behind her back (no wide, sweeping gestures here; in fact you can't even see her hands). You couldn't read or get distracted by her gestures even if you wanted to because you can't see her hands. The speaker could be saying anything, but let's imagine her reciting the pledge of allegiance. "I pledge allegiance," she says, "to the flag." There's a clear distinction between her words now. Each is an important part of the solemn ritual. Her articulation of the syllables is clearer. She doesn't ask her colleague to strike the formal hands-behind-the-back pose she's using, but when the colleague sees it, she knows something important is happening and is likely to stand up straight herself and maybe even put her own hands behind her back in unconscious mimicry.

A formal register, it turns out, bespeaks the importance of the message and causes a purposeful attentiveness in the listener. And transplanted into the classroom, that's powerful. Imagine our teacher now approaching a student with her hands clasped behind her back. She stands symmetrically and leans in ever so slightly toward the student in question. Her eyes are steady. In controlled words with distinct pauses between them, she says, "I need you to sit up." She makes no further movements. Her register communicates importance, focus, and calm authority. It supports her message. As you can probably guess, champion teachers tend to use the formal register for the great majority of their statements in which they seek control. Watch them in action, and you'll see them standing straight and symmetrically, choosing words carefully, with brief pauses between words, eyes held steady. If they make a hand gesture, it's controlled and simple, involving one movement and ending succinctly. This formal register is the wrapping that makes *Strong Voice* especially effective.

What about a sense of urgency? Imagine our two colleagues in a third conversation. The building is on fire. The first colleague enters the lunch area. She places her hands firmly on the shoulders of her colleague. "Listen," she says. "There's an emergency. I need you to come with me right away. I need you to put everything down and follow me. Do you understand? Good. Let's go." She's leaning in closer than she would in a mere formal pose, and she's punching her words. The pauses are actually more noticeable, though you might have expected her to rush. Her eyes are locked more than steady. She makes a gesture toward the fire exit with a crisp, truncated, chopping motion. She is not panicked, not blathering and rushed—just singularly focused.

Is this the tone you want to use in your classroom to ensure compliance? Maybe and maybe not.

If the chips are truly down—if the building is, metaphorically, on fire—an urgent register can work but only if it is delivered as urgent (calm, focused, and very insistent) and not panicked (emotional, hurried, and anxious). But urgency can also be like crying wolf. It has to be saved for truly urgent situations and most control-oriented interactions should be of the garden variety: made early in the process before things become urgent. Overused, urgency shows weakness and lack of control. But in the rare situations when it's needed, it can be useful. Again, it must be distinguished from a panicky register—a "you have me rattled" register. Those are never useful.

If you watch champion teachers for long enough, you will see that a large percentage of interactions in which control is at stake happen in the formal register. Again they do not conduct every interaction in the formal register; in fact, like the five *Strong Voice* principles generally, it is not for the moments when you're discussing the Civil War, two-variable equations, or *Of Mice and Men*. It's for the moments in between when you need students attentive, ready, and focused so you can have a worthwhile discussion of the Civil War, two-variable equations, or *Of Mice and Men*.

PUTTING THE *STRONG VOICE* TECHNIQUES TOGETHER

In his third-grade classroom, Darryl Williams's *Strong Voice* drives a clear and compelling culture. He has the ability to demonstrate all five techniques within a sequence of just a few seconds to bring his class to order, as he does in this example.

Having completed a study of prefixes and suffixes at the board, Williams turns to explain what's next on the agenda. "Okay," he begins. "Let's see who's . . . ," but his voice pulls up abruptly, demonstrating a refusal to talk over students. Two or three boys are waving their hands in the air while he is talking. Two others are talking to a classmate. Someone's head is down on the desk. "Well, most of us are doing an excellent job today," he says, dropping his voice to just above a whisper. He puts the book he was holding down. He turns to face the class and places his arms behind his back in a formal Square Up pose. Quietly, slowly, and firmly, he says, "Please put your hands down," focusing the boys' attention on the request with strict economy of language. His refusal to take hands is yet another way to avoid engaging in a topic other than the one of his own choosing.

The distractions are gone now. The room is silent. All eyes are on him. For Williams, though, there's one more step: the task of making his actions transparent and benign. "Thank you," he says, showing his appreciation for their rapid return to full attentiveness. "The reason I can't answer all your questions right now . . . I would like to, and I love it when you tell me intelligent things. But we don't have a lot of time. We still need to read our story and then . . ." For Williams, the strength is not just in the control but in the caring. His explanation of the rationale behind his authority ensures his ability to sustain that control, with students' buy-in, for the long haul.

TECHNIQUE 39
DO IT AGAIN

Getting lots of practice helps students improve, so giving them more practice is the perfect response to a situation where they show they're not up to speed at a simple task. That's the idea behind **Do It Again**. When students fail to successfully complete a basic task that you've shown them how to do—line up, come in quietly—doing it again and doing it right, or better, or perfectly is often the best consequence.

Do It Again is especially effective for seven reasons:

1. *It shortens the feedback loop.* Behavioral science has shown that the shorter the time lag between an action and a response, the more effective the response will be in changing the behavior. Having kids stay in for recess three hours after the action that caused that consequence is less likely to create a disincentive than is a response, even an apparently lesser one, that happens right away. If the reaction comes immediately after, while the original action is fresh in a student's mind, the two will be more deeply associated in his or her memory. *Doing It Again* shortens the feedback loop in comparison to almost any other consequence.

2. *It sets a standard of excellence, not just compliance.* Do It Again is appropriate not just for times when students fail to do something or do it in a way

that's wrong; it's ideal for times when students do something acceptably but could do it better. Saying, "That was good; but I want great," or "In this class, we do everything as well as we can, including lining up," allows a teacher to set a standard of excellence, where good can always be better and better can always shoot for best. At its best, this can drive your classroom culture by replacing acceptable with excellent, first in the small things and then in all things.

3. *There is no administrative follow-up. Do It Again* is a consequence that requires no forms to be filled out, no parent phone calls, no briefing for administrators. The consequence is done as soon as the goal is reached. In the life of a busy teacher, that's a blessing. And because it requires no detention policy or schoolwide rewards systems, *Do It Again* is almost completely free-standing. It can be used in any classroom.

4. *There is group accountability.* Though individuals can easily be asked to *Do It Again*, the technique is especially effective as a group consequence. One or two students talk while everyone is lining up, and they all try it again. This holds the group accountable in a reasonable, nonpunitive way for the behavior of all of its individuals. It builds incentives for individuals to behave positively since it makes them accountable to their peers as well as their teacher.

5. *It ends with success.* The last thing you remember of an event often shapes your perception of it more broadly. *Do It Again* ends not with punishment or failure but with success. The last thing students do in a sequence is to do an activity the right way. This helps engrain the perception and memory of what right looks like. It also helps build muscle memory. Students built the habit of doing it right, over and over.

6. *There are logical consequences.* Ideal consequences are logically related to the behavior that precedes them. The idea is that this connection helps students to understand what they did wrong and what's expected of them in terms of doing it better or differently. A consequence of lining up again and lining up better is more logically related to a failure to line up well than is a consequence of staying in at recess.

7. *It is reusable. Do It Again* can be reused. You can *Do It Again* and then do it another time if necessary. And you can do the same thing again ten minutes later. Within reason, it doesn't lose its legs. You don't need to keep

inventing new consequences. You can be positive in administering the third iteration: "I still think we can do this even better. Let's give it one more shot!" Add a stopwatch to some routines and the challenge of *Do It Again* and better only gets more powerful.

DO IT AGAIN SCENARIOS

- A class transitioning from math to lunch

- A class transitioning from writing in their journals to reading aloud

- A class transitioning from gym to reading class

- A class that needs to track the speaker

- A class that gives a halfhearted *Call and Response* (technique 23)

- A class moving from their desks to a small group reading area

Given these advantages, it's no wonder that champion teachers use *Do It Again* so often. However, it's important to do the technique well. *Do It Again* should be positive whenever possible, with a keen focus on getting better and, in a great classroom, informed by a constant narrative of "good, better, best." That is, just doing it gets replaced by doing it well. In fact one colleague suggested that a better name for this technique was *Do It Better* as it better captured the idea that doing things over again to be as good as you can be is what school is about. The goal, again, is not mere compliance but excellence, even in the little things.

One colleague suggested that a better name for this technique is Do It Better *as it better captures the idea that doing things over again to be as good as you can be is what school is about. The goal is not mere compliance but excellence, even in the little things.*

Do It Again can be an effective tool for managing affect. Sometimes people's attitudes change from the outside in. Asking a low-energy class to repeat something with enthusiasm (especially, and critically, while modeling those attributes yourself) can start to be a self-fulfilling prophecy. *Do It Again* is a great opportunity to challenge students positively to show you their best at something. Saying, "Oooh, let's line up again and prove why we're the best reading group in the school," is often better that saying, "Class, that was very sloppy. We're going to do it again until we get it exactly right," even if the purpose is to *Do It Again* until you get it exactly right.

KEY IDEA

DO IT AGAIN

Doing it again and doing it right, or better, or perfect is often the best consequence.

And here's one additional hint about using *Do It Again*. Teachers tend to think that they need to wait until an entire routine or activity is done before asking the class to try it again. In fact, you should have students go back and try it again as soon as you know the level of execution will not meet the standard you set for it. Don't wait for the routine to end. Again, this will better connect the stimulus to the response. Let's say students are lining up for lunch, and the drill is to stand up quietly, push in their chairs, turn to face the door, and then follow the table leader to the door. If students forget to push in their chairs, have them sit back down and try it again right then. Don't wait until you get to the door to announce that some students forgot to push in their chairs. This saves time and reinforces instant accountability.

SEE IT IN ACTION: CLIP 18

DO IT AGAIN

In clip 18 on the DVD, Suzanne Vera of Leadership Prep Bedford Stuyvesant demonstrates *Do It Again*. She's also investing in discipline by teaching her students the right way to do things and practice. Her practice is designed to ensure that they practice successfully by simplifying the first few times. Vega has cleverly arranged to practice first without materials ("Pretend you're drawing!") that might distract her students and get in the way the first few times she teaches a procedure.

You'll probably notice right away in the clip how positive Vera's tone is. Vera tells her students, "That was good but it could be great," before they try it the second time. She also gives them specific feedback about how to be better by describing the solution and not the problem: "You need to be looking at me"; "Remember that you turn your neck if you can't see me." The feedback lives in the now.

Consider two last thoughts about this wonderful clip. First, some teachers might assume that students would naturally grouse about having to do basic tasks over and over again to get better at them. As it happens, and as Vera's teaching ably demonstrates, students are more often quite happy practicing and getting better, especially when the practice is framed positively, because they enjoy being successful and getting better at things. If you don't believe that, watch how these kids react. Second, notice that Vega's use of the stopwatch makes an implicit challenge to kids that she is set up to make explicit in the future: "Yesterday we cleaned up in twelve seconds; let's see if we can do it in ten today!"

You can read more about how teachers like Suzanne Vera make their correction so upbeat in *Positive Framing* (technique 43 in Chapter Seven).

TECHNIQUE 40

SWEAT THE DETAILS

In any environment, countless apparently minor details signal the expectations for conduct and behavior to residents, even if those individuals don't recognize that they are responding. This is the idea behind the broken windows theory of policing. Erase graffiti, fix broken windows, and combat minor but common disruptions in lawfulness, and people perceive their environment to be orderly and safe. They will then act to preserve it, not degrade it.

Sweat the Details puts this theory to work in your classroom. To reach the highest standards, you must create the perception of order. Clean up clutter, keep desk rows tidy, make sure shirts are tucked in and hats are off, and you will decrease the likelihood that you will have to deal with more serious issues because you will decrease your students' perception that those things might be permissible. If students think the front line of their struggle to test the rules is seeing what color socks they can get away with under uniform guidelines, they are far less likely to consider other ways of testing the rules.

The key to *Sweat the Details* is preparation. Planning for orderliness means putting systems in place in advance that make accomplishing the goal quick and easy.

- *Want your students' desks in neat rows?* (The answer should be yes.) Try putting tape marks on the floor so you can instruct students to "check their desks" and move them onto their marks.

- *Want your students to do neat and tidy homework?* Give students a homework standards rubric and occasionally (or frequently) collect assignments one at a time from each student's desk when they complete independent work, giving brief feedback on neatness to students as you circulate. "I don't see a name on this, Charles." "Is this your best work, Tani?" "You know I won't accept this with fringe on the paper, Danny." This will eliminate the anonymity of turning in homework and make students feel personally accountable.

- *Want your students to keep their materials neatly in their binders and never lose them?* Put materials in binders in a group the first fifty times, teaching the students how to do it as you go: "We're going to put these at the front of your vocabulary section. Get ready, and we'll open our binders on three. Ready?"

- *Want your students to work carefully on their seat work?* Circulate as they work, offering brief corrections as you go. "Check your spelling of *daily*, James." "One of your first two sentences isn't complete, Mehmet."

- *Want your students to raise their hands quietly and crisply to foster orderly participation?* Teach them how to raise their hands and remind them "how we raise our hands here" frequently.

In planning for these kinds of actions, you will not only solve persistent low-level issues that plague classrooms but will change students' perception about your classroom, making it seem an orderly and organized place where it's hard to imagine disorder rearing its head.

TECHNIQUE 41

THRESHOLD

The most important moment to set expectations in your classroom is the minute when your classroom students enter or, if they are transitioning within a classroom, when they formally begin their lesson. The first minute, when students cross the threshold into the classroom, you must remind them of the expectations. It's the critical time to establish rapport, set the tone, and reinforce the first steps in a routine that makes excellence habitual. With culture, getting it right and keeping it right is much easier than fixing it once it's gone wrong. **Threshold** ensures that you make a habit of getting it right from the outset each day.

Ideally you will find a way to greet your students by standing in the physical threshold of the classroom—astride the door, taking the opportunity to remind students where they are (they are with you now; no matter what the expectations are elsewhere, you will always expect their best), where they are going (to college), and what you will demand of them (excellence and effort). Typically each student who enters shakes your hand, looks you in the eye, and offers a civil and cordial greeting. (Some teachers use more informal variations on this.)

Use the greeting to engage students briefly and build rapport: "Loved your homework, David"; "Nice game last night, Shayna"; "Looking for great things from you today, Mr. Williams!"; "Oh my gosh, your hair looks great, Shanice!" You can occasionally (or always) greet the procession of students through the doorway with a description of what's to come and a reminder of what's expected: "We have a quiz today. Be sure to prepare your materials, then begin the *Do Now*. It will help you review. Okay, let's go." You should also use the threshold to set expectations by correcting weak handshakes, untidy attire, or lack of eye contact. Fortunately, this is easy to do since *Threshold* allows for its own simple implicit consequence. Get it wrong, and you go back in the line and try it again, and when you meet the expectations of the room, you enter on good terms. Incidentally, this is another reason for using a handshake: it allows you to control access to the room. If a student walks past with head down and without a greeting, you can always just hold on to his or her hand and not let go until the resulting eye contact allows you to gently correct the behavior.

Threshold will naturally take on a tone and feel in keeping with your own tone and style: it can be outgoing or quiet, warm or crisp. Yet no matter the affect, *Threshold* should always accomplish two things: (1) establish a personal connection between you and your students by a brief personal check-in (ideally one in which you greet each student by name), and (2) reinforce your classroom expectations.

Dacia Toll adds a slightly different flavor to the greeting she offers each of her sixth-grade writing students at New Haven's Amistad Academy. "Good morning, Sisuelas," she says to one student as she shakes her hand. "Nice to see you again, Sandria." Her air of conviviality expresses to each student her genuine interest in and enjoyment of their presence. When one student greets her with a slightly-too-informal, "Hey, what up?" she responds, warmly, " 'What up' is not appropriate," gently holding his hand as he passes and directing him to the back of the line. A few seconds later, he greets her with a "good morning" and, without retribution, she nods: "Good morning, Jabali." Her tone remains warm and kind. His test of the limits is utterly natural, she knows, and her response explains her expectations rather than chastising or punishing. Having the chance to try it again is the benign consequence, and he enters the class smiling as well.

At North Star Academy in Newark, New Jersey, Jamey Verilli adds a few wrinkles of his own. As his students wait outside the classroom, he quizzes them on last night's vocabulary words. "Okay, *tilled*. Who would do tilling, and what kind of work was it?" Verilli asks. The message is powerful: every minute matters; we are in school even when we are not in class. After a brief preamble—"Okay, gentlemen, when you come in, you need to set your desk with your homework at the top. Your *Do Now* today is going to require you to spell some of these words we've been studying. Clear?" Verilli posts himself in the door jamb. Like Toll, he offers a personal greeting as he shakes each student's hand. Verilli's version is a bit more muscular but still kindly. He refers to students by their last names: "Good afternoon, Mr. Mumford. Good afternoon, Mr. Reeves." A young Mr. Early slouches a bit and glances away. "Stand up straight and give me good grip," Verilli responds, and Mr. Early quite happily does just that. He seems to like the expectations for him, as if it signals to him his own importance. Two students later, young Mr. Smallwood approaches, wearing a new pair of glasses. "Looking sharp, Mr. Smallwood! I like it!" Verilli cheers, his upbeat demeanor all the more compelling for the tone of formality it breaks. Mr. Smallwood beams up at him, shaking his teacher's hand firmly. Things are not going quite so swimmingly for Mr. Merrick, who has been talking. "Step out [of the room]," Verilli commands, as he sends Mr. Merrick back to get his entrance to the classroom just right.

In these classrooms, the mood is warm but industrious. All of the students are hard at work just a few seconds after hitting the door—even Mr. Merrick, who is soon settled, redirected, and ready for class, compelling evidence of the power of *Threshold* to set expectations from the outset.

Occasionally teachers insist that it's impossible for them to greet their students at the door: their school forbids students to wait outside the class in the hallway, or the teacher moves to the students rather than vice versa. When a greeting at the door is impossible, invent another ritual to signify that something formal has begun: students rise, and you and they greet one another at the beginning of each class. The point is not so much the doorway as the power of ritual to help kids see that your classroom is different from the other places they go.

TECHNIQUE 42
NO WARNINGS

As a teacher, I almost always found that if I was angry with my students, I had waited too long to address issues or that I was not using consequences consistently. Using minor interventions and small consequences that you can administer fairly and without hesitation before a situation gets emotional is the key to maintaining control and earning students' respect. Relying on personal charm, emotion, or similar aspects of your relationships to get students to do what's expected of them also risks missing the point. It's not about you. Students are not supposed to behave to please you; they are supposed to behave so they can better themselves, be the best people they can be, and get the most out of school.

Your goal should be to take action rather than to get angry:

- *Act early.* Try to see the favor you are doing kids in catching off-task behavior early and using a minor intervention of consequence to prevent a major consequence later. This is a good thing.

- *Act reliably.* Be predictably consistent, sufficient to take the variable of how you will react out of the equation and focus students on the action that precipitated your response.

- *Act proportionately.* Start small when the misbehavior is small; don't go nuclear unless the situation is nuclear.

The behavior that most often gets in the way of taking action is the warning. Giving a warning is not taking action; it is threatening that you might take an action and therefore is counterproductive. Warnings tell students that a certain amount of disobedience will not only be tolerated but is expected. Teachers are in effect saying, "It's okay once. If you do it twice, I'm going to start to get annoyed. But the third time around, well then, you're at the limit." If you do this, you should expect students to take full advantage of their two free passes. If your expectations and rules are deliberately ignored and you don't take action (with an intervention that corrects it or a consequence), they are neither expectations nor rules.

I am not saying that you must use a consequence every time students fail to meet your expectations. As discussed in *What to Do,* it's critical that you not punish students when the issue is incompetence (rather than defiance). If the issue is incompetence, your response can be a consequence (a *Do It Again* or perhaps, "We don't have more time now, but let's practice what this looks like a little more after class") or a clear directive ("Put your legs under your desk, put your pencil down, and keep your eyes on me"). Either way, your response to incompetence should teach a student how to comply

It's also fine to offer a general reminder to all students about common expectations when they begin to slide. Stamina issues are not defiance issues. It's fine to offer a reminder to an individual student who may not recognize, as you do, that she is slipping off task. Students who are trying in good faith deserve the benefit of the doubt and can be corrected using management techniques (detailed, for example, in *100 Percent*).

However, once you have determined that a behavior is the result of disobedience rather than incompetence, that it is deliberate, a consequence is better than a warning. A warning countenances the fact a student disobeyed you and makes public that no consequence has resulted. It calls attention to the fact that you recognized the situation and did nothing. And if the behavior is not intentionally disobedient, a useful correction is also better than a warning since it fixes the situation. A warning merely discusses the outcome of further bad choices.

The key to delivering on consequences is developing a scaled system of incrementally larger consequences that you can deliver reliably, fairly, and without hesitation. This will allow you to be consistent, which is the only way to extinguish behavior. It will also keep you from accidentally weakening yourself. If you use your biggest consequence right away, there is nothing left to play for, and your students will know this. They will have nothing more to gain or lose, and their behavior will reflect this loss of incentives.

Spend time planning your responses in advance, even mapping out a sequence. For example you might first require students to repeat an action more appropriately. Next you might require them to apologize. Next you might take away a small piece of a privilege (part of recess) or give several minutes of detention. Next you might plan to take away an entire privilege for a period of time (no recess today; a full hour of detention) and also make a phone call to a parent. Or you might scale your responses using a consequence system like colored behavior cards (with elementary schools students), scholar dollars (with middle school students), or demerits (with high school students).

Issue consequences in these ways:

- Be calm, poised, and impersonal, not angry or vindictive (see *Emotional Constancy,* technique 47 in the next chapter). Focus on the now: "Show me your best from here on out." Move on quickly.

- Be incremental. When possible, take things away in pieces. Keep incentives in play if you can.

- Be private when you can and public when you must. If a behavior doesn't affect anyone else, deal with it privately. If a student has appeared to get away with something in front of the class, the class needs to know there was accountability. They don't need all the details, but they need to know action was taken.

In doing so, you will likely make the necessity of giving consequences more and more infrequent, which is, of course, the goal.

REFLECTION AND PRACTICE

1. For each of the common off-task behaviors listed below, write down and practice with a friend or in front a mirror a nonverbal intervention you could use while you were teaching to correct it:

   - Student slouched in his chair
   - Student with her head down on her desk, eyes up
   - Student with her head down on her desk, eyes hidden
   - Student gesturing distractingly to another student
   - Student persistently looking under his desk for an unidentified something.

2. For each of the off-task behaviors in question 1, script a positive group correction and an anonymous individual correction to address them.

3. Make a list of at least five positive student behaviors you could reinforce with nonverbal interventions. Plan a signal for each.

4. Revise the following statements using *What to Do* to make them specific, concrete, observable, and sequential:

   - "Class, you should be writing this down!"
   - "Tyson, stop fooling around."
   - "Don't get distracted, Avery."
   - "Are you paying attention, Dontae?"
   - "I'd like to get started, please, class."

5. The next time you host a social event, practice *Threshold* by greeting each guest at the door with a short, personalized greeting.

CHAPTER SEVEN

BUILDING CHARACTER AND TRUST

The meaning of a message changes subtly, drastically, and often completely depending on the setting and tone of its delivery. In a school, the challenge of effective communication is exacerbated by the sheer number of settings in which you are required to communicate, not to mention the range of topics you must cover.

Your conversation with Steven at the close of school on Wednesday, one of hundreds you hold this week, may be conducted, depending on the details, in private, in quasi-private (overheard by others), or in public. If there is an audience, they may be few or many; foes, allies, authorities, or admired peers (of yours *and* of Stevens). Your purpose may be to correct, praise, inquire, or instruct. You may be referencing previous conversations, explicit or implicitly. You may be preparing for future conversations. You may be seeking to change his perception of himself, of you, of school work, of education, of his peers, of certain values, of who he can be. You may be attempting to do this with humor, warmth, sternness, subtlety, or bluntness. Steven (and you) may be angry, elated, upset, impassive, defensive, motivated, or grateful. You may be late for class. You may urgently need to use the bathroom. Steven may not realize this, and vice versa. In this conversation, you may affect Steven's actions today, tomorrow, or next year. You may change his perceptions of you or school. You will assuredly (and without realizing it) change your perceptions of your work: Are you successful? Are you changing lives? Are you respected? Is it worth it? Should you just get your real estate license? In short, the conversation with Steven, like all others, is a high-wire act. You will need some rules, not just for the words but for the tone you strike in talking to Steven.

TECHNIQUE 43
POSITIVE FRAMING

People are motivated by the positive far more than the negative. Seeking success and happiness will spur stronger action than seeking to avoid punishment. Psychological studies repeatedly show that people are far more likely to be spurred to action by a vision of a positive outcome than they are to avoid a negative one. This fact should influence the way you teach. It doesn't mean that you shouldn't be meticulous about responding to off-task or nonconstructive behavior. You still need to fix and improve behavior, and you need to do so consistently and with clear and firm consequences when necessary. But as you do these things **Positive Framing** argues that your interventions will be far more effective if they frame positively.

Using *Positive Framing* means making interventions to correct student behavior in a positive and constructive way. It does not mean avoiding interventions so you can talk instead only about the positive behavior you see. Doing the former is teaching kids ("disciplining" them in the sense of teaching them the right way to do things) in an optimistic, upbeat, confident manner. Doing the latter is abdicating your responsibility. If David is off task, it will not be sufficient merely to praise Kelsey for being on task. Rather, you should correct David in a positive manner.

Nonetheless, some teachers might potentially interpret this technique as an admonition to avoid correcting nonproductive behavior and focus exclusively on reinforcing positive behavior. Reinforcing positive behavior matters, and it is discussed in the next technique, *Precise Praise,* but by itself reinforcing positive behavior is insufficient. The greatest power of *Positive Framing* is its capacity to allow you to talk about nonconstructive behavior consistently and correct it positively so that you guide students to improved knowledge and action. Doing that successfully takes some hard work but is in the end highly positive.

KEY IDEA

POSITIVE FRAMING

Make corrections consistently and positively. Narrate the world you want your students to see even while you are relentlessly improving it.

Positive Framing corrects and guides behavior by following six rules:

1. **Live in the now.** In public—that is, in front of your class or while your lesson is under way—avoid harping on what students can no longer fix. Talk about what should or even must happen next. If necessary, you can do this firmly and forcefully (see *What to Do*, technique 37), but you should focus corrective interactions on the things students should do right now to succeed from this point forward. There's a time and place for processing what went wrong; avoid making that time when your lesson hangs in the balance. Give instructions describing what the next move on the path to success is. Say, "Show me SLANT!" not, "You weren't SLANTing." Say, "Keana, I need your eyes forward," not, "Keana, stop looking back at Tanya."

2. **Assume the best.** Don't attribute to ill intention what could be the result of distraction, lack of practice, or genuine misunderstanding. Until you know an action was intentional, your public discussion of it should remain positive, showing that you assume your students

> *Don't attribute to ill intention what could be the result of distraction, lack of practice, or genuine misunderstanding.*

have tried (and will try) to do as you've asked. Saying, "Just a minute, class. Some people don't seem to think they have to push in their chairs when we line up," or "Just a minute, class. I asked for chairs pushed in, and some people decided not to do it," assumes that the problem had to be connected to ill intentions and negative characteristics: selfishness; deliberate disrespect, laziness. Not only is it more positive to say, "Just a minute, class. Some people seem to have forgotten to push in their chairs," or "Whoops. The chair part seems to have slipped our minds, so let's go back and get it right," to show your faith and trust in your students, but it costs you nothing since you can still deliver a consequence and in fact can deliver exactly the same consequence. You can still assume the best even while you are delivering a consequence. In fact, by no longer making intentionality a prerequisite for consequence, you uncouple consequences from much of the emotion they carry. It is no longer a judgment ("You did this on purpose, and here is my revenge") and more a tool for improvement ("We do things a certain way, and we fix it when we fail to do that, no matter why we failed").

Furthermore, assuming the worst makes you appear weak. If you show that you assume your students are always trying to comply with your wishes, you are also demonstrating the assumption that you're in charge. "If you can't sit up, Charles, I'll have to keep you in from recess," reveals your suspicion that Charles will disobey you. On the first try, say, "Show me your best SLANT, Charles," and walk away (for the moment) as if you couldn't imagine a world in which he wouldn't do it. Or say something like, "Charles, I need your eyes," which asserts nothing about Charles's intention, only what he needs to do.

One particularly effective way to assume the best is to thank students as you give them a command. This again underscores your assumption that they will follow through. "Thank you for taking your seats in 3-2-1 . . ."

3. **Allow plausible anonymity.** Allow students the opportunity to strive to reach your expectations in plausible anonymity as long as they are making a good-faith effort. Begin by correcting them without using their names when possible. If a few students struggle to follow your directions, consider making your first correction something like: "Check yourself to make sure you've done exactly what I've asked." In most cases, this will yield results faster than calling out laggards unless the laggards are deliberately flouting you. Saying to your class, "Wait a minute, Morehouse (or "Tigers" or "fifth grade" or just "guys"), I hear calling out. I need to see you quiet and ready to go!" is better than lecturing the callers-out in front of the class. And as with assuming the best, you can still administer many consequences while preserving anonymity: "Some people didn't manage to follow directions the whole way, so let's try that again." When there is no good-faith effort by students, it may no longer be possible to maintain anonymity, but naming names shouldn't be your first move. Also, it's important to remember both that you can deliver consequences anonymously and that doing so stresses shared responsibility among your students. Some students weren't doing their job and we all own the consequence.

4. **Build momentum, and narrate the positive.** In the world of sports, momentum, the force that drives some teams forward to great achievements on a tide of energy, is sometimes known as "Big Mo." Everybody wants Big Mo, but only some people know how to get it to show up. Compare the statements two teachers recently made in their respective classrooms:

> Teacher 1: (Stopping before giving a direction) I need three people. Make sure you fix it if that's you! Now I need two. We're almost there. Ah, thank you. Let's get started.

> Teacher 2: (Same setting) I need three people. And one more student doesn't seem to understand the directions, so now I need four. Some people don't appear to be listening. I am waiting, gentlemen. If I have to give detentions, I will.

In the first teacher's classroom, things appear to be moving in the right direction because the teacher narrates the evidence of his own command, of students doing as they're asked, of things getting better. He calls his students' attention to this fact, thereby normalizing it. Students are arguably more accountable for their behavior in the first room, but nobody seems to notice because failure seems so unlikely.

The second teacher is telling a story that no one wants to hear: from the outset, students can smell the fear, the weakness, and the inevitable unhappy ending. Everything is wrong and getting worse, generally without consequence. Students can hardly fear accountability when their teacher is describing their peers' impunity ("Some people don't appear to be listening"). You won't find Big Mo in that room!

Consider the same two teachers yet again:

> Teacher 1: (After giving a direction that students should begin writing in their journals) Okay, here we go! I see the pencils moving. I see those ideas rolling out. Roberto's ready to roll. Keep it up, Marcus!

> Teacher 2: (Same setting) Not everyone has begun yet. Do you need me to help you think of a topic, Roberto? Marcus, I asked you not to stop. Let me remind you, class, that this is not an optional activity.

A student in the first class seeking to do what's normal will most likely take part in the lesson. In the second class, her attention will be drawn to the litany of woes her teacher anxiously describes and to her off-task peers who seem to be gaining converts. She will likely choose that path as well.

Narrating your weakness only makes your weakness seem normal. If you say, "Some students didn't do what I asked," you have made that situation public. Now your choice is consequence or countenance.

Perception, it turns out, is reality. Great teachers conjure Big Mo by normalizing the positive. They draw attention to the good and the getting better. Narrating your weakness makes your weakness seem normal. If you say, "Some students didn't do what I asked," you have made that situation public. Now your choice is consequence or countenance. "Check yourself to make sure you've done what I asked," keeps Big Mo on your side. If you need to follow up to address a student or give a consequence, fine. Do it as privately as you can, not just to protect the scofflaw's feelings but to keep Big Mo on the move. Similarly, "I've got almost everybody now," is better than, "I don't have everybody," or, "I'm still waiting on some of you." You might as well say, "I'm very weak and implore you not to hurt me."

Big Mo loves speed. Try to use commands that multitask. Replace, "Who can tell us what 3 times 5 is? David? Everyone please track David," with the much simpler and faster, "Who can tell us what 3 times 5 is? Track . . . David."

5. **Challenge!** Kids love to be challenged, to prove they can do things, to compete, to win. So challenge them: exhort them to prove what they can do by building competition into the day. Students can be challenged as individuals or, usually better, as groups, and those groups can compete in various ways:

- Against other groups within the class
- Against other groups outside the class (the other homeroom)
- Against an impersonal foe (the clock; the test, to prove they're better than it; their age—"that was acceptable work for seventh graders but I want to see if we can kick it up to eighth-grade quality")
- Against an abstract standard ("I want to see whether you guys have what it takes!")

Here are some examples:

- "You guys have been doing a great job this week. Let's see if you can take it up a notch."

- "I love the tracking I see. I wonder what happens when I move back here."

- "Let's see if we can get these papers out in twelve seconds. Ready?!"

- "Good is not good enough. I want to see perfect today!"

- "Ms. Austin said she didn't think you guys could knock out your math tables louder than her class. And they're sitting across the hall right now. Let's show 'em what we've got."

- "Let's see which row has this information down! We'll use a little friendly wager: the row where everyone gets it correct the fastest can skip the first two problems on the homework set!"

6. **Talk expectations and aspirations.** Talk about who your students are becoming and where you're going. Frame praise in those terms. When your class looks great, tell them they look like "college scholars," and you feel as if you're sitting in the room with future presidents, doctors, and artists. While it's nice that you're proud of them and it's certainly wonderful to tell them that, the goal in the end is not for them to please you but for them to leave you behind on a long journey toward a more distant and more important goal than making you happy. It's useful if your praise sets a goal larger than your own opinion. On a more microlevel, seek opportunities that reaffirm expectations around smaller details. When you're correcting, say, "In this class, we always track," not, "Some people aren't giving us their best SLANT." Finish an activity by saying, "If you finish early, check your work. Make sure you get 100 percent today." Keep their eyes on the prize by constantly referring to it.

Keep positive by avoiding two things:

- *Rhetorical questions.* Don't ask questions that you don't want an answer to. Don't pretend to ask a question when you aren't. Don't make a charade by asking, "Would you like to join us, David?" Just say, "Thank you for joining us on the rug, David."

- *Contingencies.* Don't say, "I'll wait," unless you will. The point is that you won't. And in saying so, you give your students the power by making your actions contingent on theirs. "We [or I] need you with us" is much more productive, positive, and strong.

SEE IT IN ACTION: CLIP 19

POSITIVE FRAMING

In clip 19 on the DVD, Janelle Austin of Rochester Prep demonstrates *Positive Framing*. Notice how effectively she kicks off class by narrating the positive ("Ooooo, look at all those hands") and then narrating it a second time but mixing in a challenge ("I love the track I'm seeing right now. I wonder what happens if I move around the room").

A few moments later, Austin again narrates the positive—"I see hands up that are ready to read!"—this time mixing in a some expectations and aspirations by describing the motivation behind the hands (they want to read) to make it explicit to all students. Notice the response from her students in terms of additional hands that go up.

Later Austin again narrates the positive ("I really like the enthusiasm that I'm seeing. This column right here is really grabbing hold to it") this time combining elements of the previous two examples, making the mental state behind a raised hand explicit ("enthusiasm") and throwing down an implicit challenge to the rest of the class by identifying a group that's particularly strong ("This column right here").

This clips shows perhaps a dozen examples of *Positive Framing*; see how many you can find. This clip is a montage of short moments from Janelle's class over about a half-hour, edited so they appear in rapid proximity. The clip therefore concentrates the amount of *Positive Framing* Austin does. This is important because too much of a good thing can cheapen it. As she shows, it's often best to sprinkle it in regularly but in small amounts throughout a lesson, to use a cooking analogy, rather than dumping in a quart of it all at once. Think: "Salt to taste."

Tracking refers to students following the speaker with their eyes. See technique 32, SLANT, in Chapter Five.

TECHNIQUE 44

PRECISE PRAISE

Positive reinforcement is one of the most powerful tools in every classroom. Most experts say it should happen three times as often as criticism and correction. However, any powerful tool can be used poorly or for naught. Poorly implemented positive reinforcement is no exception. In using positive reinforcement, follow these rules of thumb for **Positive Praise**:

- **Differentiate acknowledgment and praise.** Champion teachers make a careful and intentional distinction between praise and acknowledgment, acknowledging when expectations have been met and praising when the exceptional has been achieved. Kids who meet expectations deserve to have it noticed and acknowledged as frequently as possible. In a case where expectations have been met and acknowledgment is fitting, a simple description of what the student did or even a thank-you usually suffices: "You were ready for class right on time, John." "You did it just the way I asked, Shayna. Thank you." Kids who do something truly exceptional also deserve to be told that what they did was above and beyond—that is, to be praised. Praising usually carries a judgment in addition to a mere description: "Fantastic work, John!" "Shayna's really done something amazing!" However, mixing these two responses by praising students for doing what is expected is, in the long run, not just ineffective but destructive. Consider this statement: "Great job bringing a pencil to class today, John!" Why, in the eyes of the rest of the class, is John being praised for doing what they've been doing all along? Are the rules different for John because he hasn't been bringing his pencil? Has John really been "great," as the teacher said?

There are two possible answers to this last question, and neither is especially good. The first is, no: the teacher does not sincerely think it's a great thing that John brought his pencil to class. She's just trying to be enthusiastic, positive, and encouraging. But the more enthusiasm she packs into her voice in praising John, the more she shows that her words are disingenuous. Her praise, she shows, is empty and cheap. Who wants to be great if that's all it takes? In fact, the culturewide misuse of praise has a documented perverse effect. Recent research demonstrates that students have come to interpret frequent praise as a sign that they are doing poorly and need encouragement from their teacher. They see cheap praise as a marker of failure, not success. And often they are right to do so. Since genuine praise is critically important, teachers should carefully avoid setting themselves up for such an inversion of meaning and save praise for what exceeds expectation.

The second possible answer is yes: some part of the teacher genuinely thinks it's "great" that John brought his pencil. She is pleasantly surprised. This potential reading of her words also creates a perverse effect: if the teacher is surprised that John did what she asked, her expectations are not real. She doesn't truly "expect" them to happen. She is surprised when students do what she's asked, or she knows that her difficult students won't really be able to do what she expects of the rest of the class. A translation of what she is thinking is, "In my heart, I expect you not to do what I ask much or most of the time. In my heart, I don't really think I can get all kids to do what they need to do."

In the long run, a teacher who continually praises what's expected risks trivializing both the praise and the things she really wishes to label ''great.''

In the long run, a teacher who continually praises what's expected risks trivializing both the praise and the things she really wishes to label "great." Eroding her ability to give meaningful verbal rewards and to identify behavior that is truly worthy of notice is a dangerous practice for a teacher.

In an acknowledgment, the teacher describes what a student has done, often in an approving tone and often with explicit thanks. In praise, he or she puts an exemplary value judgment on it. This does not mean that acknowledgment has to be bland or dull. In the case of John and his pencil, champion teachers of various stripes might use a mix of enthusiastic acknowledgments for example, "Johnny B.! Got his tools and coming to work today!"

- **Praise (and acknowledge) loud; fix soft.** Whispered or even nonverbal criticism or reminders assume the best about students: they allow them to self-correct without being called out in public. This is also to the teacher's benefit, even when behavior is clearly defiant, as it keeps the student offstage as much as possible and makes the teacher appear to be in control. Good news, however, is good news: make it as public as possible. A student who exceeds expectations demonstrates the art of the possible. That's something that all students should attend to, and as the section on narrating the positive in *Positive Framing* demonstrates, consistently making students who meet expectations visible normalizes it and makes it more likely to happen.

Research into praise has shown a big difference between praising a student for being smart and praising a student for working hard. The latter is a behavior easily and readily within the student's control. This student knows that he has intentionally done something worthy and can do it again. Such praise fosters effort and positive risk taking. Praising a trait has the opposite effect: students called smart were not only being praised for something they couldn't reliably replicate, but they took fewer risks as a result, since they were afraid of appearing less smart. So praise as specifically as possible and focus on exactly the behavior and action that you would like to see more of.

- **Praise must be genuine.** Early on in school, students listen for and discount insincere praise. In fact, Stanford social psychologist Carol Dweck has shown in her book *Mindset: The New Psychology of Success* that students often read praise as an indication that their work is inferior, which suggests an epidemic of insincere praise that should be rectified. The most common forms of insincere praise are those designed to artificially bolster self-esteem and those designed in interaction with a student to fix a systematic problem in the teacher's span of control. Her conversation with a child is about that child's behavior, not the behavior of the child next to him. Telling a child, "Nice job getting ready, Bill," is fine thing. But if a teacher resorts to praising Bill in order to tell Sally, next to him, to put a move on (that is, to correct her instead of to subtly encourage her by showing that Bill has earned genuine acknowledgment), she undercuts the integrity and veracity of her praise. Setting Bill up to do your work with Sally risks jeopardizing the effective relationship you have. And it does not solve your situation with Sally.

TECHNIQUE 45

WARM/STRICT

We're socialized to believe that warmth and strictness are opposites: if you're more of one, it means being less of the other. I don't know where this false conception comes from, but if you choose to believe in it, it will undercut your teaching. The fact is that the degree to which you are warm has no bearing on the degree to which you are strict, and vice versa. Just as you can be neither warm nor strict (you may teach the children of parents who are this way and see for yourself the cost), you can also be warm and strict. In fact, as this **Warm/Strict** technique shows, you must be both: caring, funny, warm, concerned, and nurturing—and also strict, by the book, relentless, and sometimes inflexible. It's not, "I care about you, but you still must serve the consequence for being late," but, "Because I care about you, you must serve the consequence for being late."

In fact, the *Warm/Strict* paradox—the fact that what we think of as opposites are in fact unrelated—runs deeper. Not only should you seek to be both; you should often seek to be both at exactly the same time. When you are clear, consistent, firm, and unrelenting and at the same time positive, enthusiastic, caring, and thoughtful, you start to send the message to students that having high expectations is part of caring for and respecting someone. This is a very powerful message.

You can make your *Warm/Strict* especially effective in these ways:

- *Explain to students why you're doing what you are* (see *Explain Everything,* technique 48 later in this chapter) and how it is designed to help them: "Priya, we don't do that in this classroom because it keeps us from making the most of our learning time. I'm going to have to try to help you remember that."

- *Distinguish between behavior and people.* Say, "Your behavior is inconsiderate," rather than, "You're inconsiderate."

- *Demonstrate that consequences are temporary.* Show a student that when he has dealt with the consequences of a mistake, it is immediately in the past. Smile and greet him naturally to show that he is starting over with a clean slate. Tell a student, regarding her consequence, "After you're done, I can't wait to have you come back and show us your best." Once you've given a consequence, your next job is to forgive. Remember that you use a consequence so you won't have to hold the grudge. Get over it quickly.

- *Use warm, nonverbal behavior.* Put your arm on a student's shoulder and kindly tell him you're sorry but he'll have to redo the homework. You just know he's capable of better. Bend down to a third grader's eye level, and explain to her firmly that she won't be allowed to talk to her classmates that way.

In balanced combination and proportions, warm (being positive, enthusiastic, caring, and thoughtful) and strict (being clear, consistent, firm, and unrelenting) together can even help students internalize apparent contradictions and overcome what Jim Collins rightly called, in his seminal book *Built to Last,* "the tyranny of the 'or.'" It reminds students that many of the either-or choices in their lives are false constructs: "I can be hip and successful; I can have fun and work hard; I can be happy and say no to self-indulgence."

TECHNIQUE 46

THE J-FACTOR

The finest teachers offer up their work with generous servings of energy, passion, enthusiasm, fun, and humor—not necessarily as the antidote to hard work but because those are some of the primary ways that hard work gets done. It turns out that finding joy in the work of learning—the **J-Factor**—is a key driver not just of a happy classroom but of a high-achieving classroom. It's useful, if not exactly a revelation, that people work harder when they enjoy working on something—not perhaps in every minute of every day, but when their work is punctuated regularly by moments of exultation and joy. The joy can take a surprisingly wide array of forms given the diversity of teachers who employ it and the diversity of

The finest teachers offer up the work with generous servings of energy, passion, enthusiasm, fun, and humor—not necessarily as the antidote to hard work but because those are some of the primary ways that hard work gets done.

moments in which they use it. *J-Factor* moments can, but need not, involve singing or dancing. Joy exists for students in all the forms it exists for adults: loud or quiet; individual, small group, or large group oriented. The common theme is for teachers to find a way to let their own genuine version of joy shine through. For some, quiet passion is the most common form; for some its humor; for others high-energy antics.

Here are five categories of *J-Factor* activities that champion teachers use in their classrooms:

- **Fun and games.** These activities draw on kids' love for challenges, competition, and play. Examples include having students compete to see who can "roll their numbers" (do repeated addition) the fastest or who can put the midwestern states in alphabetical order by last letter the fastest. Bees (spelling, geography, math), content-based around-the-worlds, relay races, and jeopardies also count here. At one school, students play their teachers in math baseball: to hit a single, you have to solve the problem faster than the teacher who's covering first base.
- **Us (and them).** Kids, like everybody else, take pleasure in belonging to things. One of the key functions of cultures—those in the classroom and more broadly—is to make members feel they belong to an important "us," a vibrant and recognizable entity that only some people get to be part of. Through unique language, names, rituals, traditions, songs, and the like, cultures establish "us"-ness. In many cases, the more inscrutable these rituals are to outsiders, the better. The inscrutability reinforces the presence of the "them" that's necessary to any "us." Champion teachers who use these activities develop markers to

remind students that they are insiders in a vibrant culture. At Rochester Prep, for example, history teacher David McBride came up with nicknames for all of his students and used them to call on students in class or to greet them in the hallways. Being greeted with, "Mornin', T-bone!" feels more special than being greeted with, "Good morning, Taylor." After all, the people who make up nicknames for you are the people who care about you most.

If you've ever watched Chris Berman dish out his hilarious nicknames for athletes on ESPN's *Sportscenter* (Greg "Crocodile" Brock; Vincent "Ultimate" Brisby; Barry "Bananas" Foster), you get the gist of what McBride did, and you also know how fun and funny such a game can be. When you watch Berman, you listen for the nicknames because you're in on the gag. "Is that guy's nickname really 'Personal?!' " If you have to ask, you're not "us."

Developing secret signals and special words is related to this. Teachers hum a secret song—for example, "We're All in This Together"—without the words. The subtext is: *This is our song; we all know the words and why we're singing it; no one on the outside needs to (or can) understand this. We are an "us."* Some classrooms even have development myths: shared stories provided by the teacher to prove a point or teach a lesson, for example, a story about "my cousin Martha, who gives up when the going gets tough" gets referenced before each test: "Don't go pulling a Martha here."

- **Drama, song, and dance.** Music, dramatic play, and movement raise spirits and also establish collective identity. This is why they exist within every identifiable ethnic or national culture on earth. The spirit lifting is all the more potent among the youthful, especially those who are chair bound. Acting things out and singing about them can be an exceptional way to remember information.

Drama, song, and dance also power-up memory. My seventh-grade Spanish teacher taught us a hokey Spanish version of "Jingle Bells." Much though I would like to forget it or keep it from occasionally rattling through my sub-conscious, I cannot. I occasionally cannot remember my own phone number, but I will always have her Spanish version of "Jingle Bells." To learn a song about something—especially one that's a tad absurd or unusual or one you sing regularly—is, for many, to know it for life. The upside of the burden my seventh-grade Spanish teacher left me is that the power of song or dance can be harnessed to instill and reinforce any specific knowledge or belief. Imagine if I had a song rattling through my head telling me when to use *ser* and *estar*, the two forms of the Spanish verb "to be," instead of "*Jingle Bells.*" My Spanish would be forever improved (not to mention various awkward moments in my life avoided). To sing is to remember.

- **Humor.** Laughter is one of the base conditions of happiness and fulfillment, which makes it a powerful tool to building an environment of happy and fulfilled students and teachers. A tool this powerful should be used, though I can't give you much of a recipe, only an example or two.

One champion teacher taught his kids a song for dozens of formulas in sixth-grade math. After they had made a habit of learning these, he told them he was working on a song to help them determine the circumference of a circle, but that what he had so far was too uncool to use. He sang a quick snippet of what he was working on: "$2\pi r$, my Lord" to the tune of "Kumbaya." His kids laughed, and he admonished them: "Don't tell anyone about that. There is no song for circumference. Is there a song for circumference? No, we've got no song for that!" Whenever studying circumference, he would ask the class: "Remind me, do we have a song for circumference?" After the class resoundingly answered, "No!" he would hum "Kumbaya" to himself, making a reliably funny inside joke that made it all but impossible not to remember the formula for circumference.

- **Suspense and surprise.** Routines are powerful drivers of efficiency and predictability. They also make occasional variations all the more fun, silly, surprising, and inspiring. If harnessed judiciously, the unexpected can be powerful. The two together make the classroom an adventure, no matter what the content.

An art teacher I know takes the samples she ordinarily shows her class—a landscape, a still life, a traditional carving—and puts them in a wrapped box like a present. She begins her lesson by saying, "I've got something in the mystery box that's really cool and exciting. I can't wait to show you because it's an example of what we're talking about today." Several times during a typical mini-lesson, she'll build the anticipation by walking over to the box and then "deciding" to wait, or by peeking in and hamming up her reaction: "Ouch, it *bit* me!" By the time she shows the kids what's in the box, they can hardly wait to see it. A math teacher does something similar with his number rolling songs: "Oh, man, you're gonna love the last verse. It's really funny. And if we keep working, we'll get to hear it soon."

A third-grade teacher occasionally hands out her vocabulary words in sealed envelopes, one to each child. "Don't open them yet," she'll whisper, "not until I say." And by the time she does, there's little in the world each of those would trade for the opportunity to see what their word is.

SEE IT IN ACTION: CLIP 20

JOY FACTOR

In clip 20 on the DVD, George Davis of Leadership Prep Bedford Stuyvesant demonstrates *Joy Factor.* This clip provides a great example of making the work fun, as opposed to making fun the antidote to the work. His kids are getting lots of at bats while they play their game. Look for elements of all five kinds of joy in this clip.

J-Factor is similar to *Vegas* (technique 27), so people often ask what the difference is. Actually there are two differences. The first is that *Vegas* is an instructional tool, explicitly reinforcing the lesson objective and drawing the children into the content. Second, although most, if not all, of *Vegas* is also *J-Factor*, the latter is a larger category and includes classroom elements devised specifically to build and include kids in the room's culture. For example, giving students nicknames doesn't reinforce academics, so it's not *Vegas*, but it does make them feel a happy sense of belonging. In that sense it's a *J-Factor* technique. Singing the nonsong for determining the circumference of a circle is both.

SEE IT IN ACTION: CLIP 21

JOY FACTOR AND TIGHT TRANSITIONS

In clip 21 on the DVD, Sultana Noormuhammad of Leadership Prep Bedford Stuyvesant demonstrates *Joy Factor.* It's not just the happiness brought about as kids sing their transition to the carpet that's so remarkable, but the fact that the song, the Homeroom Indiana "Fight Song," reinforces productive student behaviors. Moreover, Noormuhammad is able to turn it on and turn it off. As soon as the children are settled on the carpet, the room is pin-drop quiet, and Homeroom Indiana is ready to get to work.

As I hope is obvious, this clip is also a great example of *Tight Transitions* (technique 30).

TECHNIQUE 47

EMOTIONAL CONSTANCY

Here are two things to do with your emotions. First, modulate them. School is a laboratory for students; they need to be able to figure out how to behave without seeing you explode. You should expect almost anything, so act as if you expect it and have a plan to deal with it. Second, tie your emotions to student achievement, not to your own moods or the emotions of the students you teach. Again, expect their emotions to rise and fall, and be sure to control your own to compensate. Expect students to occasionally get upset, and respond calmly. Part of adolescence is experimenting with exaggerated emotions. Don't add gas to the fire by letting your own become inflamed, and hold no grudges, but view the aftermath of a consequence to be a fresh start. After all, the point of a consequence is to create a sufficient disincentive: if the disincentive is sufficient, it has done its job and the cycle is over; if the consequence was inefficient, address the use of consequences rather than get angry.

Teachers with **Emotional Constancy** tread cautiously around much of the language that other teachers use as a habit, thinking carefully about what they imply the goal of student decisions to be. For example, many teachers say things like, "I'm really disappointed in you,"

Success is in the long run about a student's consistent relationship with productive behaviors.

when their class has behaved poorly. However, it's worth asking whether the point of the rule or expectation has been to please the teacher. There may be times when the teacher's personal sense of connection and approval is something students should be concerned about, but they are far rarer than teachers' language would indicate. Merely substituting, "I expect better of you," or, "The expectation in this class is that you give your best," takes that teacher's personal emotions out of the equation and focuses the conversation on what kids did or didn't do rather than what the teacher felt. The latter factor is, in the end, almost irrelevant.

An emotionally constant teacher earns students' trust in part by having them know he is always under control. Most of all, he knows success is in the long run about a student's consistent relationship with productive behaviors. The affect he requires is productive, respectful, and orderly, and his goal when emotions run hot is to deescalate. In so doing, he not only circumscribes the sorts of conflicts that can consume a classroom but provides an emotional rudder to help his students return to productivity as soon as possible.

TECHNIQUE 48
EXPLAIN EVERYTHING

Students in a high-performing classroom understand the dynamics of personal and group accountability. They know the logic behind the rules and expectations designed for their betterment; they understand that group success depends on everyone's participation. They get these aspects of the big picture because their teachers deliberately make their expectations clear, rational, and logical. They constantly remind students why they do what they do and ground their explanations in the mission: this will help you get to college; this will help you understand how to be responsible. If there's a pace that needs to be maintained in order to achieve the day's objective, the **Explain Everything** teacher tells her students, "I'd love to spend more time talking about this, but there's a lot we've got to do." She couches conversations about misbehavior in language that explains to students why it matters and how one action or behavior affects another. In this way, students understand the logic behind decision making and will be more likely to both believe that the systems are in their best interests and make rational choices on their own.

Consider how this looks on a typical day in Darryl Williams's classroom. A third grader asks whether he can go to the nurse. Before answering, Williams asks the student to consider the logic of the situation, saying, "Do you understand that if you go to the nurse, you're not going to participate when we have recess?" The student acknowledges that his decision will affect the rest of his day. If he is too sick to learn, then he is obviously too sick to play. Williams grants him permission to go to the nurse. Later, when hands are eagerly in the air, perhaps a little too eagerly, Williams says, "Please put your hands down. I know that you all have questions, and I love it when you say intelligent things, but we have a lot to do, and right now there's not time. We still need to read our story and do workshop." In a classroom like this, the rationale behind decisions made in students' interest and the way that adults think on behalf of children is suddenly made clear.

There's at least one particular subtlety to the narrating of the why's of the classroom that bears deeper analysis here. My colleagues and I discovered this while watching a video of a lesson in which the teacher appeared to be explaining everything but not particularly successfully. The issue, we discovered, was that she was explaining why she was doing things as she was striving, with mixed success, to get control of the room: "Remember that when I call on one student to answer, we're all looking and listening. [Sternly] Charles, we're all looking and listening because we're learning from our friends, even if it's not our turn." Her last phrase reminded students that the class was not successfully meeting expectations and that the teacher was not explaining why they did what they did but trying to get them to do it in the first place. Her explanations sounded too much like pleading. Effective *Explain Everything,* it struck us, happens either in a calm moment well in advance of behavior that needs fixing ("When I ask for your attention, I'm going to expect it from every one of you every time. That way I can be sure you know everything you need to know to be successful and happy in my class!") or else after "fixing" has resulted in the meeting of expectations: "Thank you. The reason I need you to be all the way silent like that is . . ."

TECHNIQUE 49

NORMALIZE ERROR

Error followed by correction and instruction is the fundamental process of schooling. You get it wrong, and then you get it right. If getting it wrong and then getting it right is normal, teachers should **Normalize Error** and respond to both parts of this sequence as if they were totally and completely normal. After all, they are.

WRONG ANSWERS: DON'T CHASTEN; DON'T EXCUSE

Avoid chastening wrong answers, for example, "No, we already talked about this. You have to flip the sign, Ruben." And do not make excuses for students who get answers wrong: "Oh, that's okay, Charlise. That was a really hard one." In fact, if wrong answers are truly a normal and healthy part of the learning process, they don't need much narration at all.

It's better, in fact, to avoid spending a lot of time talking about wrongness and get down to the work of fixing it as quickly as possible. Although many teachers feel obligated to name every answer as right or wrong, spending time making that judgment is usually a step you can skip entirely before getting to work. For example, you could respond to a wrong answer by a student named Noah by saying, "Let's try that again, Noah. What's the first thing we have to do?" or even, "What's the first thing we have to do in solving this kind of problem, Noah?" This second situation is particularly interesting because it remains ambiguous to Noah and his classmates whether the answer was right or wrong as they start reworking the problem. There's a bit of suspense, and they will have to figure it out for themselves. When and if you do name an answer as wrong, do so quickly and simply ("not quite") and keep moving. Again, since getting it wrong is normal, you don't have to feel badly about it. In fact, if all students are getting all questions right, the work you're giving them isn't hard enough.

RIGHT ANSWERS: DON'T FLATTER; DON'T FUSS

Praising right answers can have one of two perverse effects on students. If you make too much of fuss, you suggest to students—unless it's patently obvious that an answer really is exceptional—that you're surprised that they got the answer right. And as a variety of social science research has recently documented, praising students for being "smart" perversely incents them not to take risks (apparently they worry about no longer looking smart if they get things wrong), in contrast to praising students for working hard, which incents them to take risks and take on challenges.

Thus, in most cases when a student gets an answer correct, acknowledge that the student has done the work correctly or has worked hard; then move on: "That's right, Noah. Nice work." Champion teachers show their students they expect both right and wrong to happen by not making too big a deal of either. Of course, there will be times when you want to sprinkle in stronger praise ("Such an insightful answer, Carla. Awesome"). Just do so carefully so that such praise isn't diluted by overuse.

REFLECTION AND PRACTICE

1. The following statements are negatively framed. Try rewriting them to make them positively framed.

   • "We're not going to have another day like yesterday, are we, Jason?

   • "Just a minute, Jane. Absolutely no one is giving you their full attention except Dyonte and Beth."

   • "I need the tapping to stop."

   • "I've asked you twice to stop slouching, Jasmine!"

2. Consider what specific behavioral traits (hard work, respect for peers, for example) you most want students to demonstrate in your classroom. For each, write three or four scripts you might use to reinforce them using *Precise Praise*.

3. Make a list of the situations in which you are most vulnerable to losing your emotional constancy. Script a calm and poised comment you might make to the other people involved that also reminds you to remain constant.

4. Brainstorm ten ways you could bring more *J-Factor* into your classroom. Use at least four of the types of joy described in the chapter.

CHAPTER EIGHT

IMPROVING YOUR PACING

Additional Techniques for Creating a Positive Rhythm in the Classroom

Pacing is a term most teachers are familiar with, but it lacks a clear and consistent definition. The obvious definition, that pacing is the speed at which you teach, doesn't hold up to scrutiny. Most teachers recognize a discrepancy between the actual rate at which teaching happens and the rate at which students perceive it to be happening. You can appear to race through a lesson in adding fractions with like denominators, for example, when ironically you are stretching the time you spend on the skill to ensure mastery. You double the time you actually spend on an objective but take certain steps to make it feel as if you were moving twice as quickly. Or you could spend insufficient time on an objective and thus go too fast in the academic sense, and at the same time your lesson could seem deathly slow and tedious to students. So pacing is clearly different from the rate at which you move through material.

An alternative way of defining *pacing* is "the illusion of speed." It isn't the rate at which material is presented, but rather the rate at which the lesson makes that material appear to unfold. Pacing is the skill of creating the perception that you are moving quickly. Or maybe better, since effective teaching can use a range of tempos from slow, steady reflection to bracing, energetic speed, pacing is the illusion of speed created as and when necessary. Students like to think they're doing something new more frequently than you can afford to change the topic of their learning, and pacing taps into that desire. When you're maximizing pacing, your teaching engages and interests students, giving them a sense of progress and change. Things are happening: students feel the progress and never know what's next.

Regardless of how fast you're actually flying, passengers' perception of how fast they're moving is influenced by the reference points they see (or don't see) passing.

A vignette from life outside the classroom might help to clarify the point. When my son was five, we flew to visit my parents. As the jet touched down, he asked me whether the plane flew faster when it was landing. He thought we had sped up at exactly the time we had slowed down. I asked him why he thought so. "When we're landing," he said, "I can see the buildings and the trees going by. I see that they're going past us fast, and I know that we're going fast too." This is a good analogy for pacing. Regardless of how fast you're actually flying, passengers' perception of how fast they're moving is influenced by the reference points they see (or don't see) passing. In the classroom, moments in which the activity shifts, a task is completed, or a new person enters the conversation can serve as reference points. When reference points appear to pass in rapid succession, they can make it seem like things are moving fast, regardless of your actual speed.

This chapter offers six techniques for managing the illusion of speed in your classroom.

CHANGE THE PACE

One way to create the illusion of speed is by using a variety of activities to accomplish your objective and moving from one to the other throughout the course of a lesson—that is, to use **Change the Pace**. It's worth thinking about the difference between changing topics every ten to fifteen minutes for an hour, which is distracting, confusing, and unproductive, and changing the format of the work every ten to fifteen minutes as you seek to master a single topic. The latter is likely to improve your pacing, the former to distract and confuse students. Spending ten minutes on topic sentences, fifteen minutes on subject-verb agreement, and fifteen minutes on copyediting yields an unfocused lesson.

But a lesson on topic sentences might be both focused and fast-paced in this way:

- Start with a quick *Do Now* asking students to compare different topic sentences for a paragraph on an interesting topic.

- Move directly into a mini-lesson in which you define topic sentence and provide positive and negative examples.

- Teach a short song about the criteria for a good topic sentence.

- Guide students through three or four examples where they write an effective topic sentence for a given paragraph.

- Have your class write topic sentences for each paragraph in a humorous memoir you've written, analyzing the various suggestions for each, marking them up, and improving them.

- Move to independent work of drafting topic sentences for a set of widely varying paragraphs.

- Wrap with a quick review of your topic sentence song.

- Cap with an *Exit Ticket*.

"Nothing for more than ten minutes," advises Ryan Hill, principal of the highly successful TEAM Academy in Newark. I'd asked for guidance on pacing from some colleagues, and he pointed me to brain research suggesting that people of all ages tend to begin losing focus after ten minutes and need something new to engage them.

My colleague Chi Tschang of Achievement First has taken this idea a step further, advising teachers to switch activities within the lesson based on the Age Plus Two Rule, a concept I've seen attributed to various original sources. The rule states that a student's optimal attention span equals his or her age plus two, which means that in the case of fifth graders, his rule of thumb isn't far from Ryan Hill's. However, Chi believes that even if you change activities in a lesson at the right rate, things can still go wrong. He thinks of lesson activities as active or passive, and says activities should fluctuate between these two types: "If there are two (or three) highly active kinesthetic activities in a row," he writes, "the class's energy level can shoot off the charts, and kids can lose focus. Alternatively, if there are two (or three) highly passive activities in a row, the class can lose its energy entirely and also lose its focus."

Change the Pace carries with it a powerful potential to energize the classroom, yet I can't leave the discussion without sharing one caveat. While *Change the Pace* is useful for engaging students in many lessons at many points in their academic careers, it also risks exacerbating a problem to address: the shortness of attention spans. Think of the professions that require more sustained bouts of focused, disciplined attention than age plus 2: doctor, lawyer, airline pilot, and engineer spring to mind. Even if research proves them to exist, short attention spans are just as likely to be the product of environmental factors, some of which we can mitigate. I suspect that people in the seventeenth century did not need or crave intellectual change at the same median rate we do today, which means teachers can both recognize the usefulness of responding to limited attention spans and seek to gradually and persistently extend them. One of the greatest gifts a school can give a student is to increase his or her capacity to concentrate for extended periods of time. That said, the most successful way to do that is clearly not to immerse your students in an hour of sustained note taking on the first day of school.

BRIGHTEN LINES

Every time you start an activity in a lesson, you're presented with an opportunity to **Brighten Lines**: to draw bright, clear lines at the beginning and end. Making activities begin and end crisply and clearly rather than melding together in an undifferentiated stew can have a positive effect on pacing. Beginnings and endings that are more visible to participants are more likely to be perceived as reference points and create the perception that you've done multiple discrete things. It makes the reference points you create more distinct and visible. Drawing a bright line can also improve pacing because the first and last minute of any activity play a large role in shaping students' perceptions of them. Get your activities off to a clean start, and students will perceive them to be energetic and dynamic.

A clean start is not always a fast start, however. It can be, and in fact a fast start is often fun and engaging, and moving quickly is one great way to create the illusion of speed. But you can also create the illusion of speed by adapting the language you use to introduce a quiet reflective activity from, "Take some time to answer the questions in front of you. Then we'll begin discussing the novel," to, "Take exactly three minutes to answer the questions in front of you. Then we'll begin discussing the novel." Bounding each activity with finite time limits makes it appear to be more autonomous and makes its end point clear, and using odd increments of time—three minutes rather than five—draws students' attention to the fact that you are not meandering through time with vague estimates but actively managing each minute. You could make the transition even sharper and more visible by giving a start signal, upgrading with: "Take three minutes to answer the questions in front of you. Then we'll begin discussing the novel. Ready? Go!" Now your activity has a clear start time and a specific duration. Students can see others hop to it on cue, as if they were at the starting line of a race.

You can use a variation of this as students complete their work: telling them they're done can help make another bright, clear line. You might adapt the previous scenario, for example, by saying, "When I clap my hands three times, I'll want to see hands of those of you who want to share your answer to the first question." The claps emphasize that something has ended and something else quickly begun. This line can be drawn for individuals—"You're done, Trevor. You can start in on the reading"—or for groups—"Well done, fifth grade. Three stomps on two, and we're on to the next step." Finally, looking forward makes these transitions especially exciting. Telling Trevor or the fifth grade, "Here we go!" makes a sense of excitement and anticipation pervade.

ALL HANDS

You can also create the illusion of speed by shifting rapidly among and involving a wide array of participants by using **All Hands**. This can be especially helpful when you aren't able to shift activities in your lesson as in *Change the Pace,* which you won't always be able to do. Let's say you are reading and discussing an extensive passage for much of a class period. Having multiple students read short segments from the passage and moving rapidly among them would create a sense of speed. Each time you shift among participants, you establish a reference point. Something has changed—something begun and ended—and a bit of suspense is created (Who will go next?). Using *All Hands* can help you react to and energize a lagging class quickly and simply.

To maximize your ability to use *All Hands,* several other skills and techniques may prove useful, especially *Cold Call* (technique 22), *Pepper* (technique 24), "Unbundle" and "Half-Statement" from *Ratio* (technique 17), and Control the Game (Chapter Ten). *Cold Call* and *Pepper* allow you to call on everybody, which means more people feel part of the action. They also allow you to call on participants more quickly and with less linguistic mucking around. There is no asking who would like to add to that, no awkwardly coddling folks to raise their hands. You just say a name and get started. "Unbundle" allows you to parse a potentially broad question out to more students and in smaller, and thus faster, increments. You take a slow answer from one student and make it three quick answers from three students from the far corners of the room. Half-statements allow you to involve all students quickly using *Call and Response* but at very low transaction cost. Control the Game also builds pacing.

One barrier to pacing is the long-winded and meandering student comment offered at the wrong time. You can use *All Hands* to address this challenge by socializing students to give succinct answers, using an upbeat stock phrase—"Hold it!" "Time out!" "Pause!" or "Freeze," for example—to make a quick interruption when appropriate, reminding students of the question and diverting it to another student. You can follow up with a reminder to focus on the question, answer in two sentences, or "save that thought for later" if useful. If you do this consistently, students will intuit the pacing expectations in your classroom and respond accordingly.

A final piece of *All Hands* is managing questions, requests, and comments that are either off task ("Are we going to be writing in our journals later?") or persist on a topic you are ready to dispense with ("I wanted to read what I wrote about Tabitha, too"). Such benign distractions can pose a serious threat to pacing, and even hands raised to ask questions can waste time and disrupt the energy and timing of an otherwise perfect class. The best teachers seem to be especially attentive to this, using a version of the "Do Not Engage" portion of *Strong Voice* (technique 38) and telling students "No hands right now," or something similar when the time is not right.

EVERY MINUTE MATTERS

Time is water in the desert, a teacher's most precious resource: to be husbanded, guarded, and conserved. Every minute matters. And yet in a variety of situations, we risk letting the minutes slip by. The last few minutes of class, for example, are sometimes blithely given away. We say, "We don't have time to start anything new," or "We worked hard, so I'm giving you guys a few minutes to relax." Let's say this kind of thinking applies to just the last four minutes of class. That adds up to roughly twelve and a half hours of "last few minutes" during each of perhaps six classes in each school year. If you did that every day, you'd give away seventy-five hours of instruction—several weeks of school.

Instead, use **Every Minute Matters** and reward students for their hard work with a high-energy review of all they've learned or with a challenge problem. Keep a series of short learning activities ready so you're prepared when a two-minute opportunity emerges: at the end of class, in the hallway, while waiting for buses. A walk to the bathroom is a perfect time for a vocabulary review. Packing up backpacks at the end of the day is a great opportunity for reading aloud to the students from an inspiring novel. There's no better way to keep kids from getting off task while lining up for lunch than by peppering them with multiplication problems and mental math. Getting out to the bus to go home? Have every student think of an adjective to describe the bus.

You can always be teaching.

There are roughly twelve and a half-hours of "last few minutes" during each of perhaps six classes in each school year.

Every few months I reinspire myself by watching a short video of Jamey Verilli managing his minutes one afternoon at North Star Academy. Waiting with most of his students outside a history classroom for the last few students to arrive, he begins quizzing students on their vocabulary words:

- "What does it mean to be 'bound' to do something?"

- "Can you use it in a sentence, John?"

- "Who would have been bound to the land in a Middle Ages town?"

- "What are you bound to be doing right now?"

The students are standing in a line in the hallway just outside his classroom. Class has not even started yet. Not in the classroom, not during class time and Jamey doesn't care: there's learning to be done. Meanwhile his students are excited, smiling, happy to engaged and showing off their knowledge.

LOOK FORWARD

Even mild suspense creates tension, excitement, and anticipation. You can harvest that in your classroom to make your pacing feel more vibrant by using **Look Forward**. If you put an agenda on the board for a lesson or the morning, you can start students looking forward. If you add a catchy name to some of the topics on your agenda, they seem all the more intriguing. If you call one "Mystery Activity," you can make the anticipation even more intense. You can go further by referring to it occasionally: "We're almost there. Charles thinks he knows what it is but . . . oh, no. He has no idea."

Bob Zimmerli once entranced a class of fifth graders during a lesson on place value by writing a number with twelve digits on the board and announcing, "At the end of class today, somebody's going to stand up and read this number correctly to the class. Everyone's going to be able to, but one of you is going to get to represent! You're going to march up here and show us how. Be ready. It might be you." Here are a few other ways to refer to the future:

- "Later we'll be making this really tricky, so stay with me now, even if it seems easy [or hard]."

- "By the end of class you'll be able to [or you'll know the true story behind] . . ."

- "This is the first step in a skill that you'll want to show off to all your friends."

There are simpler ways to look forward. Consider the difference in the example we looked at in *Brighten Lines* in this chapter. While, "Take exactly three minutes to answer the questions in front of you. Then we'll begin discussing the novel," is better than, "Take some time to answer the questions in front of you. Then we'll begin discussing the novel," both are better than, "Take some time to answer the questions in front of you," with no reference to what's next. After hearing the first version, the second almost pleads for an answer to, "and then what?" even if it's only, "and then we'll move on to the next step."

WORK THE CLOCK

The teachers interviewed for this book constantly talk about time in their classrooms, and they **Work the Clock**. They count it down, parcel it out in highly specific increments, often announcing an allotted time for each activity: "Take three minutes to answer the questions in front of you." They mix in frequent countdowns to pace their class in completing tasks and emphasize the importance of each second: "Pencils down and eyes on me in 5–4–3–2–1." The countdown lends a sense of urgency to class time, reminding students that time matters and hastening them along to the next step. What's more, a countdown allows them to acknowledge productive behavior in an especially effective way.

Imagine you acknowledged two students, Brooklyn and Brian, because they were ready in exactly the manner you'd asked. If you acknowledge them in the middle of a countdown (for example, by saying: "5, 4 . . . Brooklyn's ready! . . . 3, 2 . . . Brian's sitting up and ready to roll! . . . and 1. Eyes on me and away we go!"), you are calling attention to behavior that not only meets but exceeds expectations. You gave students until you reached one, but Brooklyn was ready at 4! She did more than comply with your wishes: she set the bar high. Only by counting down the seconds did you make it evident to everyone that Brooklyn and Brian were ready early. Without the countdown, calling attention to their readiness ("I see that Brooklyn is ready; Brian is ready too") leaves you sounding weak, almost as if you were pleading with other students to comply with your expectations by praising a few students who had complied or at least come close. After all there's no way to tell, without the countdown, whether you're reinforcing excellence or mediocrity.

Finally, using countdowns can allow you to continually set goals for your class's speed in meeting expectations: "I know we can do this in 10, but we're Homeroom Hamilton. Let's see if we can get ready in 6!" Now your standard can be ever-increasing success rather than more than mere compliance. In a recent lesson in Patrick Pastore's reading class at Rochester Prep, Patrick began his countdown at 10. When he got to 4, all of his students were ready, so he announced: "And we don't even need the rest. Let's get started!"

REFLECTION AND PRACTICE

1. Go through a lesson plan you're likely to use in the next week, and if you don't do this already, assign the time you think each activity is likely to take. Now that you have general parameters, go through and find every direction you'll give to your students during the lesson, and designate an amount of time you will allot to each activity. Write a short script for each that makes the amount of time available clear and gives a beginning and end prompt to brighten lines.

2. Take the biggest single block of activity in your lesson (as measured in minutes), and try to break it into two or three activities with

the same objective but with slightly different presentations. For example, if you had a section of problems for a math lesson on rounding, you might divide it in half, with a clear line between numerical and word problems. Then you might insert a brief reflection on what rounding is and why we'd do it between the two sections to make it seem like three.

CHAPTER NINE

CHALLENGING STUDENTS TO THINK CRITICALLY

Additional Techniques for Questioning and Responding to Students

Questions asked strategically of students by teachers have been the heart of teaching for about as long as there have been teachers and students. Effective questions tend to come in groups that make the whole greater than the sum of the parts, and questioning is the art of sequencing those questions in groups. Good questioning builds solid mastery of even complex ideas by uncovering and explicating each component piece of a concept in progression.

The building process is essentially the same whether there are three steps or three hundred. A bigger goal means not bigger steps but more of the same steady, manageable steps.

Assembling questioning sequences, then, is like building steps. If each step yields a steady and manageable rise and the organizing structure is sound, the staircase can lead students up any height. The building process is essentially the same whether there are three steps or three hundred. A bigger goal means not bigger steps but more of the same steady, manageable steps. By climbing steps day after day, students get good at climbing, good at systematically developing and breaking down ideas. Soon they rise without watching their feet or counting their steps as they move ably and with quickness.

Although the idea behind questioning is generally a constant, questioning can serve at least five distinct purposes in effective classrooms.

- *To guide students toward understanding when introducing material.* The purpose is to methodically build knowledge and mastery of a preplanned skill or concept (the objective) often by building gradually on a simpler idea and anticipating the places students will be confused. *Example:* "We know that we can add fractions when they have the same denominator, that $1/3$ plus $1/3$ equals $2/3$, but what about when the denominators aren't equal? Would $1/3$ plus $1/2$ equal $2/5$? Is that possible? Let's look at our answer: Is 2 more or less than half of 5? Less. So $2/5$ is more or less than $1/2$? Less? But we can't add something like $1/3$ to $1/2$ and get an answer that's *less* than $1/2$. So we must have a problem: we can't just add the numerators and the denominators."

- *To push students to do a greater share of the thinking* (increasing the *Ratio,* technique 17). The purpose is to have students own deeply and fully acknowledge information they have previously been introduced to and begun to master by forcing them to do the lion's share of the work. This form of questioning is more likely than the first to happen during the "We" or guided practice portion of the lesson, while the first is more likely to occur during the "I" part of the lesson. (See also *Ratio.*) *Example:* "So if I'm adding $1/2$ and $1/3$, what's the first thing I need to do, Kelsey? And how do I find the lowest common denominator? Is that a complete answer, James? Does it capture everything I need to do? What's missing? Okay, so now that we know what to do, what is the lowest common denominator in this problem? All right, then, what do I do next, Max?"

- *To remediate an error.* The teacher responds to a wrong answer (evidence of a student's incomplete mastery of a concept) by breaking the original concept down into smaller component parts and adding insight through more questions to build toward mastery of the original concept. These tend to be shorter, reactive questioning sequences. (See *Break It Down,* technique 16.) *Example:* "Remember that the LCD is a number that can be divided by both of the denominators. You said the LCD was 5. How many times does 3 go into 5?"

- *To stretch students.* The teacher responds to a student who has appeared to demonstrate mastery of a concept (answered one or several questions correctly) by pushing him to apply the concept at the next higher skill level or in a new setting, often to test for reliability of the correct answer. These also tend to be shorter, reactive questioning sequences. (See *Stretch It,* technique 3.) *Example:* "Nice job adding $1/2$ plus $1/3$, Mark. Tell me, what would your LCD be if you wanted to add $1/2$ to $1/7$?"

- *To check for understanding*. The teacher uses questioning to test for mastery, sampling a strategic array of students to discern how much of what she's taught students have learned. (See *Check for Understanding,* technique 18.) *Example:* "Okay, before we move on, let's see who's got it! Albert, to get my LCD, I simply add the two denominators, right?"

The line of questioning can pursue more than one of these purposes at a time. A teacher might seek to both stretch her students and check for understanding at the same time, say, by asking a student who answered correctly to explain the solution process.

Questioning is a complex and multifaceted skill that affects almost every part of teaching. Many of its most critical elements are covered at different places in this book. For example, questioning is embedded in *Stretch It* (pushing students when they've answered correctly), *Ratio* (increasing the amount of cognitive work students do), *Break It Down* (responding to student errors), and *Check for Understanding* (strategically testing for mastery). In addition to those aspects of questioning, there are a few general rules of thumb for designing effective questioning, no matter its purpose.

ONE AT A TIME

Given that questions often come in sequences, it's easy to overlook a simple but critical rule of thumb for questioning: ask one question at a time. Ironically, teachers are most at risk of asking students more than one question when they're excited about what they are teaching and when the content tempts them to push ahead too quickly. Disciplining yourself to use **One at a Time**, particularly when you're most engaged and enthused, helps focus students on developing one idea at a time

Disciplining yourself to use the One at a Time technique, particularly when you're most engaged and enthused, helps focus students on developing one idea at a time and focuses you on questioning with a specific goal or purpose in mind.

and focuses you on questioning with a specific goal or purpose in mind, not just a generalized desire to spark (any) discussion.

Consider a teacher reading *Mrs. Frisby and the Rats of NIMH* with her fifth graders. She might ask something like, "Jason, how is the rats' house different from Mrs. Frisby's, and which one do you think she would rather live in?" This question is really two, each with a distinct purpose: one asks Jason to compare and contrast specific details, and the other asks him to infer a character's point of view about an event. Unless the teacher is disciplined about attending to both questions and ensuring that each gets answered in turn, Jason will most likely choose (perhaps arbitrarily) which of the two questions to answer, and the other will fall by the wayside, never to be answered and subtly but persistently suggesting to the class that the teacher's questions are not especially important or planned. The message is not, "I have something specific and singularly important I want you to discuss," but, "I just want you to discuss the book; any of a variety topics will do equally."

In fact, if Jason is savvy, his choice of which question to answer won't be arbitrary: he'll choose either the one that's easier for him or the one he wants to answer more—not necessarily the one that would be better for him to answer. This double question essentially devolves a critical learning decision—what's the question we're answering—to accident. Comparing and contrasting and inferring a character's perspective are critical but different reading comprehension skills, and it makes sense for a teacher to make an intentional decision about which is more productive to ask Jason at that moment rather than leaving it to him to make a spur-of-the moment choice.

Furthermore, since she doesn't know which question Jason will engage, she is immediately hampered in her planning. She can't prepare—in her mind or, better, as part of her preclass lesson planning—a series of follow-up questions to make visible to students how Mrs. Frisby's character is reflected in her preference for her own simple abode because she doesn't control whether the issue reaches the discussion floor. And even if she's disciplined about asking Jason to answer both questions, she'll be able to plan follow-up to only one or the other. Thus, in the end, one of her questions is highly likely to get shorter shrift than it deserves.

One reason many teachers may be inclined to ask more than one question at a time is that it's easy to unconsciously model in classrooms the techniques of interviewing seen in popular media. Though similarly driven by questions, interviews propose to inform and entertain, not to teach, which is very different. The interviewer hopes to generate a string of interesting, revealing, or don't-touch-that-dial remarks from an individual. Trying various questions to see which draws the most interesting response is an effective strategy, so interviewers may offer several questions at a time, hoping to elicit a vibrant response. In scholastic questioning, offering a menu of questions is more likely to cause confusion or inefficiency. It is unclear which question to answer, easy to skip the hard ones, and more difficult to sustain a conversation on a specific, focused topic. In short, the ramifications of this mundane rule are far-reaching. Fortunately the solution is simple: ask one question at a time.

SIMPLE TO COMPLEX

It's effective to ask questions that progress from **Simple to Complex**. Like a good lesson plan, effective questions initially engage students' thinking about a topic in contained and concrete ways and then push them to think more deeply and broadly. In the process of answering narrower and more focused questions, students begin to activate their memory of relevant facts and details to support their opinions. They have time to develop and reflect on ideas, turning them into insights before they're called on to share them in public. As a result, they will likely answer broader and deeper questions more factually, more insightfully, and, having seen themselves succeed at initial questions, more confidently and with the willingness to take on greater risk. In a typical sequence about a novel or a historical period, for example, you might ask a few fact-based questions to ensure that your students understood the facts and details of what happened. These might be organized from simpler to harder. Then you might start asking questions that ask students to evaluate and prioritize that information: What was the most important event in the story? What did we learn that most helped us to understand the main character? What were the most important events in the historical period, and what do they tell you about people's values then? After that, you might move to a few questions that ask students to apply their ideas more broadly. How would you compare or contrast the main character's behavior in this chapter to his behavior at some other point in the novel? What are the most important lessons from this period in history that are still relevant today?

While this latter group of questions is arguably more interesting, they'll yield less value if you jump right to them without establishing and affirming both a fact base and the logical building blocks from which students can conduct their deeper thinking.

VERBATIM (NO BAIT AND SWITCH)

Some teachers unintentionally pull a Bait-and-Switch on their students, changing the question after a student has raised his hand and begun to formulate a response.

Most teachers ask a question, wait for hands, and then call on a student to answer. However, before the chosen student answers, they often restate the question. It's often useful and occasionally critical to do this, especially when asking a challenging question. However, in repeating the question, it's important to remember to ask the same question **Verbatim**. Some teachers unintentionally pull a Bait-and-Switch on their students, changing the question after a student has raised his hand and begun to formulate a response. This seems harmless but can have several negative consequences. First, the student with his hand raised is now asked to respond aloud to a question that is different from what he volunteered to speak about. He is not prepared, and the quality of the answer is likely to be lower. Even a moderate change in syntax can force a student to revise the syntax of the answer he's been preparing, leaving him confused or distracted at exactly the moment he's onstage. If you ask your students to take the risk of answering questions about which they are less than 100 percent confident (and you should ask them to take that risk), they deserve to know what the question will be, have time to consider their response, and answer the question they think they'll get to answer. In many cases, students are left in stumped silence by a change in the question that may appear insignificant to the teacher—for example, a change from, "Why do you think the author wrote this article?" to, "What was the purpose of this article?"

If your questions matter, you want students to hear them, consider them, and participate based on thoughtful reflection. Make that easier for them by keeping the question constant.

CLEAR AND CONCISE

Too often the problem with a wrong answer is not with the answer but with the question. It sounds obvious to note that students should know what you are asking them if you want them to have the chance to answer correctly. Here are five ways to use the **Clear and Concise** technique to improve the clarity of your questions:

- *Start with a question word.* When you begin a sentence with *who, when, what, where, why,* or *how,* your students instantly know it's a question and can begin thinking about a response. You also increase the likelihood that the kind of answer you want will be clear. Asking, "Can you add to that?" provides little guidance; it is unlikely to yield the kind of answer you want and to provide students with the chance to prepare a response they are confident in. Sentences that begin with *Is* are fine too, although that they often yield yes or no answers—short responses that are hard to follow up on and don't usually yield great discussion.

- *Limit them to two clauses.* Asking questions in ornate sentences that sound as if they come from a Henry James novel may work for college professors but often confuse students younger than college age. Make your questions rigorous and demanding, but limit them to two clauses most of the time so students are clear on what you're asking.

- *Write them in advance when they matter.* The best way to ask exactly the right questions is to script them in advance as part of the lesson planning process—both the initial question and your response if students aren't able to answer as you'd hoped. This is perhaps the single driver of better teaching that most developing teachers roundly ignore.

- *Ask an actual question.* Say, "Why doesn't Stewart think so?" rather than making a statement like, "But Stewart doesn't think so." If you do the latter, students have the right to be confused. Are you asking them a question?

- *Assume the answer.* Ask, "Who can tell me . . . ," not, "Can anyone tell me . . . " The first assumes someone can answer, and a student thinks, "Who can? I can!" "Can anyone" expresses doubt that anyone will, and doubt makes students less likely to assume that someone like them should put their hand up.

STOCK QUESTIONS

I recently showed a video of one of the best questioners I know, Jaimie Brillante, to a group of teachers. In the video, Brillante's questions come at students fast and furious:

"Is that a run-on sentence?"

"I think so."

"Well, how would you know?"

"There would be two subjects and two predicates."

"If I wanted to prove it, which of those would I start looking for first?"

"The predicate."

"And can you find a predicate?"

"Is it *owner*?"

"Why can't *owner* be a predicate?"

"It's not a verb."

"Well that *would* explain it. What part of speech is *owner*?" [No answer].

"Well, think of other –er words: *dancer, singer, teacher*. What are those?"

"They're all people. They all nouns."

"And does an *owner* seem the same?"

"Yes."

"And so the predicate must have what?"

"A verb."

In Brillante's lesson, students are working hard and fast, getting a serious intellectual workout demonstrating knowledge and fixing errors. Observing Brillante in action is daunting for a teacher. How can the rest of us hope to think on our feet like that and ask artful sequences of clear questions over and over again while running a class?

Afterward I asked Brillante what the secret to her questioning was. She replied, "One important thing is that I'm not making my questions up on the spot. I am asking versions of the same few questions over and over. I've drilled them to know that it's easier to find the predicate than it is to find the subject. So I always ask them, when they're testing for a complete sentence or a run-on, 'Should we try to find the predicate or the subject first?' And they know that they need to find the predicate first because verbs are easier to find. I try to have a logical approach to typical problems and then follow that approach over and over. It looks as if I am thinking of five fast questions to ask in a row, but I am really making a decision to ask one *sequence* of questions in a row."

In short, Brillante's questioning is based on theme and variation: similar sequences of questions applied over and over in different settings. Obviously these **Stock Questions** can't occur in all cases and with all material, but she is making far fewer decisions than she appears to be. She's not deciding on five questions but on one sequence of questions with five fairly predictable parts. This reduces the intellectual daunting demands of questioning and makes it practical to execute.

HIT RATE

A last aspect of questioning to attend to is **Hit Rate**: the rate at which students answer your questions correctly (or adequately and thoroughly, in the case of questions where there's no firm right answer). If your hit rate is 100 percent, that's not necessarily a good thing unless you've just wrapped up a review. Or put another way, it's good if your hit rate starts at 100 percent, but it should not remain that way for long: when kids get everything right, it's time to ask harder questions. Asking harder questions as your hit rate approaches 100 percent allows you to test the full extent of student knowledge and retain adequate rigor. By the same token, a hit rate below two out of three shows that you've got a problem with either how you presented the material you taught or how aligned your questions are to that material. Your kids are not showing you mastery, a result that should give you pause.

HOW TO REINFORCE EFFECTIVE QUESTIONING

A variety of techniques discussed elsewhere in this book are also critical to effective questioning. A brief discussion of several of them follows.

Break It Down

The capacity to break down ideas or questions that confuse students into smaller or simpler questions is arguably the critical questioning skill. Too often teachers respond to the entirely normal and useful process of student answering incorrectly in one of three inefficient ways: repeating the same question, telling the student the answer, or calling on another student to answer and not returning to the initial student. When a student fails the answer correctly, *Break It Down* (technique 16) is the best strategy. It assists the teacher in understanding what part of the question posed difficulty and causes students to both draw on and develop what knowledge they do have. A variety of *Break It Down* strategies are discussed in Chapter Two.

No Opt Out

A related technique, discussed in Chapter One, is *No Opt Out* (technique 1). In several of the variations on it, the teacher returns to a student who was unable to answer an initial question, asking her to repeat the correct answer given by another student or to use additional information provided by the other student to solve the problem herself. *No Opt Out* questions might include, "Who can tell Charlene the first step she needs to use to solve this?" "Who can tell Charlene where she could find the answer?" or "Who can tell Charlene what we mean by [a troubling concept or term]?"

Right Is Right and Stretch It

If *Break It Down* and *No Opt Out* are useful for remediating wrong answers by students, *Right Is Right* (technique 2) adds two pieces to the picture. The "All the Way Right" portion of the technique is useful for getting students who give mostly correct answers all the way there: "I think you've characterized accurately how the main character acts in public, but is there more to say about how he acts in private?" The "Answer My Question" portion of the technique is useful when students answer a question other than the one you've asked, a much more common problem than most people suspect.

Stretch It (technique 3), by contrast, improves your questioning by reminding you that the learning process doesn't end with a right answer. Pushing students with a variety of follow-up questions is one of the most valuable ways to increase the rigor of your classroom.

Ratio

Several aspects of *Ratio* (technique 17) are also useful for questioning. Unbundling is the process of taking a large, multipart question and dividing it into a series of smaller questions that are rapidly distributed to a variety of class members, usually using *Cold Call* (technique 22). Rather than asking one student what the three dimensions of volume are, for example, a teacher might unbundle by saying, "How many dimensions of volume are there, Tyra? Good, what's one of the dimensions, Keith? What's another, Carlton? And the last, Jennifer? Good. And what number do we use for pi, the last dimension, Paula?" This technique has the effect of increasing the pacing of the lesson and involving more students. It also forces students to listen carefully to their peers' responses and adjust accordingly. Carlton can't offer *length* as his answer if Keith says it first.

A second aspect of *Ratio* that's particularly useful in questioning is to feign ignorance, that is, pretend not to know the answer or make a mistake and thus require students to correct and explain the error.

Cold Call

Cold Call is especially useful in situations above and beyond unbundling. It's the fastest, most effective way to make students accountable for staying engaged with your questioning, keep the pace of your questions fast and rigorous, and ensure your capacity to use questions to check for understanding. It ensures your ability to steer any question to the student you most want to answer it at any time.

REFLECTION AND PRACTICE

1. Interview someone at a social event, and practice asking this person only one clear question at a time. What made the task easy or difficult? What can you learn that you can apply to teaching?

Two

Helping Students Get the Most Out of Reading: Critical Skills and Techniques

CHAPTER TEN

HOW ALL TEACHERS CAN (AND MUST) BE READING TEACHERS

Reading is *the* skill. Teaching students to unlock the full meaning of the texts they read is the single most powerful outcome a teacher can foster. If your students can read well, they can essentially do anything. I've included this chapter on reading in the book to help *all* teachers, not just in certain classes but across the school in every room, use the methods of champion reading teachers to structure reading in their classrooms and ensure that students do lots and lots of it, and in ways that maximize productivity. If you teach, no matter the subject, you have the opportunity and the obligation to ensure that your students read more (and better). This opportunity will result in their being both more informed regarding the topic of your instruction and more effective assimilators and analyzers of information—better readers—in the future. It's a double investment paying both short- and long-term results.

I have a friend whose father continually stressed the power of reading to him when he was growing up. To prove it, he pulled my friend out of school for several months, bought a series of books on building, even though he had previously been only moderately handy, and proceeded, with my friend alongside, to build a house from foundation to shingles. My friend recalls sitting on beams in the twilight, he and his father reading aloud with great intensity on plumbing or framing or wiring, sometimes working through the complex passages three and four times.

Schools, however, have increasingly come to teach reading in a more specific and more limited sense, as a mere noun: a specific subject area for intentional study. We train our English and literacy teachers to teach a subject called Reading. Certainly there's a great deal of value in thinking of reading as primarily a subject, particularly at the elementary level where phonics has (or should have) revolutionized the efficacy of early literacy instruction and where specialized instruction is a key lever in creating lasting reading gains among students. But the value of reading arguably lies just as much in its status as a verb, that is, students reading frequently and broadly as a key goal of schooling. Not only do the reading programs and English classes in many schools fail to include much actual reading (in the verb sense), but untapped opportunities to read more effectively occur throughout every corner of the building. Still, schools are far less likely to maximize these opportunities, and even less likely to train teachers how to take advantage of them. Nevertheless, the overall value of the additional high-quality reading you could do in a typical school day could equal or possibly exceed the value of what happens in designated reading classes. When you stop to consider how much high-quality reading students might do outside reading class, the untapped potential is massive, but for now most students simply don't read much.

Consider four of the most enduring intellects to have worked and written in the English language: Abraham Lincoln, Fredrick Douglass, Jane Austen, and Charles Dickens. They were all educated similarly, but perhaps not how you'd think. Each received little or no formal schooling. Essentially self-educated in an era when self-education meant reading, they rose to eminence by virtue of the skills and knowledge their private reading taught them.

I am not suggesting that their educations provide a model of what education should be. Still, they remind us of the almost unlimited capacity of diligent reading to teach. For all four of these exceptional people and many others, "mere" reading was sufficient to foster and develop rare genius. And as for the rest of us, we are all self-educated, to some degree or another, by virtue of the reading we have done.

Leafing back in my mind through the ideas gleaned from my private reading, I know that they have shaped me as much as my schooling has. We are what we have read and how we read it, and no other single activity has the capacity to yield so much educational value. And yet students in many schools spend precious little time actually reading. Likely, they read for less than an hour a day. Even in their reading or literature classes, they are as likely to talk about reading or respond to what they may (or may not) have read as they are to actually read. For her dissertation, a colleague followed students through their day at New York City public schools and found that they read for an average of ten minutes per day. Worse, 40 percent of them did no reading at all.

Making "mere reading" highly productive and effective in your classroom is a critical skill no matter what subject or grade level you teach, and this chapter explains how you can do that,

We are what we have read and how we read it, and no other single activity has the capacity to yield so much educational value. And yet students in many schools spend precious little actually reading. Likely, they read for less than an hour a day.

both practically (how you can ensure that classmates are reading along with a student who's reading aloud) and pedagogically (how and when you should ask what kinds of questions). It also contains guidance especially useful to English and language arts teachers whose goal is to use techniques like "strategies" to make students "readers" over and above their mastery of any specific text.

Although I've tried to provide guidance for both teachers generally and specialists, I underscore two key assumptions in this chapter: everybody in a school must be a reading teacher and the generalist techniques may be the most productive for study by specialists. In many cases, they are highly trained in the subtle arts of interpretation and textual analysis but leave value on the table due to a lack of proficiency In other words, they may fall into the trap that many other specialists—heart surgeons or data analysts, for example—face: losing sight of the basics. The point of this chapter is to bring those basics back into focus. As one excellent teacher said to me, "I'm a certified English teacher and a pretty good one at teaching kids to interpret what we read, but I don't know the first thing about what to do when a kid can't read a word."

The chapters in Part Two offer approaches for helping all students improve their reading. They cover a set of skills that is obvious to some practitioners but where the approach taken by top teachers provides guidance that is critically important for all:

- Decoding—the process of deciphering written text to identify the spoken words it represents

- Fluency—consists of automaticity, the ability to read at a rapid rate, plus expression, the ability to group words together into phrases to reflect meaning and tone

- Vocabulary—a student's base of word knowledge: how many words she knows and how well she knows them

- Comprehension—how much of what's written a student understands

Comprehension sits in a strange position within this list as it requires both a set of techniques of its own and also the mastery of the other three: you teach fluency, decoding, and vocabulary in order to ensure robust comprehension. However, when comprehension doesn't work, it may be that students weren't able to make certain inferences or distinguish trivial from critical details, but it's just as likely that the problem was that they couldn't read the passage with sufficient fluidity and automaticity to allow them to use their processing capacity to understand its subtleties. They may be using so much of their mental capacity bandwidth merely processing the words that they can't remember the beginning of the paragraph (or the sentence) by the time they get to the end. And it's important to remember that all students face this challenge. In the first year of my graduate studies in English literature, most of us were so busy trying to unpack the jargon of the field and the impenetrable syntax of academic writing that our comprehension sagged woefully—not because we couldn't grasp the ideas but because the presentation posed barriers to fluency, decoding, and vocabulary. And presentation can pose such barriers to every reader, no matter who, and often deliberately so (the novels of William Faulkner and Gabriel Garcia Márquez are good examples).

The information in Part Two focuses broadly on making reading more effective and rigorous in any classroom and for any purpose—whether you're reading "The Three Little Bears," Plato, Chapter Seven of *Cell: The Building Blocks of Life*, the directions to a math problem, or a description of the Gettysburg Address. The guidance here is equally applicable to teachers of reading as a specific subject. However, since the art of teaching reading comprehension as a fungible skill that students learn to master and apply in any future situation is also the challenging and nuanced provenance of specialists—reading teachers—Part Two also contains specific guidance for those teachers. The last chapter on comprehension also contains a discussion of aspects of reading that are more specifically (but not exclusively) relevant to language arts or reading classrooms. In particular, I discuss in this section the reading strategies so many reading teachers currently use.

MAKING READING INSTRUCTION PRODUCTIVE AND ACCOUNTABLE: CONTROL THE GAME

So how do busy teachers integrate reading instruction into their classrooms in a way that will be productive and keep students accountable? This challenge involves a set of skills that are often overlooked but are critically important. I call these skills *Control the Game*.

Imagine, for a moment, a hypothetical school. This school values reading above all other endeavors—to an exaggerated degree. In its reading classes, it provides direct, intentional instruction on reading: phonics and comprehension at the lower grade levels, intentional focus on key terms and concepts like characterization and theme at the middle school level, introduction to college prep literature at the high school level, and vocabulary at all grade levels. It has recently decided to ensure that its students spend almost all their time in school reading. In science classes, they read chapters from articles and textbooks. In history class, they read primary and secondary source materials, often for the entire class period. They do write, but usually summaries and analyses of what they've read. In math, they supplement their problem sets with reading, and new concepts are often introduced in short descriptive texts. Imagine also that teachers in the school are able to consistently ensure that students, when asked to read, actually do read and read effectively and with attentiveness. As a result, students in the school read for six or seven hours a day, plus homework.

I offer this prospect as a hypothetical model, not a proposal for actual educational programs. My goal is not to say I think it would make for a viable school model but to cause you to reflect on what the results of such a school would be. Might reading for six or seven hours a day, 190 days a year, if you could ensure the reading was of reasonable quality, achieve better outcomes than many schools today foster? Obviously

> *Might reading for six or seven hours a day, 190 days a year, if you could ensure the reading was of reasonable quality, achieve better outcomes than many schools today foster?*

there's no way to answer this question. The fact is that the answer could plausibly be yes and that the question ("If we could ensure that students read well would it be better to read?") should be on our minds as teachers. If a teacher can ensure that her students can be relied on to read well, she can always, at any time and for any duration, ensure that a high-value activity, the single most important skill of the educated citizen, will take place in her classroom. If she can do that, she can consistently invest her time at a reliable rate of return. She need never oversee a low-value activity again. She has a hurdle rate: a rate of return she must exceed on an investment of her time to make it worthwhile.

The term *hurdle rate* comes from finance. If you know you can predictably earn 10 percent on every dollar you invest in a certain bond, for example, and you know that bond is always available to you, you would naturally avoid any investment that returned you less than 10 percent since you could always do better with your bond. The question you'd ask in assessing any potential investment is not, "Will it make me money?" but, "Will it beat my hurdle rate?" That is, you'd ask whether any investment would yield a stronger return than the best alternative investment you know you could make. Businesses ask this kind of question all the time. A technology firm's owners wouldn't ask, "Would building a new factory to manufacture cell phones make us money?" if its resources are limited. If its owners invest millions in building the cell phone factory, they must choose not to do something else with that money—say, invest it in expanding their existing computer factory. Faced with the possibility of profits in cell phones, they would ask whether investing in a cell phone plant would exceed their hurdle rate. In this case, "Would building a factory to manufacture cell phones earn us more than would investing the money in expanding our current computer factories?" The decision is a choice between the return you know you can get (from your existing computer operations) and the potential of any new project (the cell phones). If you could make an 8 percent return on the cell phone factory, it would still not make sense to do it if your rate of return was 10 percent for expanding computer operations. Just because you can make money manufacturing cell phones doesn't mean you should do it.

Although we also manage finite resources as teachers—in this case, time—we rarely think this way. We ask whether our actions will result in learning, but this is the wrong question. The right question is whether our actions yield a return that exceeds our hurdle rate—that is, yield more learning per minute invested than does the best reliable alternative use of class time. And we rarely spend time thinking about developing the strongest and most reliable hurdle rate. In the classrooms of many teachers whose teaching informed this book, meaningful reading (a term I'll define in a minute) provides an exceptionally strong and reliable hurdle rate. It's a high-quality activity (when done efficiently) that can be carried out in any classroom, at any time, and with limited additional preparation or expense required. You can always invest any stretch of time, short or long, in meaningful reading and reap a strong and predictable return. Furthermore, if you know you could always be doing meaningful reading—in any class, at any time—you can examine your other investments of time critically: Do they exceed the value of meaningful reading? Are they potentially higher return but riskier and therefore should be balanced with something more reliable? As you ask these questions, you may well find that reading crowds out some of the other ways you invest your time. Surely not all of them, but probably some of them do not exceed your hurdle rate (that is, they are not reliably more productive than meaningful reading). It would be smarter to have them read meaningfully instead.

It makes sense to pause here and define the term *meaningful reading* more specifically because it is critical to this discussion. For the purposes of this book, I define *meaningful reading* as reading that is accountable, moderately expressive, and highly leveraged. By accountable, I mean that teachers are able to reliably assess whether students are actually reading (rather than, say, sitting looking at pictures or out the window daydreaming when they are supposed to be reading) and reading effectively (decoding and reading words correctly and diligently, for example, rather than reinscribing errors such as ignoring suffixes or skipping over the difficult parts of the text). Much of the reading students do in schools fails to meet this criterion. In one commonly used program, Drop Everything and Read (DEAR), for example, students are given quiet time in which they sit with books and are expected to read. It's a lovely idea, but if you observe students during this program, you will invariably see some of them sitting with books open but eyes drifting across the room or out the window. Some flip idly through pages, gazing at pictures, while others read lazily or poorly, practicing and reinscribing weak habits as they go. Unfortunately, the students reading least are often the ones who need to read the most. This fails the accountability test. As a result, the rate of return on this activity may be low. Learning to invest reading with a strong dose of accountability is a key focus of this chapter.

By *moderately expressive,* I mean that students demonstrate the capacity to embed meaning in words as they read, to show in their inflection that they are processing the words at a level beyond the most basic level. We're not talking about Sir John Gielgud here—just the basics: nonrobotic reading with demonstrated recognition of punctuation and periodic recognition (by emphasis) of key words. Although expressive reading is insufficient to the final task of a full and rich understanding of a text, it is highly efficient as an indicator of basic understanding. Expressing the meaning and register of the words in the manner you are reading them demonstrates comprehension, the end goal of reading instruction.

Many teachers scorn the idea of allowing a single student to read aloud during class time. "What are the other kids doing?" they ask. In meaningful reading, the answer is that they are also reading—to themselves, in step with the student reading aloud. I call the degree to which other students are reading "leverage," and it's the third critical element of meaningful reading. If one student is reading aloud and her classmates are listening passively, there's a leverage factor of 1, signifying a highly inefficient activity. However, if one student is reading aloud and twenty-five students are silently but accountably reading along with her at their desks, you have a leverage factor of twenty-six. Twenty-six people reading makes for a highly efficient and worthwhile activity. If twenty-six people are reading, your hurdle rate is much, much higher so the question becomes very quickly, How do you get that leverage? The Control the Game skills explain how to get and sustain consistently high rates of leverage. When they are reading, everyone reads, and reads accountably, with the result being an especially high hurdle rate and, over time, consistently higher-value activities in the classroom because the hurdle rate raises the investment criteria for their time.

Skeptics about the efficacy of having a single student reading out loud might ask how the text could be appropriately leveled for the whole class or whether it was injurious to students' self-esteem if they struggled publicly. Without engaging in an extended philosophical debate, I would argue that there is nothing inherently injurious to self-esteem about getting something wrong, especially if students learn to do it successfully over time. In that case, the opposite is probably the outcome. Regardless, as Roy Baumeister has demonstrated in his excellent article on the topic, "Rethinking Self-Esteem: Why Nonprofits Should Stop Pushing Self-Esteem and Start Endorsing Self-Control" (*Stanford Social Innovation Review*, Winter 2005), there's little to support the idea that enhancing self-esteem is a worthy goal in schools. The best you can say is that it correlates to (rather than causes) achievement. That is, when students achieve, they believe in themselves, not the other way around. As for leveled texts, many to most of the top-performing urban charter schools of which I'm aware buck the otherwise orthodox belief in heterogeneous classroom grouping and solve this problem by homogeneously grouping classes. That said, even if you do or cannot homogeneously group, a bit of prescreening can help you target sections of the text to appropriate readers or even to prepare struggling readers by introducing phrases and words in advance for them.

Once you've mastered Control the Game and can reliably achieve a fully leveraged and meaningful read, you too can use that skill to set your hurdle rate and rigorously assess whether your classroom activities exceed it in value. I am confident that you will find many such things. You will do a lot more than just read. But you should always seek to consider your hurdle rate and subject every other activity to a comparison. Furthermore, I acknowledge that as students gain in maturity and proficiency, the definition of meaningful reading may change: silent individual reading that doesn't test as explicitly for accountability may become more frequent, for example. But the skills described in this chapter are critical because they get students to the point in their academic careers where high-value independent reading is possible, and they increase the value of those sessions if invested in systematically. Also, most urban public schools probably fail to get the majority of their students to the point where their independent reading is fully meaningful and productive. In those schools, reading falls victim to the logistical problems of poor accountability and low leverage. I fervently hope your classroom reaches the point where Control the Game is unnecessary and less productive than mere silent reading. It will be a joyous day when more classrooms do not need to manage reading in this way. I would merely caution you against assuming you have that classroom without further evidence from and training of your students, possibly over multiple years.

CONTROL THE GAME SKILLS

Keep Durations Unpredictable

When you ask a student to read aloud during class, that student is the primary reader. As the designation suggests, this student is not the only reader. While the practice the primary reader gets is critical, the actions and focus of all other students are also critical: they must become secondary readers. So when you identify your primary reader, don't specify how long you want him to read before he actually begins. "Start reading for me please, James," or "Pick up please, James," is far better than is, "Read the next paragraph for me, James." This ensures that other students in the class don't know when a new reader will be asked to pick up and therefore provides them with a strong incentive to follow along carefully. This makes them more likely to be secondary readers.

In addition, keeping duration unpredictable allows you to address an over-matched primary reader in a noninvasive manner. A primary reader who struggles mightily with a long paragraph risks losing the engagement and concentration of his or her peers, who may lose track of the narrative thread. This reduces leverage. When you've committed to a full paragraph, you lose your ability to cut a primary reader's session short and have him or her try again with a better passage without it becoming obvious. If you don't specify the length of the read, you can shorten or lengthen as you need to in the interest of both the primary reader and the rest of the class.

Keep the Identity of the Next Reader Unpredictable

If you move quickly from one primary reader to another, students focus more closely on following along. This is doubly true if they don't know who the next primary reader will be. A teacher who announces that she'll go around the room in a predictable fashion gives away this part of her leverage. Students can tune out until their turn is near. Holding on to your ability to choose the next reader also allows you to match students to passages more effectively. Retaining unpredictability makes for better leverage and better reading.

Keep Durations Short

Reading for short segments maximizes the concentration of the primary reader. It allows students to invest expressive energy in reading and focus intently on and sustain fluent and even dramatic reading. This yields higher-quality oral reading and makes the lesson more engaging. Moving quickly among primary readers also keeps the pacing lively. The lesson feels quick and energetic as a result rather than tedious and slow. Knowing that segments tend to be short and may end at any time because they aren't predictable also reinforces for secondary readers that they will likely soon get a chance themselves to read, and this keeps them from tuning out. Keeping durations short allows you to take better advantage of a crucial form of data: every time you switch readers, you gather data about your leverage. When you say, "Pick up please, Charles," and Charles jumps in with the next sentence without missing a beat, you know Charles was reading alongside the previous reader on his own. Ideally, you want this sort of seamless transition every time you switch readers, and switching frequently allows you to gather and manage this more frequently and broadly. The more data you have, the more information and tools you will have to help you ensure leverage.

Reduce Transaction Costs

A transaction cost is the amount of resources needed to execute an exchange; it can be economic, verbal, or something else. If it takes you three days of driving to different stores to find the best price on a TV, your transaction cost is high (three days of your time)—possibly higher in dollar value than the potential savings you'd get from buying the less expensive TV. When you manage finite resources like time and attention, as teachers do, transaction costs are both critically important and easy to miss. A shopper spending three days searching for a twenty-dollar savings on a TV might think he's gotten a steal, but if he spent one of those days working and then bought the more expensive TV, he'd have both more than ten dollars and two days left over.

A transaction cost is implicit in every transition in the classroom, especially in transitions you make frequently, like moving from one reader to the next. Still, many teachers fail to recognize their significance. A transaction that takes more than a few seconds steals reading time and risks interrupting the continuity of what students are reading,

> *A transaction cost is implicit in every transition in the classroom, especially in transitions you make frequently, like moving from one reader to the next.*

thus affecting how well students follow and comprehend the text.

Make it your goal to transition from one primary reader to another quickly and with a minimum of words—and ideally in a consistent way. "Susan, pick up," is a much more efficient transition than, "Thank you, Stephen. Nicely read. Susan will you begin reading, please?" Since it's more than three times as quick, the first transaction reduces threefold the amount of time students are not reading. It also keeps the narrative thread vibrant and alive in students' minds since it's subject to less interruption. Because it's quick, it also allows you to step in and use it at almost any natural pause in the text, which gives you more control over when to choose a new primary reader.

Use Bridging to Maintain Continuity

In bridging, a teacher reads a short segment of text—a bridge—between primary student readers. In a typical sequence of bridging, a teacher might allow Stewart to read for three sentences and then read one sentence herself. Then she might allow Mary to read four sentences and read two sentences herself before asking John to read for six sentences and reading one herself and then passing off to Jane. The benefit of this method is that it moves the story along quickly and keeps the narrative thread alive, while interspersing teacher-quality expressive reading, which maximizes comprehension. I am arguing for discretionary bridging when it's important to keep the narrative thread alive and create more opportunities to model. Generally the harder the text, the more you might consider bridging. But you needn't necessarily always bridge.

Oral Cloze

I learned the oral cloze technique from watching Roberto de Leon teach reading to third-grade boys at Excellence Charter School for Boys in Bedford Stuyvesant. In one example, de Leon kicked off his reading of *Phantom of the Opera* by leaving a word out at the end of his first sentence: "Carlotta had the . . . ," he read, snapping quietly on the word *the* to alert his students that they should fill in the blank. On the day in question, only a handful of his boys chimed in "leading role" exactly on cue. So Rob started over, "Ooh, some boys weren't quite with us. Let's try that again. 'Carlotta had the . . . ,'" and all his boys chimed in with "leading role" demonstrating that they were now following along. This quick device, which de Leon uses throughout his lessons, allows him to quickly and simply assess leverage.

Rely on a Placeholder

As the best reading teachers move between reading and questioning their students about what they read, they use quick and reliable prompts to ensure that their students recognize the transition and react promptly. I call this prompt a *placeholder,* because it is used to ensure that students retain their place in the text so they can quickly and immediately transition *back* to reading after discussion. "Hold your place. Track me," announces Patrick Pastore, modeling for his sixth graders how to point to the spot where they left off reading *Esperanza Rising,* close their books partway, and engage his eyes to show they are ready to discuss. After a brief discussion of why Esperanza and Miguel react differently to a train ride, he instructs, "Pick up reading please, Melanie." In less than two seconds, she and her classmates are back into the book at almost no transaction cost.

"Finger in your book; close your book," intones de Leon as he prepares his students to discuss *Phantom of the Opera* and also prepares them to end that discussion and return to the book efficiently. Leadership Prep's Hannah Lofthus uses a similar expression ("finger freeze"), with her third graders, modeling for them how to keep their place when the reading is interrupted.

SEE IT IN ACTION: CLIP 22

CONTROL THE GAME

In clip 22 on the DVD, Hilary Lewis of Leadership Prep Bedford Stuyvesant demonstrates Control the Game. As she bounces quickly and unpredictably from reader to reader, all six students she calls on (using just their names to signal the change, which results in an ultra-low transaction cost) are able to pick up reading right away. The data tell us that Lewis's leverage is high: students are reading along with the primary reader. In addition to exemplary modeling of the elements of Control the Game, you'll also see Hilary Lewis marking the spot on occasional decoding errors (for example, "Try that again please").

Want to read more? Check out the interview with Hilary Lewis in the Appendix of this book.

CHAPTER ELEVEN

THE FUNDAMENTALS

Teaching Decoding, Vocabulary Development, and Fluency

Once you've mastered the skills in Chapter Ten and have your students reading more frequently and with greater leverage, mastering the methods of champion teachers in three core elements of literacy instruction—decoding, vocabulary, and fluency—can increase the quality and productivity of your students' reading, making them more attentive, more expressive readers and building a foundation that will increase the comprehension they take from their reading, no matter what subject you teach.

DECODING

Decoding is the process of deciphering written text to identify the spoken words it represents. Although decoding might appear at first to be a mundane, lower-order skill, its mastery is a prerequisite to all reading comprehension and thus to most learning. It's the foundation. Incomplete mastery of decoding can persist well beyond the elementary grades and detract from the success of even apparently advanced students. If a third-grade student labors over just two or three of the words in a sentence, concentrating his energy on piecing together each letter's contribution, he will likely have little memory left over to absorb the meaning of the sentence or even to remember the beginning by the time he reaches the end. If a middle school student in history class reads a passage about the causes of the Civil War but leaves the *s* off the verbs, the syntax of the sentence will erode. The student may remember pieces of the main point but will fail to develop a cohesive understanding. If a high school student allocates much of her mental energy to sounding out new terms in a passage about representative government—*filibuster, cloture,* and *perquisite*—she may fail to attend to much else or even imprint the words' meanings. If she gets the names or words wrong or breezes over them with only the roughest approximations, she may fail to recognize them in future discussion, conversation, or reading.

Given the bedrock importance of decoding at every level, teachers should strive to correct decoding errors whenever possible, no matter what subject or grade level they teach. Since these errors often indicate a broader lack of knowledge or skills, reinforcing general rules and ensuring that students practice decoding are the antidotes. However, many teachers who correct decoding errors fail to do either of these, opting instead to correct the error and ask the student to make an "echo correction"—that is, to repeat the correct word without decoding it. There are times when an echo correction is necessary, but it only gets the student through the word in the immediate situation. It doesn't increase the likelihood of success the next time the student encounters the word.

So what sorts of actions are better than an echo correction? If a student can't read *might,* the best way to correct such a decoding error may be to improve her knowledge of the rules. After all, she's likely to struggle with *sight* and *tight* as well. Rather than saying, "That word is *might,*" the teacher might say, "–i-g-h-t says 'ite.' Now try that word again." This has two benefits: it requires the student to incorporate the new information and then decode the original word successfully, and it reinforces a rule she can use on other high-frequency words. The next time the teacher corrects, he or she might say, "'-i-g-h-t' says . . . ?" and ask the student to recall and then apply the rule. In most cases, asking students to self-correct by applying a rule or new information—"That vowel is a long *a.* Now try that word again," is another typical example—is powerful because it addresses the cause, not just the symptom, and thus contributes to a long-term solution.

Even so, exceptions are the rule in English—arguably one of our language's most distinguishing characteristics. Many words are simply impossible or unrewarding to decode. In fact, sight words are often learned by rote specifically because rules do not apply to them. Where the ideal of self-correcting isn't possible, the key is to recognize such cases quickly so as not to waste time and create confusion.

Transaction Costs and Decoding

A transaction cost is the amount of resources it takes to execute an exchange—be it economic, verbal, or something else. Think again of the ten dollar "savings" on the TV in the example in Chapter Ten. Transaction costs are most important in those interactions that happen frequently since frequency multiplies the importance of efficiency. This makes managing transaction costs especially relevant to addressing decoding errors.

Decoding errors are common and usually of short duration—a student reads "hope" as "hop" and the whole sequence, whether it gets corrected or not, lasts just a second or two. Correcting decoding errors consistently is important in helping your students build strong reading habits and reducing the transaction cost of your corrections is arguably the most important factor in your success—not just in improving students' decoding skills but in ensuring a successful lesson overall. Except in cases where your lesson objective focuses on decoding skills, you should strive for the lowest possible transaction cost in making corrections. This requires rigorous economy of language. Consider these two corrections of a student's decoding error:

> Teacher 1: You said in-SPEAK-tion. Can you go back to the beginning of the sentence and read that word again?

> Teacher 2: In-*SPEAK*-tion?

The difference between these corrections may seem trivial but is in fact huge. Time how long it takes you to say each of these statements aloud. The time it takes to say the first phrase—the transaction cost—is at least five times greater than the transaction cost of the second. Every extra word the first teacher says takes time and disrupts the flow of student concentration on the story. Thus, every extra word potentially disrupts comprehension. If you used the second phrase to correct, you could make three or four interventions in the time you could make just one with the first phrase. While you should correct consistently to help students decode effectively, doing so quickly and seamlessly is the only way to make correction viable. Like the second teacher, you should strive to make a habit of using the simplest and quickest intervention. If you are consistent in the manner that you do so, your students will get in the habit of self-correcting quickly and efficiently.

Two of the most efficient correction methods in terms of transaction cost are "punch the error" (quickly repeating the misread word back to the student while inflecting your voice to make it a question) and "mark the spot" (rereading the three or four words prior to the word on which the student made the error, and inflecting your voice to show that the student should continue the reading from the point where you stop).

An echo correction makes for a very low transaction cost, but as I have noted, it does not ask the student to decode. Echo corrections may be worthwhile when you're reading an especially important section of a text and can't afford even a minimal distraction. Otherwise, these corrections are best for sight words that defy the rules and logic of decoding.

Address Decoding Errors Even When Students "Know" the Rule

A certain proportion of reading errors are due to carelessness, haste, or sloppy reading habits. For example, some students habitually leave the *s* or other ending sounds off words, even though they know they are supposed to read them. These errors remain important to correct nonetheless. They still interfere with comprehension and, to paraphrase Mark Twain, the student who does not read words correctly has little advantage over the student who cannot read them correctly. This is yet another argument for lowering your transaction cost: in many cases, the key part is not so much the added information as the reminder to go back and reread more carefully, an important habit to build.

Techniques for Addressing Decoding Errors

Observing champion reading teachers in action has allowed me to develop what I hope is a clear and actionable list of the specific methods they use most often in correcting decoding errors. These methods allow you to correct errors consistently, with a minimal transaction cost, and in a manner that causes students to self-correct. Because these approaches are all relatively straightforward, you should be able to do them reliably and consistently with just a little bit of practice.

In many cases, the examples of various correction techniques provided in this section are wordier (they have a higher transaction cost) than they would be in actual classroom use. I've done this to make them clearer, but teachers should always strive to streamline. In the two examples, in Punch the Error, which follows, I encourage dropping the phrases, "Can you get the last part?" and "Try it again," as soon as students come to understand that those parts of the directions are implicit.

Punch the Error

- Repeat the word a student misread back to him or her, replicating and putting emphasis on the part where the error occurred. *Examples:* "Is that word in-SPEEK-tion??" "CARE-pet??"

- After a student makes a decoding error, repeat or describe the part of the word he or she read correctly. *Examples:* "You got the first two sounds." "*Express* is right. Can you get the last part?"

- Sometimes students get the right sounds in the wrong order. Punch this error by identifying the correct order of sounds. *Example:* "The *i* comes before the *r.* Try it again."

Mark the Spot

- Reread the three or four words immediately prior to the word on which the student was unable to decode, inflecting your voice (usually by extending the last syllable or two of the last word) to show that the student should pick up there. *Example:* When the student reads, "He ran though the door," the teacher corrects with, "He ran . . ."

Name the Sound

- Name the sound a letter should make, and ask students to repeat and apply it.
  - Identify the sound a vowel is making, especially whether it is making a long or short sound, and ask students to apply it. *Examples:* "[That's a] long *a.*" "Long vowels say their name." "Read that again: a long *a.*"
  - Identify the sound a consonant is making, especially whether a *C, G,* or *S* is making a hard or soft sound, and ask the student to apply it. *Examples:* "[That's a] soft *c.*" "Hard *c* like cat/soft *c* like city." "Hard *g* like golf/soft *g* like gym."

- Name the sound a group of letters is making, and ask students to repeat and apply. *Examples:* "-*TCH* says 'chuh' " [with the instruction to try again understood]. "-*EA* says 'ay.' "

- If there's a clear and identifiable rule, remind students of it, and ask them to apply it. Examples: "E at the end makes the vowel says its name." "Silent E makes that a long *a.*"

- Here are the most common rules that every teacher should be prepared to reinforce:

  - *Long vowels:* In a long vowel sound, a letter says its name (e.g., the *a* in cape). With the exception of times when they're followed by the letter *r,* long vowel sounds are very consistent. You should be able to prompt students with: "Long *e*" and have them self-correct.

  - *Short vowels:* In a short vowel sound, a letter says something, well, shorter than its long form (e.g., the *a* in cap). With the exception of times when they're followed by the letter *r*, short vowel sounds are consistent (almost as consistent as long vowels). You should be able to prompt students with: "Short *e*" and have them self-correct.

  - *Silent* e *(makes the vowel say its name):* When a word's pattern is vowel-consonant-e, the *e* is almost always silent and the preceding vowel is long (says its name). You should be able to prompt students "Silent *e*" (or "Tricky *e*") and have them self-correct.

  - *Bossy* r *(makes her first car turn):* Vowels followed by *r* usually make their own sound—distinct from the long or short sound and often similar to other "*r*-controlled" vowel sounds. The sounds in *first* and *turn* are the same; the *a* in car isn't short *or* long! You should be able to prompt students to remember "bossy *r*" and have them self-correct.

  - *Soft/hard* C: Hard *c* says *car*. Soft *c* says *cent*. You should be able to prompt students "Soft *c*" (or "Hard *c*") and have them self-correct.

  - *Soft/hard* G: Hard *g* says *gas*. Soft *g* says *gentleman*. You should be able to prompt students "Soft *g*"(or "Hard *g*") and have them self-correct.

  - -tion *says* shun: You should be able to prompt students "-*tion* says *shun*" and have them self-correct.

  - -ight *says* ite: You should be able to prompt students "-*ight* says *ite*" and have them self-correct.

  - -igh *says* I: You should be able to prompt students "-*igh* says *I*" and have them self-correct.

  - *Slyly:* When a word ends in −*y*, it most often makes an *i* sound if the word is one syllable and an *e* sound if it has multiple syllables. Think *dry* and *democracy* or *sly* and *slyly*. Because it contains both, use *slyly* as your cue. You should be able to prompt students *slyly* and have them self-correct.

- Give the student a more familiar example of a troubling letter sequence from which to model. *Example:* For a student struggling to read the word *would:* "You know *could,* so this must be . . . ?"

Chunk It

- Help students chunk difficult words by recognizing familiar patterns and words-within-words. *Examples:* If a student struggles to read the word *hope-less:* "Do you see a part of that you already know?" "The first four letters are a word you know." "Cover the '–less,' and read what you have."

- Affirm and reiterate what the student got right, focusing him on the problem chunk. *Example:* "You got *hope*, but the second part isn't '-ing.' "

- Ask students to read a confusing word without a suffix or prefix first. *Example:* " 'Re'– is a prefix. Try reading the word without it. Cover up the *r* and the *e*. Now what do you have?"

Speed the Exceptions

- When a word does not conform to standard rules, identify the correct pro-nunciation quickly and directly. *Example:* "That word is written 'bury' but pronounced 'berry.' We'll just have to remember it." "That word is *through*."

- If a student should know a word's distinctive pronunciation (it is a sight word or has recently been discussed), quickly identify it as an exception. *Example:* "That's one of our sight words." "That word doesn't follow the rules, but we studied it yesterday."

- If there's a specific rule the word breaks, identify that rule if you can to make the reasoning clear. *Example:* "We'd expect the *e* to make that *I* say "g-IVE" [as in *hive*] but this word is an exception."

It's also important to use quick and simple positive reinforcement when students read a word correctly not only because it encourages them but it also lets them know explicitly that they got it right. Since correction of mispronunciation and misreading is inconsistent at best in their lives, they may not know when they've gotten a word correct. As students continue reading, say "yup," "perfect," "you got it," "nice," and so on. You can also increase efficiency by reducing the amount of time students spend pausing and wondering whether they've gotten a tough word correct. Obviously you want this method to speed, not slow, your reading. You can minimize your transaction costs by making the phrases you use to reinforce both quick and consistent (too much variation draws too much attention to your words).

Cueing Systems

Good readers often begin to read a word incorrectly but arrive at the right pronunciation by using knowledge of letters and sounds, grammar and syntax, and context to develop plausible options. Experts call these *cueing systems* because they are three separate ways students infer information about words.

Experienced teachers and reading specialists should carefully encourage students to use and develop these cueing systems to address decoding errors:

Letter and Sound Cueing

Text reads: "The dog growls."

Student reads: "The dog barks."

Teacher says: "If it was *bark*, there would be a *b* at the beginning. [pointing to the letter *g*] Is this a *b*?"

Grammar and Syntax Cueing

Text reads: "The boys wore their coats."

Student reads: "The boys wore their coat."

Teacher says: "The boys all shared one coat? Is that correct?"

Although using students' knowledge of grammar and syntax can be useful, teachers should avoid instructing students to use what "sounds right" since what sounds right to readers who have not internalized standard rules of grammar is unreliable at best.

Meaning and Context Cueing

Text reads: "Clowns wear makeup and fake noses."

Student reads: "Clowns wear makeup and face noses."

Teacher says: "Does it makes sense that they would wear face noses?"

Poor readers often rely excessively on meaning and context cueing systems. Be careful not to encourage them to rely exclusively on techniques that do not reinforce actual letter and sound decoding.

VOCABULARY

Students need a rich vocabulary to understand what they read, and the importance of word knowledge is redoubled by the fact that, as E. D. Hirsch, whose books on cultural literacy led to the founding of the Core Knowledge program, points out its effect compounds over time. Whether a student learns the word *taiga* as she's reading a passage about subarctic climates may depend in part on whether she knows what *tundra* means. In his book *The Knowledge Deficit,* Hirsch describes this as a Matthew effect. Simply put with vocabulary, the rich get richer and the poor get poorer. The term was first coined by sociologist Robert K. Merton in 1968 and takes its name from a line in the biblical Gospel of Matthew:

> *For to all those who have, more will be given, and they will have an abundance; but from those who have nothing, even what they have will be taken away.*

Students who know more words learn more words. In fact, research suggests that a ten-thousand-word vocabulary gap exists between students of privilege and students from less advantaged backgrounds by the time they reach tenth grade. This disparity in and of itself may account for a significant part of the learning gap.

But while teaching vocabulary is critically important, all types of teaching vocabulary are not equal. Good vocabulary instruction starts with a student-friendly definition that's simple and clear. While some teachers believe that arriving at the definition is the goal of vocabulary work, champion teachers start there and spend their time having students practice using words widely and richly *after* they know the basic meaning. They recognize that knowing a definition is a long way from being able to use a word effectively in writing or thought. They recognize that it is more powerful to ask students, "How would you use it?" When would you use it?" or "How is it different from [a similar word]?" than to guess, "What do you think that might mean?" In fact, a correct guess may be a dangerous false positive, suggesting that a student knows what a word means, when in reality, she understands it only at the most basic, and therefore insufficient, level.

Many teachers also use a synonym model in teaching vocabulary: defining a word by finding a viable synonym. This technique has critical flaws, however (*Bringing Words to Life: Robust Vocabulary Instruction* by Isabel L. Beck, Margaret G. McKeown, and Linda Kucan). Even if two words overlap significantly in their meaning, they are not the same, and it is the difference between the two that matters. Consider *mimic* and *imitate*, two words that might be taught as synonyms. *Mimicry* usually implies mocking, often for humorous effect, while *imitation* can be neutral or negative. However, even when negative, it implies something cheap and not the derisive sense that *mimic* carries. This difference accounts for a disproportionately large share of the meaning either word contributes to a written passage. A scene in which Billy *mimics* his teacher makes for a very different story than does one in which he *imitates* her. A student who sees these words as interchangeable misses that critical difference not just in the words but in the passage as well. Teaching deep word knowledge means helping students understand how a word is similar to and different from similar words, and it unlocks shades of meaning in the author's word choice. That is, focusing on difference prepares students to use vocabulary functionally and increase their reading comprehension.

Although the skill of inferring vocabulary from context appears frequently on state assessments, teaching vocabulary primarily by context clues is also far less effective in the long run. Contexts can be vague, nondirective, or misdirective. Even if students learn to infer word meaning correctly much of the time, they are still essentially making guesses, and often erroneous ones at that. More significant, deep word knowledge, a better predictor of achievement than broad word knowledge, can rarely be grasped from context-based instruction. Strong vocabulary must be systematically and directly taught.

Finally, since good vocabulary instruction requires a significant investment of time, choices of which words to invest in are important. Some words are more worthy of investment than others. Generally teachers should invest time in teaching tier 2 words, which are relevant to student's lives, likely to appear again, and respond well to instruction. Tier 1 words such as *awesome* and *cafeteria* are basic words that students at a given grade level should know. They appear frequently in oral rather than written language and are too common or easy to warrant significant investment of a teacher's time. Tier 3 words such as *microbe* and *piccolo* have a low frequency of use, and they tend to be used in specific domains. They are less worthy of investment because they are least likely to appear again in other parts of a student's life.

If there are too many tier 2 words to teach (there often are), invest in words that relate best to what you're teaching (either the content of what you're reading or other vocabulary words). If you're reading a passage on the Civil War, *hostility* might be especially useful (and memorable). If you're reading a novel about social class, the word *dignified* might be a strong choice. And teaching *dignified* might make a strong case for including words like *haughty* and *aspire* since they could be compared, contrasted, and used as a group, making the whole larger than sum of their parts.

Since the approach described here involves intentional teaching of vocabulary—that is, teaching words regularly, consistently, and often before (or even regardless of whether) they come up in an authentic text—it's worth looking at a possible road map for introducing vocabulary words.

Six Techniques to Reinforce Strong Vocabulary

Observing champion reading teachers in action has allowed me to develop what I hope is a clear and actionable list of the specific methods they use to reinforce vocabulary, especially depth of word knowledge. These methods allow you to reinforce word knowledge, in a variety of settings. Because these approaches are all relatively straightforward, you should be able to do them reliably and consistently with just a little bit of practice.

1. **Multiple takes.** To enter a word into their functioning memory, students need to hear a word (and ideally its pronunciation) multiple times. Try to get them myriad quick exposures after introducing a word.

- Have students practice using a word in different settings and situations and give an example of a time when they might use it.
  - "What animal would you most want for a companion?"
  - "What's the most nutritious thing you've eaten today?"
  - "Can you think of a character in a movie or on TV who wears a disguise?"
  - "When would it be especially important to be precise?"
- Circle back to words you previously taught—yesterday, last week, or last month.
  - "Who can recall a vocabulary word we've studied this month that means not having enough of something?"
- Give students a sentence stem with a vocabulary word, and ask them to finish it.
  - "My mother stared at me with astonishment; she never imagined that . . ."
- Have students practice saying words correctly.
  - "That word is pronounced 'FLOO-Id.' Everybody say that."
  - "What vocabulary word did we have that can refer to a liquid?"

2. **Compare, combine, contrast.** Beware the "synonym model." It's the difference between similar words that creates meaning in a passage.

- Ask students to distinguish between or compare two different words; focus on nuances of meaning.

  "Can anyone describe how *indifferent* is different from *apathetic*?"

- Ask students to describe how and whether they could combine vocabulary words.

  "Could a tyrant ever be humble?"

  "What kind of disguise could be vibrant?"

- Ask students to apply and discuss a change (ideally to a similar word).

  "How would the meaning of what Mr. Beasley said change if he used the word *furious*?"

  "How would it make James different if he mimicked Sue instead of imitating her?"

  "What does *mimic* have in common with *spiteful*?"

3. **Upgrade.** Find opportunities to use richer and more specific words whenever possible.

- Ask students to use recently introduced words in class discussions.

  "We have a vocabulary word for weather that's hot and damp. Can you use it?"

  "Who can summarize the first chapter using the word *desolate*?"

- Ask explicitly for a better word.

  "Can you use a better word than *big*?"

  "James is upset when he's speaking. Let me hear me hear you describe how he talked with a better word than *said*."

4. **Stress the syntax.** Students often struggle to use new words in different settings. They know *inadvertent* but can't turn it onto *inadvertently*. They say, "I am feeling inadvertent."

- Ask students to identify or change a word's part of speech.

  "What part of speech is *stride* here, Susan?"

  "Can you use *stride* as a noun instead?"

  "How would I make *inadvertent* an adverb?"

- Ask students to identify or change a word's tense.

    "Can you think of a sentence that uses *cower* in the past tense?"

    "Can you put that sentence in the third person?"

5. **Back to roots.** Stress the foundational knowledge of roots so students can apply their understanding to new words.

- Ask students to identify roots or affixes and describe how they relate to meaning.

    "Why is the root *ped-* in the word *pedestrian*?"

    "What might *monolith* and *lithograph* have to do with a stone?"

- Ask students to identify other words containing a root.

    "*Telepathy* is sending or reading thoughts and feelings from far away. What other *tele-* words have 'far away' in their meaning?"

6. **Picture this.** Create a multidimensional image of each new word by using pictures and actions.

- Help students visualize words by giving them a picture that exemplifies a word they've learned. Or have students draw their own picture of a word.

- Ask students to act out or personify a word.

    "Show me what you would look like if you were furious."

    "Who can swagger across the room?"

- Have students develop gestures to help them remember words. Give them the word, and ask for the gesture. Give them the gesture, and have them provide the word. *Example:* For the word *idyllic*, students skip once to signify skipping through the woods, an exaggeratedly idyllic way to spend an afternoon.

Vocabulary Methods for Specialists

Reading and language arts teachers take on the additional challenge of introducing vocabulary instruction more systematically into their classes. Teachers at one high-performing middle school use the following sequence to introduce vocabulary words. It applies many of the techniques above and requires ten to fifteen minutes at the outset of each class to teach one or two new words as follows:

1. Provide the definition and part of speech of a new vocabulary word.

2. Provide a similar word, ideally one with which students are familiar, and explain how the vocabulary word is similar but different. Have students suggest times when they might use the word in question and why.

3. Show students a picture that portrays the vocabulary word. Explain why the picture is a representation of the word.

4. Create a sentence, written by the class with your guidance, that reflects the word's meaning in a complete thought.

5. List and discuss variations on the word, identifying their part of speech: "*Apathetic* can be a noun, *apathy*. Or I could make it an adverb by adding a suffix. What suffix would I add to make *apathetic* an adverb?"

6. Play vocabulary-reinforcing activities and games using multiple takes and compare, combine, contrast.

7. Write a sentence independently (usually as homework) using the word correctly and according to standards for quality vocabulary sentences.

FLUENCY

In the standard definition, *fluency* consists of automaticity (the ability to read at a rapid rate without error) and expression (the ability to group words together into phrases to reflect meaning, emphasize important words, and express tone and register). You could argue, however, that fluency consists of automaticity plus expression plus comprehension. That is, to read a text expressively, the reader has to comprehend it. What are the register, tone, and mood like? Which words deserve special emphasis? How does the punctuation shape the meaning? In short, fluency isn't more than fast reading; it's reading with the meaning made audible.

True expressive and fluent reading demonstrates comprehension—in some cases, more efficiently than talking about or describing that understanding. It embeds the understanding in the action of fluent reading. And while many teachers think of fluency as a skill that's most relevant in the elementary grades, the opposite may be true. Developing students' ability to comprehend the full amount of information carried within the text relies on an "expressive ear" that can extract meaning from subtext, tone, register, innuendo, and analogy. Mature books rely even more heavily for their meaning on the portion of the argument carried by these subtextual elements. Unlocking those forms of meaning must be continually practiced and modeled even, and especially, in the later years. The best way to truly understand Shakespeare, experts will tell you, is to read it aloud. And of course the other key to understanding Shakespeare—or any other text—is to be able to read it quickly and efficiently and with sufficient brain cells left over for thinking about things other than what the words were.

Four Techniques to Reinforce Strong Fluency

Observing champion reading teachers in action has allowed me to develop what I hope is a clear and actionable list of the specific methods they use most often to reinforce fluent and expressive reading. These methods allow you to reinforce both automaticity and comprehension in a way that most students will find enjoyable. Because these approaches are all relatively straightforward, you should be able to do them reliably and consistently with just a little bit of practice.

• **Show some spunk.** Read aloud to your students regularly. When you do, model strong reading and expressive emphasis. This may involve some risk taking—if you're not inclined to drama—but not only will you show them how to unlock the expressive parts of language, you'll make it safe for them to take the risk of reading with spirit and vigor. This is equally important whether you are reading *War and Peace*, *Owl at Home*, "A Summary of the Oxygen Cycle," or the directions to a word problem. In fact, students may be least familiar with how to extract meaning from the last two examples and thus may get the most out of hearing those read aloud.

A particularly important time to show some spunk is at the start of a longer section of oral reading or when starting up again after a break for discussion. Reading the first few sentences yourself models expressiveness, normalizing it and helping to sustain and engage interest in the text by getting it off to an exciting start. The verve and energy you bring to oral reading will be modeled in your students' oral (and silent) reading.

Talking about modeling effective reading raises questions, however, about what to model and how. Here are two thoughts. The first is to group the words. Reading is like making music. The notes and rests have different lengths, both in how they are written and in the subtleties of how they are played. In the sentence, "Reading is like making music," for example, the words *making* and *music* run together slightly more than the other words for most readers. Readers tend to group those words for emphasis and rhythm, and the sentence's meaning shifts subtly as a result. As with music, some of the meaning is made visible by punctuation; other aspects are less obvious. When you read, help students recognize how the music in reading is played by grouping consciously. Seek to model stringing words together in fluid groups—the longer the better. For example, look for words in prepositional phrases to stick together, for a drop in the voice, and a slight acceleration for a parenthetical.

Another technique to follow in modeling oral reading is to identify especially important words in a passage and emphasize them. One benefit of this technique is that when students implement it, they are required to engage their full intellectual faculties in deciding what words are in fact most important. Their choices present a fruitful topic for discussion and a valuable source of data about their reading. One Shakespearean expert I know proposed that the best way to read the Bard is to find and emphasize contrast words and emphasize the tension between them as you read. You can start students off more simply by having them look for transition words (*after, instead, suddenly*) and comparative and superlatives (*darker, faster, saddest, fullest*) to emphasize.

• **Ask for some drama.** Just as your reading expressively is good for students, so too is asking students to read expressively. It forces them to practice looking for the depth of meaning in words. To make oral reading more systematically expressive, try the following:

- Identify (by telling students or helping them to infer it) the kind of expression your students should impart to the passage and ask them to apply it. "Wilbur is upset, Diamond. Can you read that sentence in a way that shows that?" You could also ask students to first infer Wilbur's mood and then ask them to model: "How is Wilbur feeling right now? What emotion is he feeling? Good. Can you show me that?"

- Call students' attention to dialogue tags and their role as "stage directions." "The passage says, '"I don't want any," Mr. Malone said sharply.' Read that again so his words are sharp." You can make this technique even more effective by modeling the applicable tone when you read the dialogue tag and asking students to apply it to the sentence they are reading. In other words, in the example, you would say the word *sharply* in a sharp tone of voice that students could mimic and apply to the sentence.

- Ask students to identify the two or three most important words in a sentence (or the two or three most important ideas in a passage) and place special emphasis on them.

- Ask students to add to or extract something particular to or from the text by choosing a key descriptive word from the surrounding passage or even a vocabulary word and asking students to read the passage in a way that emphasized that word. For example, in a lesson at Excellence Charter School in Brooklyn, third-grade teacher Roberto de Leon responded to a student's reading of a passage from *Phantom of the Opera* by saying, "Stop. Repeat that line, and read it as though he wanted to make her obey him." *Obey* was one of the classes vocabulary words, and as he gave this instruction, de Leon held up a note card with *obey* written on it. The student reread the passage focusing on incorporating the emphasis that de Leon suggested. In another example, a teacher asked her students to read aloud from a scene in C. S. Lewis's *Prince Caspian.* After the first reading, she noted, "Look back a few sentences. It says the children are feeling gloomy as they sit and wait for the train. Can you read that again to show that the children are gloomy?" Obviously it can be especially rigorous when your line of questioning forces students to infer what tone or mood the words should carry from subtler clues. "Who can tell Danielle what kind of tone to use in reading these lines? Why do you say that?" You might even add, "Did everyone read it that way?" before asking Danielle to model the tone in her reading.

- Ask students to provide other possible interpretations of a line that a student read. De Leon is a master of this. "Oh, I love it!" he replied to a student's expressive reading. "Who else wants to read that line expressively? Maybe in a slightly different way?"

SEE IT IN ACTION: CLIP 23

FLUENCY

In clip 23 on the DVD, Roberto de Leon of Excellence Charter School of Bedford Stuyvesant demonstrates exemplary teaching of fluency. He begins this inspirational clip by using the oral cloze technique from Control the Game to test for leverage. He quickly finds he needs to restart to ensure that his students are not just listening but reading along with him (or a student reader). From here it's all fluency.

De Leon demonstrates Show Some Spunk by modeling for his students the kind of expressive reading that embeds meaning and shows comprehension. Notice how effective his pass-off is to the student who reads with the mask. Roberto models the tone of the letter he asks the student to read with the first two words and then passes off to his student midsentence. The student can now practice applying the tone Roberto has set to his own reading simply by trying to continue it—something the student does extremely successfully. The student probably wouldn't have taken the risk of reading so expressively if de Leon hadn't done so himself first. Show

Some Spunk and Ask for Some Drama are permanently and inherently connected!

Finally, notice the way Roberto uses Lather, Rinse, Repeat so effectively, embedding it within lots of positive feedback but asking the student to reread with a new emphasis: embedding the application of the vocabulary word *obey*.

In this clip, de Leon is both developing his students' reading ear and teaching them to use their reading to demonstrate comprehension. This in turn will make his evaluation of their comprehension more efficient. He'll be able to hear it.

- **Check the mechanics.** Students may see punctuation but not grasp what it is telling them to do in terms of meaning or inflection. Make explicit reference to punctuation, and ask students to demonstrate their understanding of it in their oral reading. "There's a period there. Did you stop?" "I want you to pause and breathe whenever you see a comma." "Someone is talking there, right?" Emphasize the importance of syntax—the relationship of the pieces of a sentence and its effect on meaning, which is often lost on weak readers—and the idea that *though* sets the rest of the sentence in contrast to the initial phrase is a critical part of effective reading. Ask students to identify which words told them a sentence was a question or which words told them that the two men were not alike.

- **Lather, rinse, repeat.** Don't just have students read frequently; have them reread frequently. Once students have made basic sense of the words in a sentence, ask them to go back and reread specifically for fluency. Here are three particular reasons for a reread:

- *To smooth out an original read that was wooden or required mechanical correction.* "Okay, now that you've got the words, let's go back and read it with energy. This is an exciting part of the book!"

- *To emphasize some aspect of meaning or incorporate feedback.* "Okay, good. Now read that sentence [or passage] again, and try to show how scared they are." "Can you go back and put special emphasis on the words that show the boys are scared?"

- *For fun or because the original read was especially good.* "Oh that was great! Can you read it again so we can all hear how surly you made it sound?"

SEE IT IN ACTION: CLIP 24

FLUENCY

In clip 24 on the DVD, Hannah Lofthus of Leadership Prep Bedford Stuyvesant demonstrates exemplary teaching of fluency. In this clip you'll hear in her student readers the clear results of the consistent use of Ask for Some Drama, but the epiphany I take away from this clip is how powerful Lather, Rinse, Repeat can be when it's used to give positive in addition to constructive feedback. Lofthus asks her student to read the passage again because he showed "fantastic expression," both celebrating and analyzing a great student read with the rest of the class. The expressiveness the final reader brings to her reading as the clip closes just can't be a coincidence.

For fans of *Strong Voice* (technique 38 in Chapter Six) you'll also notice Lofthus using the self-interrupt method of ensuring that she doesn't talk over students. It might be interesting to compare and contrast it to Sultana Noormuhammad's self-interrupt in clip 17.

CHAPTER TWELVE

COMPREHENSION

Teaching Students to Understand What They Read

Comprehension—understanding a text's full meaning and relevance—is the ultimate aim of reading. Comprehension is often difficult to teach directly, however, because it encompasses so much and relies on so many different skills. Still, one theme reflected in this chapter is the importance of testing the assumption that when students cannot answer questions that test an understanding of a text's full meaning and relevance, the problem is that they don't grasp the broader concepts those questions directly address. In fact, many times students cannot answer deeper questions not because they don't know how to think in a broad or abstract manner but because they failed to understand what they read fully and are trying to make cognitive leaps from a faulty base of underlying knowledge.

Champion teachers, I have observed, do ask rigorous and challenging questions to assess students' knowledge of a text's full meaning and relevance, but they also put intensive focus on often unacknowledged barriers to comprehension. Word- and phrase-level questions are a prime example. Failure to understand colloquial expressions and phrases or the syntax of a complex sentence (who, for example, a certain pronoun refers back to) is common among students who arrive in class with underdeveloped language skills. Therefore asking questions like "Who's 'he' in that sentence?" or "What does the author mean when she writes that Harry 'flashed his teeth,' and what does that tell you about him?" are effective questions not just for ensuring solid comprehension of basic facts in a passage but because they are necessary to higher-level comprehension. In a key scene in C. S. Lewis's *The Lion, the Witch and the Wardrobe,* for example, Aslan, the heroic lion, "turns on" the witch. A reader who fails to understand that to "turn on" someone means to do more than to turn around but to do so with the intent to attack will miss the building tension in the scene and fail to understand it. I am not arguing for an exclusive focus on word- and phrase-level questions but for the recognition that such questions are as necessary to understanding gaps in student comprehension as broader and deeper questions that appear to better assess their knowledge of the big picture.

> *In a nutshell, the assumption that's broken down by watching champion teachers in action is the idea that instruction that teaches comprehension skills should necessarily look like instruction that relies on those skills once established.*

In a nutshell, the assumption that's broken down by watching champion teachers in action is the idea that instruction that teaches comprehension skills should necessarily look like instruction that relies on those skills once established. This challenge is exacerbated by the fact that so many of us became acclimated to teaching that relies on established comprehension skills in college (and often high school). Its look and feel have been normalized for us and literature classes have replaced reading classes in our minds' eye. As a result, many teachers skip over steps like confirming understanding of key phrases and events in a test in order to get to "deeper" conversations about a book's place in the world on the assumption that the latter discussions are more rigorous. However, this is not necessarily true, as classrooms that build strong comprehension skills rather than using them to engage in interpretation maintain higher standards for the use of evidence to support opinions, for example.

TECHNIQUES FOR BUILDING COMPREHENSION

I've described some of the key methods champion teachers use and adapt to teach comprehension following. I've grouped them into three categories according to when in the reading process they take place: before, during, or after reading.

Prereading Techniques

Top reading teachers often begin the reading process by preteaching students critical facts and context they'll need to understand in order to make sense of the text they're about to read. If students don't really know what a Nazi is when they start reading, they're not going to get what they need to out of *Number the Stars* or *Diary of Anne Frank*. Preteaching background material is usually more efficient than stopping and providing explanation and detail during reading because it prevents misunderstandings before they crop up rather than remediating them afterward. Although the argument for preteaching seems self-evident, the manner in which top teachers approach it is distinct from what's often "typical," and informed by a greater emphasis on efficiency and intentionality.

For example, when I was first teaching, we were socialized, as many teachers are today, to coax contextual information out of students with KWL charts. We would list in two columns (1) things students said they already knew and (2) things they said they wanted to learn. The "Things I Know" column, I came to realize, asked students to make unsubstantiated guesses about the things they knew least about or led to our developing a wide-ranging list of "facts" of varying degrees of importance and accuracy. The "Want to Know" column was similarly grounded in lack of knowledge—often idiosyncratic or distracting from the things that were most important for students to master and many of which would never be addressed, causing me to play a shell game of pretending to be open to talking about whatever my students wanted when this was illogical and impossible. I found with some relief, then, that observation of top teachers suggested the power of delivering the necessary preliminary information in a direct, clear, and organized manner at the outset and saving the earnest list of what I want to understand for during and after the reading. Ten minutes of teacher-driven background and then getting right to reading is usually worth an hour of, "Who can tell me what Nazis were?" Efficiency matters.

The tricky part lies so much in the background knowledge you know your students will lack but the knowledge they lack that you may not realize. We've probably all experienced a version of this. We sweep a text for tricky vocabulary words before reading it with a class, for example, only to find on teaching it that a word we missed (once, twice, even several times during planning) is an obvious barrier to comprehension. In retrospect we ask: How could I have failed to see that? And of course the same thing happens with other forms of important prior knowledge. We don't always recognize the places where our students' gaps exist. You know they won't know what a Nazi was but don't realize that they know almost nothing about World War II, or the proximity and relative size of Denmark and Germany, or that Danes and Germans don't speak the same language.

What follows are some ways to ensure that prereading sets the most powerful basis for knowledge possible.

Contexting   The most basic approach to helping students comprehend a text is to give them context on it—to take them methodically through key information that will help them enter into it as informed readers, for example, what they need to know about history or science or baseball or Japan to follow the action. Contexting can take place before the introduction of a text or before reading a specific section, a chapter, say, as Lisa Delfavero of Rochester Prep recently did in preparing her fifth-graders to read one of the key scenes in Gary Paulsen's novel *Hatchet.* Lisa led off by showing her students three or four slides of a moose with full antlers. "I don't want to give too much away but it will be important for you to understand how fierce and intimidating a moose can be," she said. She wisely recognized that her students, many of whom had never left Rochester, would need that context to understand the key scene (a standoff with a moose) and accomplished the task in less than thirty seconds.

Top teachers strive for efficiency in their contexting, delivering the information directly and letting the experience of the book yield the deeper engagement. At the same time they are aggressive about finding and addressing areas where contexting might work. As E. D. Hirsch has pointed out, lack of prior knowledge is one of the key barriers to comprehension for at-risk students and it affects all aspects of reading, even fluency and decoding, as struggling with gaps soaks up the brain's processing capacity. "Prior knowledge about the topic speeds up basic comprehension and leaves working memory free to make connections between the new material and previously learned information, to draw inferences, and to ponder implications. A big difference between an expert and a novice reader—indeed between an expert and a novice in any field—is the ability to take in basic features very fast, thereby leaving the mind free to concentrate on important features" ("Reading Comprehension Requires Knowledge of Words and the World," *America Educator,* Spring 2003, p. 13).

Focal Points   Reading a rich text is like visiting a state fair or perhaps a circus, with action in every direction and full of sensory detail, voices, events, and images—maybe too many, in fact, for a reader to attend to them all. By college or even the latter years of high school, many of us find this to be the exciting part of interpretation, with each reader uncovering a unique version of events or focusing on different events in arriving at a different meaning.

Many teachers therefore model their classes on approaches to meaning similar to the ones they enjoyed so much in college. However, this aspect of reading often poses a challenge to developing readers. You learn to determine what's worthy of attention only with time and practice. Without years of practice, readers often make questionable or nonstrategic decisions about what to attend to. They notice something of tangential relevance but miss the crucial moment. The trapeze artists are in full swing, and they can't stop looking at the cotton candy seller. They see three details but fail to connect them to one another.

To help students manage the complexity of a text, champion teachers steer them in advance toward key ideas, concepts, and themes to look for. Which characters will turn out to be most important? What idea will be most relevant to the story discussion? In addition, they advise students what's secondary, not that important, or can be ignored for now. "There's a lot of discussion of their clothing. That would have told us a lot about them in the eighteenth century, but we're not going worry too much about it."

In a lesson I observed, a teacher read the short story "The Substitute" by David Lubar with her fifth graders. The story's ending is both unexpected and requires a significant inference to understand. As and even before she read, the teacher began calling students' attention to key lines and details that would help them understand the end when it arrived: "The word *conductivity* is going to be very important to understanding what happens in the story, so let's define it carefully now." "Ooh, that line is extra-important. Let's underline it. The fact that he was picked on by his students is going to prove very important in the end." By the time her students arrived at the finale, they didn't know what the surprise would be, but they had paid special attention to the key pieces of evidence and were fully prepared to make the inference that comprehending the story required.

In a lesson in his third grade classroom at Excellence Charter School of Bedford Stuyvesant, Rob de Leon set his students up for their study of *Akimbo and the Elephants* with an elegant introduction that used focal points on several levels. First Rob told his students to get ready to be surprised by the book. "One of the things you'll find about great books as you read them all your life is that they change your thinking," he told them. "This book is going to change your thinking about elephants, about poachers, and about the idea of bravery." Then to accentuate not only a theme like bravery but also their own change of opinions, he asked them to write answers to a few quick prereading questions that forced them to state their opinions about issues raised in the book (e.g., "True or false: it is acceptable to take any paying job to feed your family, even if it hurts animals") so they could track their own changing perceptions as they read.

Front-loading   In addition to introducing key ideas in advance of students reading them, the best teachers introduce key scenes before their students read them, much like movie studios make sure their multimillion-dollar bets pay off by prescreens for us in the form of previews, a series of exciting, fascinating, mysterious, or otherwise intriguing scenes from the movie. The scenes they show aren't always in narrative order. They are often quick and disconnected, designed to excite our interest and awaken suspense rather than offer a logical précis of the story to come. They front-load our exposure to critical scenes so we feel connected to the story before we begin and so we give special attention to those scenes when we come across them. We've been tipped off that they are especially dramatic and important. For a reading teacher front-loading scenes can also excite interest and increase comprehension by making the narrative seem more familiar at key points. When you encounter a scene you've seen previewed in the midst of the movie and feel as if you've seen it before or recognize that it is of primary importance, further meaning is unlocked in some of the same ways that seeing a movie or reading a text for the second or third time does.

As with a movie preview you don't necessarily need to front-load in the same order scenes will appear in the book or even with full explanation; a little mystery can help too. You goal is for your student, reading *Macbeth* for the first time, to encounter the scene where Macbeth tries to wash the blood he imagines on his hands and say, "Oh, here it is! My teacher told me about this scene!" and read it with special attention.

Here are a few examples of front-loading and focal points:

- "You're going to meet just about the cleverest and nastiest crocodile you've ever seen. Not only is he surly and mean, but wait to you see him try to disguise himself as a palm tree!"

- "For the rest of your life, you'll hear people refer to the idea of having 'blood on your hands,' and they'll mean not literal blood but the inescapable weight of guilt. That expression, that idea, was coined by Shakespeare four hundred years ago in this play. So when you see Macbeth talking about the blood on his hands, you'll know that you're reading a scene people have found unforgettable for centuries."

- "There's a big storm coming in this chapter. And the children are going to be scared. But watch and see how Sarah reacts. It's one of the moments that shows her character, so it's very important."

Prereading Summary   Summarizing occurs before, after, and during reading. I've included it here because it is especially effective as a jumping-off point for any given day's reading to summarize the previous day's. If you're using your summary to quickly prepare students to read a new section of the text, try combining questioning and narrative in a fast-paced summary. Start summarizing the reading yourself to cover key sections quickly. Stop at critical points and ask students highly focused questions to fill in the blanks: "So the two heroes fight a bloody battle. And where do they fight it, Janice? And who wins the battle, Paul? And what happens to the loser, Steven?" Obviously these questions are not as rigorous or as in-depth as summary questions you might ask after reading, but their purpose is different: to activate memory of prior reading.

The narrative portions of these summaries are often especially effective when they are quasi-dramatized in an energetic play-by-play that captures the thrill and energy of the original text by describing it in a tone that reflects the mood of the events, that is, modeling excitement when summarizing sections when characters were excited and modeling anger when characters were angry.

Prereading in Action   When reading teacher Dinah Shepherd at Roxbury Prep in Boston prepared her students to encounter *Animal Farm* by reading an article on the Russian Revolution, she talked students through a basic understanding of industrialization and communism (*contexting*). They talked briefly about how the initial idealism of communist revolutions was quickly co-opted. Shepherd directed her students to pay particular attention to the characteristics of Trotsky, Lenin, and Stalin since they would be portrayed, in allegory, in *Animal Farm* (*focal points*). As she did this, she dropped in intriguing references to scenes from the book: "When you see the pigs walking around talking . . . when you see the horse flipping her mane with blue ribbons in her hair . . . , you'll know this is no ordinary farm. That's how you know this story is an allegory" (*prescreening*). When her students began reading the novel, they did so with a keen sense of carefully honed anticipation.

During-Reading Techniques

Although an intentional approach to instruction before reading is critical to success, the types of questions you ask while students are reading are of critical importance. It's easy to assume that this importance should always mean asking broad and abstract questions. Although such questions are important, champion teachers are diligent in maintaining a balanced approach to their questions.

Don't Wait   Among the most potent facts about top teachers is that they constantly check for understanding by asking students questions to see if they "get it" frequently and throughout the passages they read. They read a few sentences or perhaps a few paragraphs and pause to ask a quick question or two, assessing whether students are following the narrative and guarding against unexpected barriers to comprehension. Their questions are often relatively straightforward. Did students absorb a key detail, make a key inference, understand a word? In asking they are careful to keep discussion limited. The goal in their questions is in fact not to discuss but to confirm understanding so students with additional thoughts are often asked to save them until a clearer discussion point.

Perhaps this sounds obvious, but watch enough instruction and you will frequently see teachers slog through a passage of several pages, holding their questions for the end and never stopping to confirm that students are still with them. An ancillary benefit of Don't Wait, by the way, is the fact that in allowing you to recognize comprehension gaps as soon as they emerge, it allows you to gather better data about the root causes of your students' comprehension difficulties. If you waited until the end of a passage, you'd likely never know the source of the problem. What's more, catching a misunderstanding is more effective as soon as it happens, in this case as soon as the sentence is misunderstood rather than several minutes later or even at the end of a paragraph and after three subsequent sentences of misunderstanding have accrued. Asking questions every few sentences rather than waiting until the end of a selection accomplishes this task, with the caveat that it is extremely important to recognize that frequent breaks for questions can interrupt the flow of the narrative, making it fragmented and interfering with comprehension if they are not extremely brief. It's critical to return to the reading quickly.

To use this technique effectively, combine the frequency of questions with brevity. Ask quickly to ensure comprehension and attention, and then get right back to reading. While you read, lots of short, focused discussion breaks maximize comprehension in the moment. This isn't to say that there's no place for broader and deeper conversations. They are merely different from what you ask to ensure that students grasp the full detail and depth of what they're reading as they are reading it.

Here's an example of what Don't Wait might look like during a reading of a short section from the first chapter of Madeline L'Engle's *A Wrinkle in Time*. The example is adapted from watching the lessons of several top teachers. I've inserted the teacher's questions in roman type within the text of the book, which I am assuming students would be reading aloud. If you're not familiar with *A Wrinkle in Time,* the passage occurs just after the protagonist, Meg Murry, has come down from her bedroom in a state of anxiety and fear in the middle of a dark and stormy night. She finds her little brother, Charles Wallace, waiting there.

In the kitchen a light was already on, and Charles Wallace was sitting at the table drinking milk and eating bread and jam. He looked very small and vulnerable sitting there alone in the big old-fashioned kitchen, a blond little boy in faded blue Dr. Denton's, his feet swinging a good six inches above the floor.

"Hi," he said cheerfully. "I've been waiting for you."

Teacher: Is Meg's brother younger or older than she is? What does it tell you about him that he says he's been "waiting for her"?

From under the table where he was lying at Charles Wallace's feet, hoping for a crumb or two, Fortinbras raised his slender dark head in greeting to Meg and his tail thumped against the floor. Fortinbras had arrived on their doorstep, a half-grown puppy, scrawny and abandoned, one winter night. He was, Meg's father had decided, part Llewellyn setter and part greyhound, and he had a slender, dark beauty that was all his own.

"Why didn't you come up to the attic?" Meg asked her brother, speaking as though he were at least her own age. "I've been scared stiff."

"Too windy up in that attic of yours," the little boy said. "I knew you'd be down. I put some milk on the stove for you. It ought to be hot by now."

Teacher: Who's calmer right now, Meg or her little brother?

How did Charles Wallace always know about her? How could he always tell? He never knew—or seemed to care—what Dennys or Sandy were thinking. It was his mother's mind, and Meg's, that he probed with a frightening accuracy.

Teacher: Who is "he" in that sentence? [After correct identification of Charles Wallace as "he":] What does it mean that Charles Wallace probed their minds with frightening accuracy?

Was it because people were a little afraid of him that they whispered about the Murry's youngest child, who was rumored to be not quite bright? "I've heard that clever people often have subnormal children," Meg had once overheard. "The two boys seem to be nice, regular children, but that unattractive girl and the baby boy certainly aren't all there."

Teacher: What do people mean when they say Meg and Charles "aren't all there"? Are they "subnormal"?

One question you might ask, after reviewing the preceding sequence, is how do I balance Don't Wait with other methods of developing reading skills from previous chapters, such as Fluency or Control the Game? Although this sequence could be integrated with such approaches as is, it could also be coordinated via two separate readings. That is, you might have students read once for fluency and then read a second time with questions embedded.

Lower the Level   Questions about a text can refer to any of (at least) four levels of meaning:

- Word or phrase level of meaning: "What does the word *forlorn* mean here? Why might the author have chosen that word?" "The author says, 'It was the worst thing imaginable.' What's the 'it' she's referring to there?" "What does it mean that Aslan 'turned on' the witch? What else beyond just turning around?"

- Sentence level of meaning: "Can you take that sentence and put it in simpler language?" "How might we express an idea like that today?"

- Passage level of meaning: "What part of this paragraph tells you that Mohi is mean spirited?"

- Story level of meaning: "What's the purpose of this essay?"

It's easy to assume that the goal is to get to the story level as quickly as possible and ask as great a proportion of story-level questions as possible. In fact, the lower levels of meaning (word and sentence) are critical to ensuring firm story-level understanding. Misunderstandings about big issues often start as misunderstandings about smaller things: who "them" is in a sentence, for example. Students will be more successful in story-level discussions when they have a firm grasp of sentence and word-level meaning. Remember to ask constantly about the lower levels and ensure that meaning is built reliably up from small units to larger ones.

Here are the questions from the *Wrinkle in Time* transcript I included in Don't Wait with each identified according to the level it focuses on. To be clear, I would expect the teacher to ask more story and passage level questions after concluding the passage but only on the assumption that they are balanced by plenty of word-phrase and sentence-level questions during (and even after) the reading.

Is Meg's brother younger or older than she is? [Passage level]

What does it tell you about him that he says he's been "waiting for her"? [Phrase level]

Who's calmer right now, Meg or her little brother? [Passage level]

Who is "he" in that sentence? [Word level]

What does it mean that Charles Wallace probed their minds with frightening accuracy? [Phrase level]

What do people mean when they say Meg and Charles "aren't all there"? [Phrase level]

Are Meg and Charles Wallace "subnormal"? [Passage level]

Evidence-Based Questioning Top reading teachers constantly emphasize groundedness in the text, even on subjective and opinion questions, by asking evidence-based questions—that is, questions where students must make reference to a fact or event from the text. One of the primary advantages is that evidence-based questions are "testable" in that you can much more clearly tell whether students have understood (or done) the reading. It's easier to get a line on how well (and even whether) a student grasped what she just read if a question pins her down to something concrete in the text. You can fake your response to a question about a story's theme by listening to the discussion and offering a vague summary in support. You can offer a judgment ("What did you think was the most exciting scene, Sarah?") with only the thinnest engagement in what you've read. But you can't nearly as easily fake "What happened on page 157?" "What words in the sentences tell you there's trouble brewing?" "Find me the sentence that proves who took Carlton's watch."

It's important to observe that evidence-based questions need not be narrow or concrete. You could just as easily ask students to find a sentence or a passage that supports the argument that a certain idea is the theme of a story. Further, evidence can be used in two ways: to induce and deduce. You could ask students to find three pieces of evidence that characters in Greek mythology are punished for doing things to excess or you could cite three examples of characters getting punished for their excess and ask student to draw the relevant conclusion.

To provide some examples, I've taken some of the questions from the *A Wrinkle in Time* sequence in the sections above and revised them to show how they might be made more evidence based.

Original: Is Meg's brother younger or older than she is?

Revised: Who can read me a sentence from the text that shows that Meg's brother is younger than she is? Who can find me more evidence, this time with an example that helps us guess his age.

Original: What does it tell you about him that he says he's been "waiting for her"?

Revised: Who can find other examples of places where Charles Wallace appears to know what Meg is thinking?

Original: Who's calmer right now, Meg or her little brother?

Revised: What details in this scene help show us that Charles Wallace is cooler and calmer than his sister? I'll want you to find the exact words.

Original: What does it mean that Charles Wallace probed their minds with frightening accuracy?

Revised: On the next page we're going to see Mrs. Whatsit read Meg's mind. What can you conclude about their relationship from these two strange incidents?

Postreading Techniques

A good experience with a text doesn't end when the reading ends. Here are some observations about the types of questions champion teachers ask as they push discussion onto broader or more analytical topics after completing a text (or a day's reading).

Summarize Summarizing is especially important as a tool to process at the end of a session of reading and is most effective when it forces students to prioritize information separating important from peripheral points and rephrasing and condensing key ideas to ensure that they "own" the material. When summarizing is unsuccessful it's often because a teacher fails to stress the difference between retelling (rewriting or restating details) and summarizing (retelling while condensing and prioritizing the important parts). When teaching students to summarize, ask questions like, "Who can describe the chapter by recapping its three most important events?" or "Can you summarize the author's two major arguments in support of his thesis?" These questions are powerful because they ask students to prioritize information. Until students fully understand the nuances of effective summary, asking questions requiring specific elements of summary such as prioritization are often most effective as teaching tools.

Another particularly effective strategy is to provide students with an ever-decreasing word limit for their summaries (for example, "Summarize this chapter in fifty words. Now summarize the chapter in a single sentence with fewer than fifteen words"). This always proves challenging: shortening accurately and effectively is a lot harder than just shortening because it requires true comprehension and insight to prioritize information. There are, as far as I can tell, two ways to shorten a summary: reduce the number of topics you are trying to include and reduce the number of words you use to describe the topics you include. These tips may help get students closer to efficient and effective summaries:

- Ask students to go back through their initial summary and eliminate every word that's not absolutely necessary. As students get more proficient at this skill, suggest that they eliminate adjectives and replace them with stronger, more potent verbs, boiling "ran as quick as she could" down to "sprinted." You can take this a step further by then suggesting words for them to eliminate (and expanding their conception of how to drop verbiage) or having them suggest unnecessary verbiage in one another's summaries.

- Ask students to prioritize the events in a summarized section. They will get only so far in making tighter and tighter descriptions of all the events in a section but will ultimately have to choose to leave some out entirely. Rank-ordering the events or material to be summarized forces that process along. (Discussing that order can be an effective conversation as well.) Jackie Robinson once said that a life is not important except in the impact it has on other lives. You can use the same criterion for deciding which events belong in a summary: "An event is most important in the impact it has [or is likely to have] on other scenes in the story. If you know or think it will affect the outcome of the book, include it in the summary; if not, drop it."

BETTER CONNECTIONS

When asking students to make connections beyond a text, champion teachers recognize that certain types of questions are usually more rigorous (and more likely to reinforce reading comprehension) than others. The types of questions are listed next in priority order according to their relative rigor, with the more rigorous question formats at the top (be aware that this order may be contrary to what many teachers expect or assume):

- **Text-to-text.** These are preferable to text-to-world and text-to-self because they reinforce testable ideas rather than judgments, opinions, and stories that students may not be able to access ("That happened once to my mom!"). They can include within-the-text questions ("When else in the book have we seen someone act this way?") and across-text questions ("Can anyone think of a character in another book we've read who was similar?" or "How is the suspense in this chapter like or unlike the suspense at the end of *Fantastic Mr. Fox*?").

- **Text-to-world.** Asking students to relate an issue in a story to some event or person in their world is a valid exercise. This is so especially when it asks students to connect specific aspects of a text to specific aspects of the broader world rather than allowing them to discuss any connection they see to any event in the world.

  Some of the most common text-to-world connections are text-to-media connections in which students connect something in the text with television shows or movies they have seen. Text-to-media connections can often take conversations about texts off track. It may be best to tell students that you are not looking for text-to-media connections. However, assuming a student's text-to-media connection is a valid one, the best follow-up question is something like this: "How does the connection you are making between our hero in the text and Spider Man help you to understand the text?" or "What specifically about Mr. Fox is similar to Spider Man?"

- **Text-to-self.** These questions are inevitable and valid, but they are also more limited in their relevance to other students and comprehension of texts. Although engaging, they can often lead classes astray. They are best when they focus on the specific elements of the text being read ("How would you feel if you were in a position like Donovan, Charles?") rather than sweeping in their breadth ("Did anyone else have a time when they felt scared?").

Keep in mind that connections are not an end in and of themselves. For example, while reading a story about a birthday party, a student may say, "I went to my cousin's birthday party last week." It is important not to accept this connection without further questioning: "What happened at your cousin's birthday party that reminds you of this story?" or "What kinds of things happened at your cousin's birthday party that might also happen here?" Students should be encouraged to use their connection to develop an understanding of the text, and to do that, you should bring the connection back to the text: "So how does that help us understand what's happening here?"

Teaching literary structures and conventions is especially productive in helping students make worthy connections. The basic idea is that conventions describe the ways stories usually or often work: the degree to which a story conforms to or diverges from convention (what most stories do) is a deeply productive line for connecting. But to do so, students need lots of study of other texts and the idea of structures and conventions. Point out that they can and should look for connections to text, particularly text-to-text connections and connections based on structures, conventions, and methods. Ensuring a rich collection of shared books that the whole class or school has read is one good way to enable this.

STANDARD-ALIGNED QUESTIONS

Most state standards articulate a dozen or so core types of questions students need to be able to answer. If they don't do so explicitly, the assessment portfolio your school uses (state tests, SATs, and whatever additional assessments you add) do it implicitly. For example, New York essentially asks four types of character study questions: character change ("How did x change during the story?"), character perspective ("Which of these statements would x probably agree with?"), character motivation (Why did x decide to walk home from school?"), and character traits (X could best be described as . . ."").

Although it's easy for teachers to fall into the habit of asking the same three or four types of questions over and over, their students need to practice the full array of question types, both to ensure their success on assessments that stand between them and college (and college readiness) and to make sure they are comfortable demonstrating a wide range of skills. Discipline yourself to ask questions that mirror the kinds of comprehension questions students need to master, thus providing practice at all skills and enforcing diversity on you and your students. Top teachers are intentional about this in several ways, often making an inclusive list and mapping them into their unit plans so they are constantly focusing on a different type of questions. They also study the different formats of questions used on assessments to better understand how the questions are asked and ensure that their own questions are at least as rigorous as the questions that control access to college.

SEE IT IN ACTION: CLIP 25

VOCABULARY AND COMPREHENSION

In clip 25 on the DVD, Roberto de Leon of Excellence Charter School of Bedford Stuyvesant demonstrates exemplary teaching of vocabulary and comprehension. He is preteaching vocabulary words that are critical to the story. Notice that students get multiple opportunities to use and hear *decoy* in a variety of settings, including one that intentionally front-loads the story they are about to read, thus allowing them to apply their vocabulary to explain and react to the book. De Leon is careful to differentiate between words that are the same and words that are similar. Contrasting the subtle differences between words is at least as important as discussing their similarities.

READING STRATEGIES AND THE TECHNIQUES OF CHAMPION TEACHERS

In the Introduction to this book, I discussed the difference between techniques and strategies. I recognize in drawing this distinction that many teachers of reading use what they refer to as "reading strategies" to guide their teaching. These strategies draw from the work of several authors who propose similar conceptualizations of the strategies students need to achieve full comprehension. They usually include a group of skills like the following: noticing, connecting, picturing, wondering, predicting, inferencing, and summarizing.

Given the prominence of strategies-based instruction in the professional discourse of reading teachers, I'll describe how the techniques here can overlap and interface with common approaches to "reading strategies." Although a variety of authors write about reading strategies, I will use Nancy Boyles's book, *Constructing Meaning Through Kid-Friendly Comprehension Strategy Instruction* (2004), for this discussion because it is among the clearest and most effective.

In the analysis here, I am frankly critical of some aspects of strategies instruction and the manner in which it can be employed. Therefore I want to make it clear that I believe that well-implemented, strategies-based reading instruction can be effective and that the work of authors like Boyles has advanced the quality of the teaching of reading. At the same time, a series of significant pitfalls can erode its effectiveness, and a wide disparity exists in effectiveness among the strategies. With that in mind, I make some general observations about strategies and then look at each of the most common strategies individually.

Risks and Challenges of Strategies Instruction

Relying heavily on reading strategies poses risks and challenges. One challenge is that the "strategies" involved are often too broadly defined. The strategy "noticing," which Boyles defines as "keying-in to important verbal clues: words, sentences, and paragraphs that offer evidence of the text's meaning" (p. 10), is an example. By that definition, what comment about a text, even one only tangentially related to it, would not be an example of noticing? And because nearly every response to a book requires an act of noticing *something*, teachers risk reinforcing the idea that any observation is worthwhile or that all observations are equally productive. However, all comments can't be equally useful, so the necessary and often unresolved question quickly becomes, How can teachers identify and help students understand the things that are most worthy of notice, and how can they systematically be identified and modeled?

A second challenge in strategies-based reading instruction is a confusion of correlation and cause. This is reflected in the basic argument behind strategies-based instruction: that if good readers do *x,* then those who do *x* will become good readers. Good readers may picture what they are reading in their minds as they read it, but this may well be an effect rather than a cause of good reading. Is this really a significant issue? Surely a study of proficient readers could reveal that strong readers all like to sit in comfortable chairs when they read. If this were the case, there would be a strong correlation between comfort and reading. But if we assumed a causal relationship (as strategies theory sometimes advises), we would likely approach reading by making the seating of students in more comfortable chairs a major priority, which would clearly be a mistake (and an expensive one at that!). Similarly, it's a larger logical leap than it may appear to suggest that practicing picturing will make you a better reader. In fact two examples Boyles provides suggest how tenuous this assumption is. In the first example, Boyles writes:

> To help students understand the value of using the picturing strategy while reading, I ask them to remember a time when they received big news, whether it was good news or bad news. "Where were you when you got the news?" I ask. "What was the weather like at the time? Who was with you?" Chances are you can answer all of these questions. The content of that message, the big news you received, is forever embedded in the context in which you received the news, a context that is made of many different sensory impressions. [p. 8]

Ironically, Boyles's example may prove only that students already have the capacity to picture. She assumes that if she asks them to recall an intense memory, they will have a strong visual memory of it. The problem, then, may not be that the students don't know how to picture. It may be that if they understand what they read and have excess processing capacity left over after figuring out the words and the basic fact of the description, they will picture it naturally. That, Boyles appears to assume, is what their minds naturally do. In that case, teaching them to read fluently and attend carefully to mundane details might be more effective than investing time in intentionally "teaching" them to picture, something they appear to know how to do. They just need a clear sense of what to picture.

In a similar example, Boyles writes:

> *"Readers figure out different kinds of things as they read," I tell my students, holding up the "figuring out" mini-poster.... "For example, the author might write that a certain character calls people names and teases kids who are younger, and this character picks fights, too. The author wants us to* figure out *that this kid is a ... How would you fill in that blank?" I ask my students.*
> *"Bully!" everyone choruses. "He's a bully." [p. 12]*

The fact that Boyles assumes that her students already have the capacity to figure out a story before she's taught them strategies (as long as the basic narrative is presented to them as simple, clear formulation) suggests that the problem may not be in their capacity to figure out but in their capacity to understand enough of the details of the story to engage their "figuring-out" skills fully. In short, good readers may "figure out," but the problem for bad readers may not be that they don't know how to figure out but rather that they don't understand what they've read enough to use those skills.

Another challenge to strategies instruction, a challenge to which the techniques in this book are not immune, is that the easier a strategy is to understand and use, the more likely teachers may be to use it. However, something easier to use is not necessarily more conducive to student achievement. Connecting, picturing, and predicting are especially tangible and specific. Their clarity may tacitly encourage teachers to use them more often. This may not be justified, however, because they have significant downsides, which are discussed later in this section, particularly in regards to "picturing," a technique easily overused and therefore particularly distracting.

In addition, reading strategies can be used to promote both engagement and comprehension, which are different goals, and teachers sometimes do not recognize the difference between the two. Boyles writes, "If we try really hard to think of ways a story connects to us and our lives... we're more likely to stick with the story. That's one reason it's so important to look for connections. Making connections with the text will help us to keep reading it" (p. 7). Although it's certainly worthwhile to try to engage students in texts so they want to read them, it's also important to note that making students want to read a book and ensuring that they comprehend it are different issues. Picturing what they're reading may engage students and cause them to persist in reading, but this is a different issue from whether they understand what they are reading. For all you know, the picture they've made in their minds is erroneous! Strategies-based instruction can frequently fail to make this distinction.

Finally, there is a large caveat regarding fluency that generally does not get fully acknowledged in discussions of strategies instruction. Boyles writes, "Teaching reading comprehension strategies can benefit just about any student operating at a reasonable level of reading fluency (second grade or above)" (p. xiv). It's worth noting that many students in high-poverty schools aren't at that level, and Boyles's assertion that a second-grade level of fluency is the cut-off point for determining the efficacy of strategies instruction appears to be arbitrary. What if it's fifth grade? What if it's "sufficient to the level of the book you're trying to read" and the book is hard? With any technique, the question we should ask is not whether its use can help students learn to read but whether it can help students learn to read better and more efficiently than reading. Whether this is the case with strategies instruction remains an unanswered question. It is almost assuredly the case in some instances and assuredly not the case in others.

The unintended consequence of any teaching approach is the tendency to make the approach (not comprehension) the purpose. For example, a student makes a useful comment, but the teacher says: "You're not visualizing! I asked you to visualize." This risk is especially acute in strategies-based instruction because the strategies are actions students are supposed to enact, and this public aspect means there's an incentive to misapply the approach more aggressively and broadly.

This is equally true with the techniques in this book. Ben Marcovitz, principal of the successful Sci Academy Charter School in New Orleans, described how to think about this paradox in a panel presentation: "My teachers are accountable for results. The techniques can get them there. They have for others. But the point is to succeed—not to use the techniques no matter what. If they can find some other way to get great results, I don't have a problem with that."

SPECIFIC STRATEGIES AND THEIR RELATIONSHIP TO THE TECHNIQUES IN THIS BOOK

In this section, I discuss each of several common reading strategies and analyze both areas of concern and their connection to the techniques described in this book.

Noticing

In further describing the strategy of noticing, Boyles writes, "When we find clues in the text, we should file them away carefully in our mind so we can pull them out later and see how they all fit together—as main ideas and themes" (p. 11).

While noticing things is critical to becoming an effective reader, it is far too broadly and vaguely defined to be useful as a tool for teaching. What comment, observation, or moment of engaged attention would not be an example of noticing something about a text? Since every response to a book requires an act of noticing something, teachers risk reinforcing that any observation is worthwhile or that all observations are equally productive. Or they risk telling students to notice without giving them useful guidance on what to notice. The question is: What are the things students should notice most, and how can they systematically be identified and modeled?

One place where the techniques I've described in this section can be especially useful is in helping students to notice better. What kind of observations can students make to use their noticing in the most productive way?

- Observations that relate to and advance understanding of the most important ideas in what you are reading. This sounds obvious but can be greatly improved with a bit of discipline and advanced planning. Use focal points, for example, to draw students' attention to some critical themes or ideas in what you're reading and ask them to try to notice, as they are reading, the things that make Macbeth's ambition destroy him or that allow Charlotte's goodness to change and Wilbur to mature. In short, don't just have students read; have them read for something. Alternatively, and especially if you prefer a style that's less proscriptive about what the most important themes might be, use front-loading to draw students' attention to scenes of special importance so that you can discuss critical watershed moments in special depth.

- Observations that relate to and advance understanding of skills (that is, learning standards) you're teaching at the time. Using standards-aligned questioning is especially effective to develop students' skills at noticing a wide variety of powerful things about a text. If you are studying characterization, for example, ask them to notice how the characters are changing, or are described, or speak. Many students are most inclined to notice in the ways that are most natural and intuitive for them. Asking them to employ specific skills in noticing forces them out of their comfort zones and builds their ability to notice in a wider variety of ways.

- Evidence-based observations. Noticing the evidence that supports the opinion is as important as the opinion itself, or even more important, "What makes you mistrust him?" is usually a better question than, "Do you trust the main character?" Use evidence-based questioning to stress this aspect of noticing.

- Observations drawing on different levels of noticing. The thing about not noticing is secondary ignorance. By its definition, you don't usually know that you didn't notice something. A lower-level technique can cause students to notice more systematically by stressing and causing them to practice different types of things to notice about a text. Observing what a tricky phrase means or how an author cleverly crafted a sentence to make the subject of the action unclear is often just as important as noticing that the main character is probably untrustworthy. Certainly students need to practice noticing at all of these levels. Ask them; then try to notice things about the colloquial phrases an author uses; her word choice; or how she likes to start or finish her chapters; or, ideally, how her word choice and use of phrases show that she's trying to do something particular with the beginning of chapters.

Connecting

When connecting (or making connections) students are socialized to think of ways the text they are reading is similar to some previous or familiar experience. Readers can connect with another text (a text-to-text connection), the world (a text-to-world connection), or themselves (a text-to-self connection). One of the benefits Boyles describes of connecting is that it engages students in the text. "If we try really hard to think of ways a story connects to us and our lives . . . we're more likely to stick with the story" (p. 7). This is certainly true and significant, though it's also worth observing that while getting students to engage is an important and worthy goal, it is a different goal from their comprehending.

Thoughtful connections can often be the jumping-off place for inferences about the text. They can help students begin to understand the text by tapping into what they already know about a topic. Effective connections can also help students see the story from a character's point of view by accessing their own analogous experience. But they don't necessarily do this, and in many

> *Thoughtful connections can often be the jumping-off place for inferences about the text. They can help students begin to understand the text by tapping into what they already know about a topic.*

cases, the connections students are most likely to make ("Hey, this is just like something that happened to my family!") are least rigorous and least useful to engendering long-term reading comprehension. ("Hey, this is just like the introduction to the other book we read," is probably a more useful connection in the long term than is a text-to-self connection.) Furthermore, students (or teachers) can infer that the point is simply to make any kind of connection to the text. That shouldn't be the end. Connections aren't inherently valuable; only good connections are. A good connection serves to help readers understand something about the text, not the thing connected to—in most cases, having the discipline to use the world to understand the text rather than the text to understand the world. Students can also potentially let their connection project onto the text. That is, they can replace actual details with imagined details or contradictory or confusing details as when a student who once lost an article of clothing and was upset about it infers that a character who lost her sweater was also upset, even while the text has clues showing that the character was happy about it. Finally, connections can be off task and waste time, and clever students can use them to co-opt discussion onto easier or more convenient topics.

It may also be that people naturally make connections, and so the skill doesn't need to be taught so much as managed and guided. The skill is in making connections effective and focused. In light of that, you should be clear about linking connections back to the text to understand what light the connection sheds on what you're reading.

These and other aspects of making effective connections are discussed in the Better Connections section above.

Picturing

In picturing, Boyles writes, students are taught to use clues from the text to create an image of what is described. This helps students remember what they've read and engage in the text. "The pictures we have in our mind help us respond to the text at an emotional level" (p. 8), Boyles writes, and this is almost certainly true.

Generally, however, picturing is among the most overused and poorly used strategies, and this is significant because it can be among the most destructive in its application. The use of picturing as a comprehension strategy may be confused by some teachers as validating visual literacy generally and make it more common for them to use visual images more frequently to aid in comprehension. This may seem benign, but the result is a compensatory strategy for effective reading. In teaching students to picture, some teachers feel encouraged to draw on actual pictures to make inferences about the story in a way that crowds out reading. When a teacher says, "What do you think is about to happen? Look at the picture if you need help!" she is allowing students to "read" the story by drawing enough information from pictures to keep them from having to read the words to succeed. This results in their learning to circumvent their poor reading skills.

Teachers may also overuse the picturing strategy because it is so accessible. As a result, they may spend valuable time visualizing rather than reading or asking more productive and rigorous questions. Teachers often make it a point to take a simple passage from a book and ask students to visualize it so they understand it. " 'He went to his desk, opened the drawer and pulled out a marker.' Class let's try to visualize what that looked like. What was in the drawer? How did he walk across the room?" This can be useful. But it's also worth noting that this could be a scene where the author didn't think it was important to create a sensory image. More important, picturing can be incorrect. Students who are asked to picture an image can and often do introduce erroneous details. In this example, the student might create a false image of when and why the character went to the drawer and what he found there.

Finally, it's also possible that intentionally visualizing doesn't help students learn to comprehend what they read that much. As Boyles points out in her book, people seem to naturally visualize when they understand something, so we could ask whether picturing is a strategy the causes comprehension or is the result of it, with better picturing resulting from better comprehension.

The most productive applications of visualizing I've seen teachers use are to ask students to draw or picture a scene in order to clear up what's confusing about it. For example, a teacher I observed teaching *Macbeth* drew separate pictures of Birnam Wood and Dunsinane and then sketched how soldiers cut down the branches and marched to the latter location, thus proving the impossible prophecy of Macbeth's dream true. This is different from asking students to share what they are visualizing. Another effective use of visualizing is to ask students to create a picture using details they have read in the book. This is actually a version of an evidence-based question, and when teachers do it well,

> *The most productive application of visualizing is when a teacher asks students to draw or picture a scene in order to clear up what's confusing about it.*

they ask students to point out specific aspects of the story and or where they found certain details that gave them their picture.

Wondering

In wondering, students ask questions of the text as they read. Examples, Boyles writes, might include wondering "what might happen next in the story or how the story might end" (p. 9). This technique is also sometimes called "asking questions." As with noticing, however, the technique is at times vague. Wonder about what? Anything? All things equally? Having students develop questions about what they are reading encourages them to be active readers and may motivate them to know more about a text. Moreover, wonderment and curiosity are usually very good things. The point is that there are myriad forms of wondering, and they aren't all inherently of equal value. Students' private experience, in which what they want to wonder about is their own to determine, and public experience, in which a group of people chooses certain wonderings to discuss, are different kettles of fish. There are settings for both, and in the latter, a class deserves criteria about what wonderings they'll engage most. "Here are the kinds of things we're going to talk and wonder about today to increase our understanding of the story [or our skills at understanding stories]." I realize this may seem either vague or directive (Is he telling us to shut down kids' imaginations? some readers may ask), but encouraging students to wonder on the premise that it is inherently among the most valuable things they could be doing regardless of how and what they wonder about is a false premise.

Wondering can be especially effective when modeled by a teacher, especially in a soliloquy form. "I'm wondering, here, what might make Donald want to give his dog away. I'm thinking back to the earlier chapters, and I know Donald loves his dog. The author told us he would 'never do anything to hurt him.' So I'm wondering: Why might a boy give away a dog he loves?" While this strategy of making thoughts visible can model how to think about books effectively, it can also result in teachers' doing most of the work. Rather than involving students and working to transfer thinking skills to students, they are merely performing a public literary analysis.

Predicting

Boyles writes that "predicting sets the stage for students to monitor their own understanding of the text" (p. 10). In its most basic and common form, it involves teachers asking students what they think is going to happen next. Its benefits include engagement. It gets students to focus on what they are reading next to see if their prediction is confirmed. When done well, it can also help them monitor their understanding of the text based on whether their predictions came true. That's the best possible outcome of predicting, but to make that effective, you should make a habit of circling back to intentionally discuss whether predictions came true and why. This last step makes predicting a relatively productive activity, but unfortunately, the last step often doesn't happen, perhaps because many teachers don't recognize the particular value of this aspect of predicting. You can augment the strength of your predicting if you use the evidence-based questioning technique. This will cause you to consistently ask more productive questions. In the immediate follow-up to each prediction, you can ask: "Why do you think will happen next?" and "What in the text makes that seem likely to happen?" In the postprediction follow-up you can ask: "Why did you think so?" "What fooled you?" and "What made you know this would happen?"

Two other challenges pose barriers to predicting and can often make it an ineffective use of time. First, students can make wild predictions unrelated to the text or more related to their lives or experiences than to the text. Alternatively they can narrate the obvious and make predicting facile. The best defense against this is once again to focus on evidence-based questioning. This forces students to ground their predictions in the text.

Figuring Out and Inferring

The last strategy common to most reading teachers is alternatively called figuring out or inferring. Boyles refers to figuring out as pushing students to go "beyond the construction of basic meaning to a deeper understanding of the text" (p. 12). This strategy attempts to focus on what is by all rights the heavy hitter of comprehension: understanding what's between the lines, left unsaid, hinted at. In short, this is the strategy that asks students to go beyond the basic, literal understanding of the text to apply higher-order thinking. But its importance belies the difficulty of applying it. Obviously, merely asking a student to make an inference won't do. You can't tell a student, "Read this page and figure something out that you can share with the class." Inference happens but can't be commanded.

Stop and ask a student to reread a line, unpack a key phrase, define a word, underline a crucial piece of evidence.

To make inference successful you must set the table, often by meticulous work with both the Lower Your Level and Don't Wait techniques. When your students are learning to make inferences, you can surreptitiously assemble the key pieces they need to make their leap forward by stopping frequently with short discussions of and directives to attend to the key pieces of guidance in the pages or lines before. Stop and ask a student to reread a line, unpack a key phrase, define a word, underline a crucial piece of evidence. Focus on words and phrases; the building blocks that make or break the inference often start at the mundane level. Ironically, strong instruction on the literal meaning of the text, including vocabulary and focus on important details, doesn't distract from higher-order thinking. It makes it possible.

Summarizing

Advocates of strategies-based instruction sometimes also include summarizing as a key strategy. For this strategy I see nearly 100 percent overlap with the techniques in this book. For a further discussion, see *100 Percent* (technique 36 in Chapter Six).

CONCLUSION

THE END IS THE BEGINNING

In the Introduction to this book, I addressed the differences between techniques and strategies. A strategy, you may recall, is a decision, and a technique is something you practice, hone, and adapt throughout your life. Artists, athletes, musicians, surgeons, and performers of a thousand other varieties achieve greatness only by their attention to the details of their technique. Their constant refinement of it perpetually renews their passion for the craft and allows them to seek the grail of better performance, expression that sings, the ability to make the greatest possible difference. This focus on technique and its constant refinement is also the path to excellence for teachers.

Approaching teaching as an art—meaning by that phrase that it is difficult and requires finesse and discretion in the application, craftsmanship, and careful and attentive development of technique to master it—is the path to success. That path is different for each teacher. The techniques developed by champion teachers and described in this book were not mine to start with, but they can belong to any teacher who embraces the concept of constant attentive refinement of techniques. Only that approach, coupled with the aggregated wisdom of the teachers compiled in this book, will be sufficient to change the equation of opportunity in our schools and close the achievement gap at scale. Adapted, refined, improved, and, perhaps in a few cases, ignored because not everything in this book can be right for you, these techniques can transform your classroom.

A colleague of mine, Ben Markovitz, recently founded a new school in New Orleans. Sci Academy achieved exemplary first-year results with high school students who had not previously been successful. This school has made extensive and focused use of the techniques in this book, with dozens of staff meetings and training sessions. Yet when Ben was recently asked how he ensures that his teachers use this material, he observed that he doesn't. He manages his teachers for results and provides these techniques to get them there. They are free to use them or not. All of them do, with an energy and vigor I am humbled by, but Ben insists that the tools here are a means to results, not an end in themselves. I wholeheartedly agree with Ben. In fact, I would like this fact to distinguish this book from so many others: it starts with and is justified by the results it helps teachers achieve, not by its fealty to some ideological principle. The result to aim for is not the loyal adaptation of these techniques for their own sake but their application in the service of increased student achievement. Too many ideas, even good ones, go bad when they become an end and not a means.

The techniques I've written about were derived from observing outstanding teachers at work. But more exciting than that fact is that way this book has changed over the years as I have been writing it. During that time, it has evolved from an informal document within Uncommon Schools to a more explicit guide to instruction that I have shared with colleagues and offered trainings on, to this book you've now read. It has changed and evolved and gained the depth that I hope has made it worthy of your time. What gives this book its depth and focus is the unrelenting application of the ideas by remarkable teachers. What I first wrote was a skeleton of what now appears; the techniques that appeared in it were described in insufficient terms and short aspirational paragraphs. Only when other teachers tried them, applied them, adapted them, and improved them (and let me videotape them doing it) did the truly useful parts of this book emerge. In short, what's good here is good only because of the process of constantly refining and adapting techniques in the relentless and restless drive for excellence. That observation seems a fitting one with which to end.

BEHIND-THE-SCENES INTERVIEWS

Many of the teachers and school leaders I've worked with in sharing the material in this book have asked for more information, particularly in response to the incredibly powerful accompanying videos, which show champion teachers in action. It instantly became clear that answers to many of the excellent questions teachers asked about the videos could only be provided by the teachers themselves. In response, my colleague Max Tuefferd, who analyzes video and develops training activities for Uncommon Schools, began interviewing many of the top teachers we'd videotaped, asking them to explain in their own words what they were doing in their videos, why they were doing it, and how they thought about and prepared to do the things they did.

The resulting feedback was overwhelming. People loved the interviews. Not surprisingly, it turns out, champion teachers are far more articulate than I could be in describing their work. With that in mind, what follows are the transcripts of four of Max's interviews.

INTERVIEW WITH JASON ARMSTRONG, DVD CLIP 3

INTERVIEWER: Discuss how the concept of *Right Is Right* works in your classroom.

ARMSTRONG: Students see me use a lot of specific vocabulary in class, and I expect them to use it when appropriate. They learn that there are differences between related mathematical objects and that this is reflected in vocabulary.

When students have answered questions in writing, I have them read their written responses verbatim, and I often write those responses for all to see so that we can critique and edit them before moving on. I regularly call on students to explain their answers or the answers of peers they agree with. I place as much value on the accuracy of explanations as I do on the accuracy of the answers.

INTERVIEWER: There are three examples of *Right Is Right* in this video clip: Answer the Question, Hold Out for All the Way, and Use Technical Vocabulary. Discuss each of these moments separately. What is your point of view on how you are using each technique?

ARMSTRONG: For Answer the Question, the response from Mark was a pretty easy one to deflect—I think students can easily be alerted to the difference between a calculation and a definition. What I like about my response is that I did not say no but rather just described what Mark did and then described what I wanted.

Hold Out for All the Way: I would try to use some *Ratio* if I were to do this again, polling the students for other examples of cubic units rather than listing them myself. Now that I am in my fifth year and using a SMART Board [an interactive computer-assisted whiteboard] for each lesson, I can write more neatly and quickly by typing in responses, so in this case, I might type student responses on the board so that other students could both hear and see what I am about to correct. These days, I sometimes put up several similar or contradictory answers so that students can see the differences.

Use Technical Vocabulary: Here's a situation where I don't have a big problem with "takes up." In fact, I think students need to have access to a common phrase like that while they get used to something like "occupies"—as long as "takes up" is sufficiently rigorous. This is where I like calling "occupies" the "other word" rather than the "only word."

INTERVIEWER: What standards and expectations do you have for your students that lead to these three *Right Is Right* examples?

ARMSTRONG: I love the fact that mathematics has terms like *minuend, isosceles,* and *vinculum,* because different terms indicate different functions; for example, a minuend is different from a subtrahend because they have different roles in subtraction, whereas all the terms in an addition problem are called addends because they do not differ significantly in their function. Most math words have etymologies related to their meanings, and these etymologies can help students memorize vocabulary; for example, *isosceles* means "same legs"—a helpful way for students to remember the word and later look for "iso" in other disciplines.

Since so much of success in math depends on facility with symbols, having terms for those symbols can give students a foothold. For example, once students know what a vinculum is, they can point to a fraction or repeating decimal and talk about the vinculum instead of the "bar" or "line" or "thingy."

Since I have a personal expectation that I use this knowledge with accuracy, having a lower expectation for my students would feel dishonest.

INTERVIEWER: What are the most common ways that your students get off track or evade the question?

ARMSTRONG: Often I call on a student who has had a hand up and get, "Oh, I have a question." My typical response is, "I need my question answered first," and I usually remember to come back to the student's question.

Occasionally students with a thorough understanding of what we're talking about will get ahead of the pace I am establishing for a topic (this is "Right answer, right time"). The biggest difficulty is that a student who moves ahead to the end of an explanation will shift the discussion from the entire class to a one-on-one between me and him or her. To counter it, I will either tell the student that we need to make sure everyone is with us, or I might interrupt the student to restate, more slowly, one part of the explanation, and then reengage the entire class.

INTERVIEWER: When is right almost right, and when is wrong just wrong?

ARMSTRONG: I think the "just wrong" case—I'm interpreting this as a time when it's appropriate to say no—is when it is clear that I am asking for specific knowledge that I expect students to recall with no difficulty, for example, a multiplication fact. Mark's response from the clip is also wrong, but that's because he understandably confused *algorithm* with *definition*, and so the appropriate response is simply to point out that confusion, Mark is not incorrect, just confused about what question to answer. I think the "almost right" cases are those that call for Use Technical Vocabulary or Hold Out All the Way—when a student doesn't use the level of rigor I want or gets close enough to the right answer that I should not throw it out.

INTERVIEWER: Is there any background on students that we see in these clips that you wish to add?

ARMSTRONG: I think it's worth mentioning that those students were not at the top of their class in terms of achievement, and so I think it was important that they be treated to the same level of expectation as their more accomplished peers.

INTERVIEWER: Are there any moments in these clips that you wish to draw attention to?

ARMSTRONG: Watching this clip, I get self-conscious about how quickly and unintelligibly I can talk. I'm better about it now. One way to correct that habit is to say less and make the students say more—a trade-off of efficiency and speed for clarity and student participation. This example walks a fine line in terms of pacing. Defining volume was not the aim of the lesson, and this was not the first time we had done so. Therefore, I think a quick pace and my assuming a lot of the intellectual burden were appropriate.

INTERVIEW WITH JAIMIE BRILLANTE, DVD CLIP 15

INTERVIEWER: Describe how the concept of *100 Percent* works in your classroom and in this clip.

BRILLANTE: *100 Percent* in my classroom means that everyone is doing everything 100 percent of the time. I tell my students that everything we do is designed to make them great writers. I expect you to do it because I know it will make you a great writer. Everyone wants to be smarter, so everyone works hard.

INTERVIEWER: How do you balance your use of *100 Percent* with the need to maintain pacing in your class?

BRILLANTE: Achieving 100 percent is an intentional focus at the start of the year. I use a variety of teacher tricks to get all students participating. Proximity, nonverbal gestures, wait time or countdowns, positive framing, and, if necessary, deductions help students see the expectation that I have. It takes longer the first few weeks of the year. Once the precedent is set, the students know what to expect, and it does not usually affect the pacing for the remainder of the year. If there is a time where I do not have 100 percent in a reasonable amount of time, I tend to make the time for it because it is a sign to me as the teacher that something else is not working in the lesson. If I let it go, that student is going to think that, one, I do not see them or, two, their actions don't matter. There are moments due to student personality or in my attempt to maintain whole class engagement that I might not address someone in the moment. Usually if I make this decision, it is because the rest of the class is unaware that someone is not with us. I don't want other students to see someone off task and think that it's okay. If I don't address it in the moment, I try to address it at some point within the lesson. I want all students to be thinking, "She sees me." This helps maintain the expectation of 100 percent without negatively impacting pacing.

INTERVIEWER: Discuss your radar and awareness of student engagement and how you are able to see what is going on at any given moment.

BRILLANTE: In order to have strong radar I have to know my lesson. I can't look at my lesson plan and look at the students at the same time. I tend to use a combination of cold calling and high-paced questioning near the start of each lesson to create and measure student engagement. Then within the I and We portion of the lesson, I sprinkle in moments of independent work. For example, I might say, "Do number 1 and then SLANT." While they are working on number 1, I am silently observing. If I am bent down talking to an individual student, I am often looking at everyone else while listening to the individual student. During these sprinkles, I intentionally walk the border of the room looking at their work. The work they produce is the clue that someone might not be on task. A few moments later when the class has come back together, my radar will be focusing in their area.

INTERVIEWER: Why did you choose to make this moment a private individual correction?

BRILLANTE: Although she was off task two separate times, the rest of the class was unaware of her behavior. It was more effective to make the correction privately because I only wanted to correct her. The rest of the class was working independently, so they had no idea what I was whispering to her. This allows her to avoid any unnecessary embarrassment that could have led to even more distraction on her part. I also wanted to avoid distracting the whole class from their independent work by talking aloud. I also didn't want to advertise to the whole class that someone was off task. I didn't want to plant that seed in someone else's mind.

INTERVIEWER: You give your student in this clip some very specific feedback ("there were two times when you did not track the speaker"). How does this specificity play into this private individual correction?

BRILLANTE: I was so specific because in the moment, I did not stop the flow of the lesson to gain her sight. Yet I wanted her to know that I saw her and that it was not acceptable. She was cold called during the lesson and answered incorrectly. I wanted her to see the connection that by not tracking, she was not learning what she needed to be successful.

INTERVIEWER: How do you keep track of the moments when you don't intervene or intervene differently?

BRILLANTE: I am not exactly sure if I understand this question. I determine whether to make a private correction based on the student's personality, the particular moment within the lesson, and the behavior that the student is exhibiting. There are moments when I do not intervene publicly because it will affect the pacing, it will bring negative attention to a student who is seeking it, or because it can escalate a particular problem. Generally if an individual correction can't be done in a few seconds or with a few gestures, I would prefer to make it privately.

INTERVIEWER: Explain how both your unaggressive approach and immediate walk away are an important part of this interaction.

BRILLANTE: My approach to this student was designed to mimic a typical conversation I would have with any student during independent work time. I didn't want it to look or feel like I was reprimanding her. I wanted it to be seen as a moment where I let her know the problem because I was concerned. I am here to help you learn and you did not learn in that moment. This is what I saw and this is how you are going to fix it. I try to walk away immediately because it implies that I expect you to understand and comply with my request. It also eliminates any power struggle situation. When I walk away, it's because I know you are going to do this and I will give you the time and space to prove it.

INTERVIEW WITH BOB ZIMMERLI, DVD CLIP 16

INTERVIEWER: Describe how the concept of *100 Percent* works in your classroom and in this clip.

ZIMMERLI: *100 Percent* is crucial to achieve within your classroom, especially when you have asked for it when you use words like "everybody," "everyone," "repeat after me," or any other nonverbal *Call and Response* technique. You must stop what you are doing when the students do not demonstrate *100 Percent,* or you are signaling to the students that you actually do not mean what you say, at least not all the time. It almost embeds a sense of power within the students to feel as if they are part of the lesson and part of such a strong voice going forth. It also sets students up for success because they are expected to do the small things with all their energy, focus, and attention. It kind of carries over to the objective for the day and feeds into the rigor around the academic work.

INTERVIEWER: How do you balance *100 Percent* with a need to maintain pacing in the class?

ZIMMERLI: Pacing is one of those things that is completely within the teacher's control. You just manipulate it like you would a throttle on a motorcycle. If you feel as if the pace is dying down, you just crank it up in a variety of different ways. Expecting *100 Percent* does not need to take much time at any one given moment. You might need to expect it thirty times or more in a lesson, but each instance might require anywhere from three to five seconds. A quick statement of, "Show me SLANT," will work wonders. If you are missing someone, then, "Josh, minus two. Please SLANT." The more students get used to your expectations, the less the frequency of interventions as the year progresses.

INTERVIEWER: Are you really going for 100 percent at any given time, or is 90 percent close enough in reality?

ZIMMERLI: I am a stickler for 100 percent. If you accept 90 percent, then you are already on your way to 80 percent or 70 percent. The students also see the same things you see. If you know you are taking less, then so do they.

INTERVIEWER: Part of the *100 Percent* technique is about awareness. Discuss your own radar or awareness of student engagement and how you see everything that is going on at any moment.

ZIMMERLI: You cannot become preoccupied with any one thing. Your eyes have to see what is happening and beyond and on either side. I believe this can be one of the most difficult things for new teachers. The more you need to have a lesson plan right in front of you, the more you get caught off guard with an unexpected question, the more you get rattled by a behavior that you were not expecting, the more difficult it is to be aware of the nonacademic warning signs that are going on all around you at the same time.

I play out my lesson in my head from the time I am in the shower that morning, during my ride in to school, and continually until I actually am teaching it. It kind of gives you a "been there, done that" approach even if it is your first time teaching to that objective. You have already thought of the potential pitfalls, the areas where the pacing might be a bit slower, the questions the students will have at each segment of the lesson, when you will get students up at the board, what all the other students will be doing at that point, what you will be doing when that child is up there, etc. This allows your mind to not get bogged down during the delivery of the lesson. For example, if a student has a question, nine times out of ten I already know what the question is going to be and how I am going to approach answering it. That way, while the question is still being asked, my mind is free to still stay engaged with the rest of the class. My eyes are rarely on the student who is asking the question; instead, they are looking all around the rest of the room making sure everyone else is SLANTing, tracking the speaker, not looking out the window, or trying to poke someone else in the back. The bottom line: the more unsure you are of your content and the lesson, the less effective your radar will always be. Your mind can't do both effectively at the same time, and usually content wins and radar loses.

INTERVIEWER: In this clip you are describing a kind of momentum that is occurring. In one part you point out that you don't have Marisa but you do have Jasmine; in another, you remark that you don't have three people and you "want them back." How does this play out in the classroom and lend itself to getting 100 percent engagement from your students?

ZIMMERLI: At times I simply tell them that I am very jealous of their attention and I don't want to share it with anyone. I think this lends itself to *Strong Voice* as well. From the minute you step into that classroom, you want the students to feel a shift in the atmosphere. I know it sounds hokey, but I am completely serious here. You want them to know that you have arrived and you mean business. I don't mean in a hostile or negative way, but in my mind, a very effective teacher is a performer—not a dog-and-pony show, but someone who uses the classroom as his or her stage and has an agenda that will be accomplished and a set script already in mind. It has been rehearsed many times already, leading up to the time you walk in and there is an anxious expectation to bring it forth. They need to feel like they don't want to miss a minute of anything that happens, much like they would feel at the movie theater waiting for a movie to start.

INTERVIEWER: There seem to be several significant moments in the clip, namely, the way you position yourself in front of Marisa, when you take two scholar dollars from the student in the front right and when you bring your voice down to a whisper. Discuss how you decide what the appropriate response to any particular moment is.

ZIMMERLI: You need to be able to play off the atmosphere you are in and constantly compare it to the atmosphere you want to be in or the one you are trying to create. Sometimes you want to make the whole class aware of a particular problem and you act accordingly. If pace is low and you still have one or two students off task or not with you, it is a much different approach. You pull out different teacher tricks like proximity, a long stare at that individual student as you are addressing the whole class (but the misbehaving student feels like there is no one in the room except you and him, since you have not taken your eyes off of him as you are continuing with what you are saying), squaring up, leaning in on his desk, simply including his name in the sentence you are using, snapping your fingers, or simply stopping in midsentence. A good way to transition out of one of these moments and back to the lesson is simply changing the inflection of your voice, as if to signal a turning of a page. If I was louder, I'll get quiet. If I was already quiet, I'll start speaking noticeably louder.

INTERVIEWER: In the clip, there are at least four of the six interventions described in the taxonomy for *100 Percent*. I see nonverbal correction, a positive group correction, a lightning quick public correction, and then an anonymous individual correction. Describe why you choose to present these in any given moment and how effective they are.

ZIMMERLI: Nonverbal is always for an individual and always when I need to maintain pace. Positive group is used to not lose the mojo and keep things at a more positive level. Lightning quick public correction—again to maintain pace, but I am beginning to see something brewing that needs to be addressed before it really gets to a much larger scale. Anonymous individual correction—I usually use this when I know that I don't need to specifically address the students and they will be able to self-correct within the time frame of being named, or, sometimes at a possible volatile moment with a specific student where any public use of their name might actually backfire and force me into a much more severe consequence.

INTERVIEW WITH HILARY LEWIS, DVD CLIP 22

INTERVIEWER: How does Control the Game fit into your general reading strategy and expectation?

LEWIS: Control the Game [CTG] lends itself to guided reading instructional time and reading mastery, as it focuses directly on students reading out loud and teachers assessing students' reading behaviors. CTG allows teachers to assess student fluency and a student's decoding strategies, and monitor mistakes that students make while reading aloud. CTG as a taxonomy element also requires the planning, preparation, and implementation of a strong reading culture in the classroom. Throughout the first-grade classrooms, reading is a fun and special time that requires a lot of work and can be a lot of fun. Teachers' expectations during reading time are that students work hard, use the strategies, and work on learning new skills to make themselves better readers. Since everyone is working hard to become better readers, the culture of the reading group makes all readers, primary or secondary, feel comfortable with working on challenging tasks.

INTERVIEWER: Discuss how CTG works in your classroom and this clip.

LEWIS: In this clip, I begin the lesson by setting up my expectations for reading. All students know that their finger must be on the first word of the text in order to be ready to read. Since the scholars have no idea who I will call on to read first, all scholars want to be ready to read. Keeping the identity of the reader unpredictable truly does maximize students' incentive—all scholars were ready to read.

At this time, students are reading a very short passage in their *Reading Mastery* book. Students are seated in a horseshoe format so I may easily track their reading and reading behaviors.

As students read, I'm first noticing the movement of their fingers—also called tracking—to ensure that all scholars are following along with the text. At the same time, I'm listening for the reading behaviors of each student, asking myself, "What words are they stuck on?" "What strategies are they using?" "Which strategies have they not yet mastered?"

During this clip I keep the reader unpredictable for students, but my sequence is planned. Whenever I ask my group to read, I always begin with a stronger reader to set the pace. I will always follow a struggling reader with a stronger reader and prepare a struggling reader with a stronger reader to build leverage. By giving a struggling reader the chance to hear the text read smoothly, it allows that reader to enter into the passage with more knowledge about what the text is about and might give them some key vocabulary that will present itself in their section of the text.

INTERVIEWER: There are many nuanced moments in this clip. Explain a little more about working with your students and your use of finger follow/finger freeze.

LEWIS: Finger freeze is a quick verbal cue to remind scholars to stop their finger from moving in the text when they have stopped reading. This behavior has to be taught explicitly to students as often students will lose their place while reading. When students lose their place while reading, transaction costs go up, and there is more wait time. When there is more wait time, students lose engagement. When all students have their fingers frozen on the last word that was read, they can come back to the text seamlessly.

INTERVIEWER: Low transaction costs?

LEWIS: Again, low transaction costs keep students engaged. Since students have no idea who I will call on next, they are all ready and prepared to read. I am also checking who is ready to read by looking at their tracking in the text. If students are not in the right place, I'll silently guide them to the right word and make sure their tracking is consistent with what is being read.

INTERVIEWER: *Call and Response* spot checks?

LEWIS: The *Call and Response* spot checks allow two things to happen. First, they allow students to maintain engagement with the text while I check to see who is following along, and second, *Call and Response* checks help my struggling readers with tricky vocabulary words or concepts in the text.

INTERVIEWER: How do you prepare your students for the quick transitions from reader to reader?

LEWIS: At the beginning of the year, I taught students to notice the end of the sentence by looking at the punctuation. Once students were comfortable with that, I asked students to read one sentence at a time, and then I would call on a new student. I explained that as readers, we need to keep our eyes on the text and be ready to read at any moment. Students knew that when they heard their name, it was time for them to pick up where the last reader left off. These transitions were not quick at first; it took weeks of practice before students could juggle tracking with their finger, listening to the reader, and comprehending what was going on in the story. But over time, I could see that scholars were truly engaged in the text, mastering tracking and listening when they would pick up the next sentence right away—eager to find out what would happen next in the story.

INTERVIEWER: How many of your readers do you decide on ahead of time, and on what basis do you choose them and the length of their read out loud?

LEWIS: I always keep in mind who is in need of more modeling and support and the readers who can be great models for my struggling readers. I plan in advance who I would like to open up the story (typically a strong reader) and who should follow (usually a weaker reader). Staggering the levels of readers allows the pace to stay up while maintaining accountability for all readers.

Every reader gets a chance to read. For my stronger readers, they will read longer passages, while my struggling readers will read shorter sentences, more often, throughout a longer text.

INTERVIEWER: What are your most effective tools for gaining leverage among young readers?

LEWIS: It always starts with joy. If I'm excited to read, then students are excited to read. If I model that it's okay to make a mistake, students will be okay with making mistakes while reading. Modeling what great readers do, including what adult readers do, gives students leverage in their own reading.

Within my reading group, I also built leverage by building in support when a student has a tricky time with reading. For example, in the clip, one reader made a mistake on a character's name. Without acknowledging that it was a mistake, the whole group was held accountable for saying the name out loud correctly: "Jan." When the group did not say the correct name at first, I quickly asked again, and students knew to check their answer. Their response—"Jan"—was correct, and we were able to move on. When one student makes a mistake, all of the readers knew they could support that scholar and learn something too.

For readers who are particularly shy or have serious decoding deficiencies, I would supply them with a copy of the reading passage the night before so they could practice and have exposure to the tricky words in the text. The next day, the scholars would feel more comfortable reading in front of the group and got the practice they needed.

INTERVIEWER: At the end of the clip, you announce that you are circling back around in the text to read for both expression and comprehension. How does CTG help you gain both leverage and meaning with your students?

LEWIS: In *Reading Mastery,* we always read the story at least two times. The first time allows scholars to work through their decoding, use their strategies, and get a sense of the text. The second time we read, after we've tackled the decoding, allows scholars to now make meaning of the text by using expression. Expression is taught as a reading skill by using clue words in the text to figure out the tone of the story. I am able to listen and see which scholars are reading with expression because they know what is going on in the text. Reading with expression adds joy to the text and keeps students engaged. Leverage goes up when students are able to interact with the text with feeling and emotion. Other scholars are more engaged and listen more attentively to the text when it's read with expression. Students are able to make meaning when the words are read with feeling. CTG allows all scholars to be part of making that meaning in the text and holds them accountable for listening to their own reading and the reading of others.

INTERVIEWER: What role does positive framing play in the use of CTG and building strong readers?

LEWIS: First, I always narrate the positive in reading groups, especially when students are modeling great reading behaviors like, "I love how X has her finger on the first word," which shows me students are ready to read.

I use positive framing by giving students a challenge: reading with expression means that not only do you have to decode words correctly and read with fluency, a reader must listen carefully to what's going on and use clue words to help themselves make meaning of the text. My readers know they have a lot to accomplish, they know they have a challenge, but I make it positive and exciting and encourage them by making it fun.

Whenever a student makes a mistake, I use plausible anonymity. I simply say, "Try again" or ask the group in a nonjudgmental tone to help figure out the word. I also ask students to reread, even when they've read a passage correctly, to emphasize a portion of a passage. Students get comfortable with rereading, and in my own modeling, I reread as well to show scholars that checking for errors and rereading is a reading strategy.

INTERVIEWER: What challenges do you face when it comes to CTG, particularly with young readers?

LEWIS: Major challenges for young readers and beginning teachers would include keeping the pace up, maintaining patience, and sustaining comprehension. When students are working hard on decoding, pacing, patience, and comprehension tend to run low. When this happens, it's important to remember that to keep pacing up, we can supply students with shorter passages and prepare them to read the night before or just before their reading session with a highlighted section of the story. When patience runs low, we must model for scholars what to do when we make a mistake or take a while to figure out a word. Have decoding strategy cue words—for example, read through to the end of the word, chunk it, what's the first sound, etc.—to keep the pace up and give support as needed. Finally, if a student is stuck, employ the help of the reading team to say the tricky word to keep them engaged and also provide support for the reader.

Finally, infuse comprehension questions throughout reading to ensure scholars are listening and monitoring their reading. As scholars read, give them time to go back into the text to answer questions if necessary and encourage rereading as a way to build comprehension.

INTERVIEWER: What moments do you wish to highlight in this clip? Is there any background that you wish to add?

LEWIS: The reading group was the lowest performing on reading assessments. Planning comprehension questions is key; planning who to call on is also essential. This kind of planning allowed me to see which students are comprehending the text, what comprehension skills they are using, and what types of questions my readers are having difficulty with during and after reading.

Index

HOW TO USE THE DVD

SYSTEM REQUIREMENTS

PC with Microsoft Windows 2003 or later
  Mac with Apple OS version 10.1 or later

USING THE DVD WITH WINDOWS

To view the items located on the DVD, follow these steps:

1. Insert the DVD into your computer's DVD-ROM drive.

2. A window will open asking you to select the program in which you wish to view the videos. Select the program.

IN CASE OF TROUBLE

If you experience difficulty using the DVD, please follow these steps:

1. Make sure your hardware and systems configurations conform to the systems requirements noted under "System Requirements" above.

2. Review the installation procedure for your type of hardware and operating system. It is possible to reinstall the software if necessary.

To speak with someone in Product Technical Support, call 800-762-2974 or 317-572-3994 Monday through Friday from 8:30 a.m. to 5:00 p.m. EST. You can also contact Product Technical Support and get support information through our website at www.wiley.com/techsupport.

Before calling or writing, please have the following information available:

- Type of computer and operating system.
- Any error messages displayed.
- Complete description of the problem.
- DVD ID# from the front of the DVD

It is best if you are sitting at your computer when making the call.